THE EMPOWERED
PARALEGAL

CAROLINA ACADEMIC PRESS

THE EMPOWERED PARALEGAL SERIES
Robert E. Mongue

The Empowered Paralegal:
Effective, Efficient and Professional

The Empowered Paralegal: Working with the Elder Client

The Empowered Paralegal Professionalism Anthology
Forthcoming

The Empowered Paralegal Cause of Action Handbook
Forthcoming

The Empowered Paralegal: Working with the Elder Client

Robert E. Mongue
Assistant Professor of Legal Studies
University of Mississippi

Carolina Academic Press
Durham, North Carolina

Library of Congress Cataloging-in-Publication Data

Mongue, Robert E.
 The empowered paralegal: working with the elder client / Robert E. Mongue.
    p. cm.
 ISBN 978-1-59460-795-0 (alk. paper)
 1. Legal assistants--United States--Handbooks, manuals, etc. 2. Older peo-
ple--Legal status, laws, etc.--United States. I. Title.

 KF320.L4M663 2010
 340.12373--dc22

                    2010025542

CAROLINA ACADEMIC PRESS
700 Kent Street
Durham, North Carolina 27701
Telephone (919) 489-7486
Fax (919) 493-5668
www.cap-press.com

Printed in the United States of America

Dedication

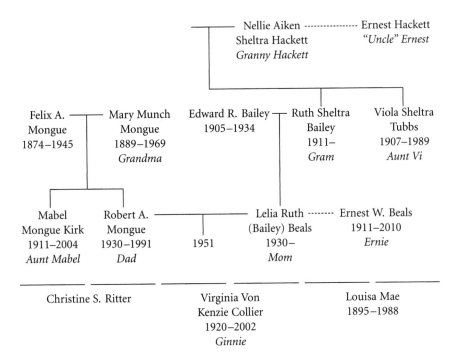

Nellie Aiken ---------------- Ernest Hackett
Sheltra Hackett   *"Uncle" Ernest*
Granny Hackett

Felix A. — Mary Munch   Edward R. Bailey — Ruth Sheltra   Viola Sheltra
Mongue   Mongue   1905–1934   Bailey   Tubbs
1874–1945   1889–1969   1911–   1907–1989
                    Grandma   *Gram*   *Aunt Vi*

Mabel   Robert A. —   Lelia Ruth -------- Ernest W. Beals
Mongue Kirk   Mongue   (Bailey) Beals   1911–2010
1911–2004   1930–1991   1951   1930–   *Ernie*
Aunt Mabel   *Dad*   *Mom*

Christine S. Ritter   Virginia Von   Louisa Mae
                                      Kenzie Collier   1895–1988
                                      1920–2002
                                      Ginnie

CONTENTS

PREFACE

My first "real job" was working as a janitor in a hospital in western Massa-chusetts. Being new to the staff, I often found myself assigned the wing of the hospital that cared for elderly patients. This was a wing in which no one on the staff wanted to work. The patients were generally senile and generally dying. They were all, of course, "old" and no one was anxious to be around old, se-nile or dying people.

Many of these patients were tied to their beds. Many had little or no sense of where they were. Some would repeat phrases or individual words endlessly. Often the repeated word was, "Nurse." Almost all had constant needs—the need to be cleaned, the need to roll over, the need to be acknowledged.

As I moved from room to room mopping and dusting, morning after morn-ing, two things came to mind. First, these people, being elderly and approaching the ends of their lives even if they were not—at that moment—dying, had a good number of commonalities. Second, however, each of them was differ-ent. Each had their own particular instance of whatever disease or ailment brought them to the hospital even if many of the other patients had the same disease or ailment. More importantly, each had his or her own personality and, if not suffering from constant dementia, their own approach or perspec-tive on their current state, their future, and their approaching death.

One of the advantages of being a janitor is that, unless there is a specific need, you are largely invisible. Being unnoticed, you can observe not only the patients but their families and the medical staff. Here to, I found commonal-ities. But among families, I saw remarkable differences not only in personali-ties and temperaments, but in *their* approach to the current status, the future, and the approach to the end of life of their loved ones. The broadest, most su-perficial commonalties arose from the mere fact that those loved ones were elderly and in the hospital. Other commonalties appeared to arise from cultural, religious, educational, and economic factors.

Our area did not have a lot of diversity. However, there was enough to see that common elements of the perspective of second generation Italian-Amer-icans from the northern-New England "Yankees" of my mother's family and the French/German influence on my father's family. The Protestant perspective was not much different from the Catholic, although the differences were perceptible. There were common factors in the approaches of the poor, distinguishable from those of the middle class, which were equally distinguishable from the rich (although the truly rich seldom found it necessary to die in the public hospital). Perspectives changed with the level of education. Combining these factors with differences in attitudes that existed between generations within each family resulted in a multitude of individual emotional and intellectual reactions to illness, aging, disability, dementia and death.

Yet, it appeared to me that medical service providers had only one approach that they applied to all of the patients and, if they paid any heed to the families at all, to those who loved and except for the duration of their hospitalization provided care for them. Caught up in the science of medicine—the machines, the charts, the new techniques, perhaps combined with a need to depersonalize the patients in order to remain objective, the approach was often one of intellectual superiority, of knowing better than the patient or their families what the patient wanted or needed, of knowing better than the patient or their families when, how, and where it was better for the patient to grow old or die. Patients appeared to be just patients, not necessarily people in the sense of individual persons.

Thus the only perspective that mattered was that of the medical providers. It is not that they did not care, often deeply, for their patients. It appeared simply that they believed there was only one way *to care* for the patients, regardless of the individual perspective and personality of the patient—*their way*. I was in high school at the time, convinced that I was going to become a doctor myself, so my focus was on the medical profession. It was not until a decade later as I began the practice of law that I realized the legal profession was often afflicted with the same narrowness.

In my last year of high school, Elizabeth Kubler-Ross published *On Death and Dying* beginning the long process of changing the medical profession's perception of the "right" way to care for the dying patients. Since then great progress has been made not only in the medical profession's approach to death and dying, but in the approach to aging and the elderly with new research assisting in the understanding of the elderly in terms of medicine, sociology, law and many other aspects of society. It is my hope in this book to digest and present much of that knowledge for the paralegal—the person in the law office most involved in interacting with the client—so that the paralegal will be empowered to best meet the needs of the elderly client and to manage that client as part of the legal team.

ACKNOWLEDGMENTS

This book would not have been possible without the support, guidance, editing, amazing knowledge of American culture, and understanding of death and dying of my wife, Denise Collier.

Jo Ann O'Quin, Professor of Social Work and Pharmacy Administration, at the University of Mississippi has been a wonderful resource on the gerontology aspects of this book. It is a much better book as a result of her assistance.

I also gratefully acknowledge Catherine V. "Ginny" Kilgore, Director of the North Mississippi Rural Legal Services Elder Project for her insight on the particular concerns of poor and frail elderly, and Billie York, one of my students and owner of "Hire A Legal Assistant," for her comments and editing.

Part I

The Elder Client

CHAPTER ONE

INTRODUCTION

A. The Empowered Paralegal

Empowerment does not come from the outside. It comes from within. It is not granted, it is earned. The empowered paralegal gains that power and the confidence that comes with being professional, by being a competent, effective and efficient member of the legal team. In *The Empowered Paralegal: Effective, Efficient and Professional* we examined some clear, concise, and easy-to-use techniques for empowering paralegals.

In addition to legal knowledge, the effective, empowered paralegal knows and uses these essential skills:

- The effective, empowered paralegal manages time well. Generally, a lawyer sells legal services, rather than a product. The value of those services is measured by the amount of time spent fulfilling a client's legal needs. It is essential, therefore, that both the paralegal and the attorney organize themselves and their time to maximize efficiency. In addition, they must keep track of, and bill for, their time in a way that makes sense for the law office and the clients.
- The effective, empowered paralegal manages the calendar well. Missed deadlines result in dissatisfied clients, malpractice claims, and attorney disciplinary procedures. It is essential that both the attorney and the paralegal be aware of upcoming deadlines and have a system in place to meet those deadlines without last-minute pressures that increase the likelihood of mistakes.
- The effective, empowered paralegal manages files well. The best crafted deeds, contracts, wills and pleadings are worthless if they cannot be found when needed. None of them can even be created if the necessary information cannot be located in a timely manner, or was never obtained in the first place. It is essential that both the paralegal and the attorney have a system in place, and use that system, for organizing, identifying, indexing and tracking files and the materials contained in the files.

3

- The effective, empowered paralegal manages clients well. The client is part of the legal team. Without the client there is no need for either the paralegal or the attorney and no money is generated to fund the law office. However, the client is the member of the team who knows the least about the law and her role in the team. It is essential that the paralegal and the attorney keep the client informed about what is being done for her and why, and what she needs to do for the outcome to be successful.
- The effective, empowered paralegal manages the paralegal's relationship with the attorney well within the legal team. Both the paralegal and attorney must know and respect their respective roles and those of the other; their abilities and those of the other. It is essential that the paralegal understand what the attorney expects of him and the attorney understand what the paralegal can and cannot do for her.
- The effective, empowered paralegal knows and applies the principles of professionalism and thereby gains recognition of his status as a professional.

Each of the essential skills was examined in detail with management of time, workload, docket, files, clients and attorneys each being the focus of their own chapter. We then put all of that knowledge to work in the context of litigation.

Certainly the paralegal who can apply those techniques to effective management of their time, workload, docket, files, clients and attorneys will be a more effective, competent, efficient and professional paralegal. As a result that paralegal will be more empowered in his or her own eyes and in those of his or her attorneys and clients. They will gain more respect and responsibility because they have earned more respect and responsibility.

Yet, the point of this book is more than just explanation and transmission of practical techniques. The point lies in the basic underlying approach — *The Empowered Paralegal* approach — to all aspects of paralegal practices based on the concept that the paralegal can manage each aspect rather than being managed by it. Paralegals can and must do so as the professional they are.

We focused on the management of specific aspects of paralegal practice, the ones that appeared to me, based on thirty years of practicing law, to be the most pervasive concerns of paralegals attempting to survive and thrive in the American law office. Because most of my career has involved litigation, much of the discussion was cast in the context of the litigation paralegal. However, the principles underlying the techniques can, and should, be applied to every aspect of paralegal practice, in every type of office in which a paralegal works (law office, government office and corporate office), and in every area of law.

As we moved through each of the chapters in *The Empowered Paralegal* dealing in turn with management of time, workload, docket, files, clients and attorneys we discussed particular techniques, but the underlying principles were the same in each. The techniques themselves are the result of applying those principles to whatever area in which the paralegal is seeking to become efficient, effective and empowered.

The first principle is to recognize and to account for the fundamental *inter*relationships and responsibilities of paralegal practice:

- The interrelationship between the facts, the file, the docket and time
- The interrelationship between the client, the paralegal and the attorney
- The joint responsibility and involvement of all members of the legal team for the facts, the file and the docket in achieving a successful outcome.

The goal for the effective, empowered paralegal is the ability to understand and manage each of the key factors.

The second principle has to do with the way the paralegal approaches any and all aspects of paralegal practice. It is a proactive rather than reactive approach. It seeks to understand and manage even those aspects of practice that the paralegal cannot control. This principle involves taking a rational empowered approach.

While the specifics were different for management of time than for files, for files than for docket and so on, in each case we identified the areas of concern, analyzed each aspect of that concern, set priorities that addressed those concerns, sought a greater understanding of the area of concern, investigated solutions and barriers to those solution, and established procedures for implementing solutions and removing or overcoming barriers to those solutions. We did so in a direct, rational and professional way. We did so in a way that honored our own need to be efficient, effective and empowered, and honored the interrelationships and responsibilities of the first principle.

When a paralegal applies these principles, that paralegal becomes empowered. The empowered paralegal is an essential member of the legal team in any office. In particular, the empowered paralegal not only survives, but thrives in the American law office.

This book applies those principles to elder law. My hope is that after reading this book, paralegals who apply these techniques will recognize in themselves the ability to manage their practice, gain the self-confidence, respect they deserve, satisfaction, and gratification of being a legal professional.

B. Understanding the Legal Team

Our discussion has to start with an understanding of who the members of the legal team are and the role each member plays in relation to the legal matter being handled by the team. A diagram of the traditional concept of the legal team looks much like a corporation or government organizational chart with a rigid hierarchy of commands, responsibilities and duties:

Figure 1-1

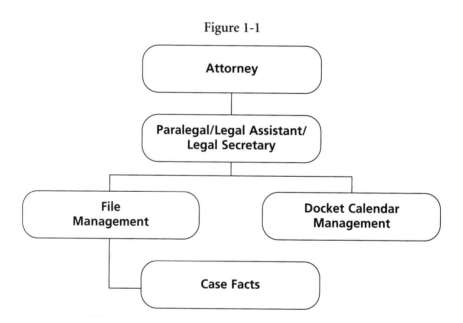

This traditional view of the legal team suffers from several flaws, the most prominent of which is that it fails to recognize any role for the client. Every law office gives some importance to the client in the sense they acknowledge that without the client there is no case and no fee. This type of recognition results in only a minor change to the chart:

Figure 1-2

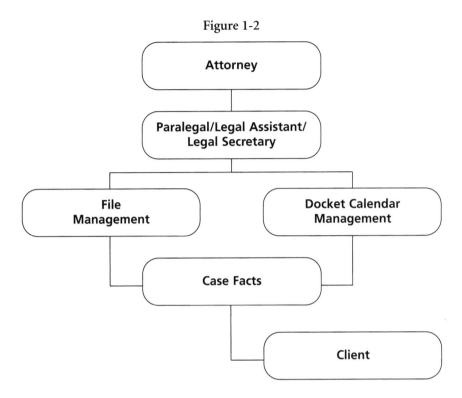

However, recognizing the importance of the client to the law office is not the same as recognizing the client as part of the legal team; rather it keeps the client apart from the team and, to a great extent, from the very legal matter which brought the client to the attorney.

As explained in the next section, we will discuss the elder client in depth in this book. For now it is necessary only that we be aware that in this book the client, the paralegal and the attorney are all members of the legal team. This conception of the roles of each member in the legal team differs from the traditional view. The conception used in this book is better illustrated by the following diagram than the traditional diagram:

Figure 1-3

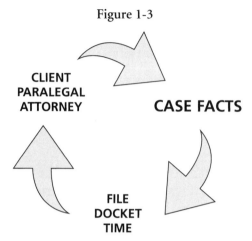

This diagram begins to account for critical and fundamental *inter*relationships and responsibilities:

- The interrelationship between the facts, the file, the docket and time
- The interrelationship between the client, the paralegal and the attorney
- The joint responsibility and involvement of all members of the legal team for the facts, the file and the docket in achieving a successful outcome.

These interrelationships and responsibilities appear more complex than they have often been characterized and will be discussed extensively in this book. The goal for the effective, empowered paralegal is the ability to understand and manage each of the key factors. It's simpler than it sounds.

Before starting we'll take an introductory look at Elder Law in the next section.

C. Introduction to Elder Law

Elder law is a dual-natured creature. It is quite like any other kind of law and, at the same time, quite unlike any other area of law. Substantively the law is law —statutes, cases, rules, and regulations, all of which must be researched, analyzed, understood and applied. Elder law attorneys and their paralegals march through the same steps of legal research and analysis as other attorneys. They use the IRAC method of writing their memoranda and briefs. They need to manage their time, workloads, files, and dockets just as any other attorney/paralegal team.

Unlike any other type of law though, elder law is not about something a client is going through—a divorce, a bankruptcy, immigration, a criminal charge, a real estate transaction. Elder law is about whom and what the client *is*—elderly. Unlike other areas of law, elder law applies to everyone. Many people go through life without running a business, buying property, getting a divorce or being charged with a crime. But everyone goes through life with the certainty of growing old. Even those who do not survive long enough to confront old age (or their survivors) must deal with elder law issues—end-of-life decisions, death, disability, probate.

So, elder law is as much focused on "elder" as it is on "law." This book is focused primarily on the elder client rather than elder law. Standard substantive law topics such as Social Security are covered but not in detail. Trained and experienced paralegals already have the skills to research, locate, analyze and apply the laws that relate to elder issues. My focus here is on understanding and working with the elder client.

Our goal is to add to those skills knowledge and understanding of elder law clients and the issues they face. These clients and their issues require some special accommodations. Managing their files requires slightly different methods, or at least slightly different focus, than other files. But all of these differences arise from the particular nature of the clients—they are elderly.

The elderly, too, are dual natured. They have uniformity in that they are at approximately the same stage in life. That stage of life entails a certain commonality of concerns as noted above—dying, death, planning for those left behind, physical changes, diminished mental capacity and vulnerability. There are even certain psychological factors that seem almost universal.

Yet, we cannot let this commonality mask the diversity of approaches to each of these concerns. Each client will perceive these issues and the law that relates to them from a unique perspective arising from years of personal experiences rooted in cultural, ethnic, religious and other influences. Thus, each will have his or her own perspective on aging, the elderly, the role of the family, dying, death, dead bodies and the other practical and legal issues that confront the elderly.

No one can hope to thoroughly understand the many different influences on our clients and their families, or the deeply personal perspective which result from those influences. However, the empowered paralegal will be aware of these differences and understand enough about them to appreciate how they affect the decisions that an elder law client will make.

Much of this book will focus on gaining that awareness and understanding. The chapters in Part I deal primarily with the client while those in Part II focus more on substantive law. In Part I we start with an introduction to the elder client, then proceed in Chapter Two with a discussion of some of the physical and psychological changes that occur as we age and the practicalities accommodating these changes when working with elderly clients. Chapter Three reviews the issues surrounding and the standards for determining competency. In Chapter Four we discuss several aspects of dealing with the client's family. Chapter Five ends Part I with consideration of various perspectives, many culturally based, on aging, death, and dying.

In Part II we begin by examining estate planning basics and intestacy in Chapter Six, and then basic estate planning tools in Chapter Seven. Planning of a different type—advanced directives regarding end-of-life decisions are covered in Chapter Eight. Chapter Nine surveys some of the laws that directly affect the elderly. Chapter Ten focuses on the growing problem of elder abuse. We end in Chapter Eleven by considering some of the ethical dilemmas faced by the elderly and the professionals who work with them.

D. Introduction to the Elder Client

Just who is considered elderly often depends on perspective. In the 1960s and 1970s, when I was well under thirty, we vowed never to trust anyone over thirty. Jefferson Airplane sang of poor Lather, whose mother lamented as Lather turned thirty, "And I should have told him, no, you're not old." As I crossed over the thirty threshold I no longer felt it was so old. Old had become 55, the magic age when "seniors" became entitled to a discount at the local pharmacy and movie theater. Now, it appears the age for elderly discounts has moved to 65, but my invitation to join the American Association for Retired Persons arrived when I was 50, although neither I nor anyone I know plans to retire before they are 65. After all I am far too young to retire—retirement is for old people![1]

The dual nature of aging shows in our attitudes towards aging. On the one hand we often look upon the elderly in terms of their diminished capacities and the changes to their physical appearance. Old age is something we fight against —to the great benefit of the companies selling wrinkle-creams and plastic surgery. On the other, we attribute to the elderly a certain respect, dignity, and

---

1. One study conducted in 1992 indicates that "old age" does indeed change depending one's own age. "On average, 16- to 24-year-olds suggested old age began at 63, while those aged 75 and over suggested it started at 76. Whereas 59 per cent of the younger group suggested old age started between the ages of 60 and 75, only 27 per cent of the older group did so. The younger respondents also seemed more readily able than the older ones to give a definite answer to the question of when old age starts." Robert Slater, *The Psychology of Growing Old: Looking Forward* 2 (Open University Press 1975).

wisdom, based solely on their longevity. Many of our feelings about aging and the aged are based on myths, stereotypes, cultural prejudices, and extrapolations to the general population based on personal experience with a select few elderly persons. As a result much of what we think about the elderly is wrong, or at least not applicable to all the elderly. Scientific study is warranted.

The study of biological, psychological, and social aspects of aging is called gerontology. Because aging affects every aspect of life, gerontologists include researchers and practitioners in such diverse fields as biology, medicine, dentistry, physical and occupational therapy, psychology, psychiatry, sociology, economics, political science, pharmacy and social work.[2] While not included in this list, there are clearly also legal aspects of aging and a growing number of legal practitioners who focus on the law that applies to elderly clients. Whether our law office consists of legal gerontology practice, a general practice or other specialty practice that includes elderly clients, we need not get too heavily involved in the debate about what it means to be "old." We should, however, take from gerontology those aspects which can be helpful to us in our practice.

Gerontologists look at aging from the viewpoint of at least four different aging processes, each of which has some import for the paralegal dealing with elderly clients: chronological aging, biological aging, psychological aging, and social aging. We will take a brief look here at each of these processes and how they relate to the law practice.

Chronological Aging

This is the simplest to understand and the one to which we are most often referring when we speak of a person's age. Chronological aging is simply a matter of counting the person's birthdays. This measure of age is important to legal personnel because eligibility for many rights and benefits available under law, and responsibility for many duties required under law are determined (almost) entirely by virtue of chronological age. Our primary concern is with those chronologically based rights, benefits, and duties that directly affect people as they get past middle age, but such rights, benefits, and duties begin when we are quite young, although the obligation to perform the duties is most often directed to our parents or guardians. For example, the right to a free public education together with the requirement to obtain vaccinations before attending school and the obligation to attend school are all based on chronological age.

---

2. Nancy R. Hooyman and H. Asuman Kiyak, *Social Gerontology: A Multidisciplinary Perspective*, 3 (7th ed., Pearson 2005).

Some of these laws are of concern to legal practitioners engaged in some aspects of elder law or those that deal with end of life issues which can arise at any age. For example, age (normally the age of eighteen) is one element in determining whether a person is entitled to make a will, execute an Advanced Health Care Directive, or make decisions under an Advanced Health Care Directive or surrogate statutes. In addition, estate planners make provisions for the eventuality that estate assets may be distributed to persons under the age of majority.

Of direct concern are laws such as those against age discrimination such as the Age Discrimination in Employment Act of 1967 (ADEA), 29 U.S.C. §6101, that protects certain applicants and employees 40 years of age and older from discrimination on the basis of age in hiring, promotion, discharge, compensation, or terms, conditions or privileges of employment. Most notable, perhaps, is the Social Security Act which currently sets the "retirement age," that is the age at which one can retire and receive full Social Security Benefits, at 66 (up from 65 in 2004, and set to go up to age 67 in 2022). The Social Security Act also sets the age requirements for Medicare coverage.

Biological Aging

As we age chronologically our bodies age. This would be simpler if there was a direct correlation between chronological age and the rate at which our bodies aged, but that is not the case. While there is no doubt that all bodies age as we grow chronologically older, each body ages at its own rate. We all have general preconceptions of what a body will look, feel, or act like at a particular chronological age, but we also frequently find ourselves saying things like, "He does not look sixty," or "She is as spry as a woman half her age." When I first started practicing law I had a client, Louisa Mae, who was able to walk right beside me as we ascended the long and steep stairs to my office, discussing the rather frustrating performance of the Boston Red Sox and of Congress as we went. (The Red Sox have fared much better recently; Congress, not so much.) My partner, who was about my age, would often be out of breath at the top. Louisa Mae, about whom you will hear more later, was not. When we first met, Louisa Mae was seventy-seven years old!

Awareness of biological aging is important to legal professionals primarily because, at least insofar as it relates to the elder client, it typically means physical changes that result in loss—loss of hearing, visual acuity (sight), mobility, and other signs of physical decline. It also generally means a greater susceptibility to certain diseases, disorders, and disabilities. As we will discuss in more depth in Chapter Two, if we are to best serve our elder clients and meet our ethical obligations to them, we must be aware of and accommodate these losses, and avoid allowing our preconceptions regarding biological aging to affect our judgment regarding them. While we must be aware that there is a general correlation between chronological aging and biological aging, each client is an individual. We must be aware of what aging means to clients, but be mindful of just how each client has aged.

Psychological Aging

As we age chronologically our minds age also. As with biological aging, there is a general but not direct correlation between chronological aging and psychological aging. And, as with biological aging, insofar as it relates to elder clients, psychological aging is most often evidenced by loss, primarily diminution in mental functioning such of memory, but also in sensory and perceptual processes. In addition, psychological aging can result in personality changes such as increased irritability and impatience.

Legal professionals need to be aware of these psychological changes. As with biological changes, we must be aware that in general there is a correlation between chronological aging and psychological aging, but that each client is an individual. We must be aware of what psychological aging means to clients, but be mindful of just how each client has aged.

In Chapter Three we will discuss the importance of this awareness in the context of serving the elder client primarily in terms of the constant need to document the capacity and competency of a client to engage in legal activities such as executing a will, transferring property and granting powers of attorney.

Social Aging

As we age chronologically, our place in the social structure changes. Our expectations of others and others' expectations of us change. When we are young we expect to be taken care of and are expected to attend school. Later, we expect to take care of our children and provide them with care. For many of us, one of the biggest changes is the change from being a paid, "productive" member of society to being retired. For others, the change from active parent to being an "empty nester" is a tremendous change.

These social changes, however, affect not only our expectations of others and their expectations of us, but our perception of others and our perception of ourselves. In fact, for some people the loss of what they viewed as their primary purpose in life whether it be their work, taking care of children, caring for a spouse, or something else, together with diminished capacity both biologically and psychologically often resulting in difficulty in retaining any clear idea of "self."

Physical disability, lessened income, death of family and contemporaries, and the like can often lead to social isolation and dependence. Far too often the elderly must depend on persons who ought not to be trusted with such reliance, leading to elder abuse. As discussed in Chapter Four, legal professionals must be mindful of the potential that even members of the family of an elder client may be taking unfair advantage of our clients' circumstances and we must take steps to prevent such actions. While we cannot substitute our judgment for theirs, it is incumbent upon us to ensure that their judgment is indeed theirs, free from undue influence, duress and fraud. We have an ethical, and, in some cases, a legal duty to take action when we have reasonable grounds to believe that elder abuse is taking place.

Stereotypes and Discrimination

As discussed above, what it means to be "old" is relative. It changes not only with one's own age, but also in some objective fashion. There is likely a maximum life span that even modern medicine will not be able to exceed, but life expectancy continues increasing albeit at a slowing rate. Fortunately, it also appears that significant strides are being made in extending the quality of life and the amount of life during which we can remain active.

Regardless of at what point each of us perceives old age to begin, we do tend to stereotype those we consider old. We need to be aware these stereotypes exist and that we are subject to buying into them. There is also a tendency to evaluate other people by comparing their group to ours. Unfortunately, when we do so, there is also a tendency for that other group to come out on the short end of the evaluation. It is especially likely that we will attribute any negative qualities of individuals within a group to the entire group. Then, we react to and treat members of the group as if they all share those attributes, rather than as individuals. I have often seen members of the legal profession do this with clients in general. They view all clients as untruthful or as whiners because a few clients are!

Failure to recognize the diversity of our clients, even elderly clients, leads to assumptions that can be harmful to our relationship with them, making it less likely we will understand their needs, and making full integration into the legal team less likely. At the same time, as with physical changes, understanding how aging can affect our clients psychologically increases our ability to provide for their legal needs. The trick is to use our understanding in the context of each individual, not in the context of stereotypes. We need to balance the commonality of issues and concerns that come with aging and the individuality of each client.

Failure to recognize the diversity of the elderly and engaging in stereotyping of people based on their age almost inevitably leads to discrimination. Of course, this is not unique to the elderly. The Age Discrimination Act of 1975 prohibits discrimination against anyone due to their age, regardless of that age, in any program or activity receiving Federal financial assistance.[3] However, there is little doubt that there is very real discrimination based on advanced age, especially in employment. This necessitated passage of the Age Discrimination in Employment Act of 1967 as noted in the Congressional findings which state:

Sec. 621. Congressional statement of findings and purpose

(a) The Congress hereby finds and declares that—
    (1) in the face of rising productivity and affluence, older workers find themselves disadvantaged in their efforts to retain employment, and especially to regain employment when displaced from jobs;
    (2) the setting of arbitrary age limits regardless of potential for job performance has become a common practice, and certain otherwise desirable practices may work to the disadvantage of older persons;
    (3) the incidence of unemployment, especially long-term unemployment with resultant deterioration of skill, morale, and employer acceptability is, relative to the younger ages, high among older workers; their numbers are great and growing; and their employment problems grave;
    (4) the existence in industries affecting commerce, of arbitrary discrimination in employment because of age, burdens commerce and the free flow of goods in commerce.

(b) It is therefore the purpose of this chapter to promote employment of older persons based on their ability rather than age; to prohibit arbitrary age discrimination in employment; to help employers and workers find ways of meeting problems arising from the impact of age on employment.[4]

---

3. 42 U.S.C. §6102: Prohibition of discrimination

Pursuant to regulations prescribed under section 6103 of this title, and except as provided by section 6103(b) of this title and section 6103(c) of this title, no person in the United States shall, on the basis of age, be excluded from participation in, be denied the benefits of, or be subjected to discrimination under, any program or activity receiving Federal financial assistance.

4. 29 U.S.C. §621.

We will not discuss these laws in detail here. At this point, it is important that we keep in mind the very real nature of this discrimination so that we do not become susceptible to it and so that we understand that a perception on the part of our clients that the discrimination exists is not the result of paranoia. As we will discuss below, this discrimination can also factor into the loss of sense of self and self-esteem that can accompany aging.

The Aging Population

There appears to be no end to the statistics showing just how old the population of the United States is becoming. These statistics are important for sociologists, policy planners, and politicians who must deal with the social and political ramifications of this trend. For example, the fact that we are living longer and, in many cases, living healthier and therefore potentially productive lives has implications for the viability of our Social Security system. Our good fortune does not bode well for survival of the system since there will be more people entering the system than leaving it and they will be staying in it longer than the system can support. With the baby boomer generation, the generation born between 1946 and 1964 about to enter the system, statisticians forecast that the Social Security Trust fund will soon be broke.[5] At the same time the fact that we are not only living longer may also provide part of the solution provided we are willing to change our concept of "retirement age" —which is now 66 years old for Social Security full-benefits purposes and set to go up to 67 in 2022.

Sociologically we must prepare for the greater number of ill and disabled elderly. Society must determine how it will deal with health care, housing, support for care-givers and many other such issues. There has to be recognition that the nature of the elderly population itself is changing, requiring different classifications in the description of the elderly. According to the U.S. Census Bureau, since World War II, the population aged 85 and older has increased more rapidly that any other age group in our country. This "oldest-old" pop-

---

5. Estimates of when funds will run out vary depending on the statistical model used. Those estimates change when actually system data differs from projections. For example, on April 28, 2010, NPR reported, "For some older Americans who lost jobs in the Great Recession, Social Security is filling the void left when unemployment benefits run out. The Social Security Administration had predicted there would be a 15 percent increase in retirement applications last year as baby boomers reached retirement age. Instead, the increase was 20 percent." http://www.npr.org/templates/story/story.php?storyId=126314707&ft=1&f=1006 (Last accessed April 28, 2010).

ulation has increased by a factor of 23 while the "old-old," aged 75–84 have increased twelvefold, and the "young-old," aged 65–74, increased eightfold.[6] This creates a far greater need for long-term care dealing with the multiple problems resulting from the psychological, biological and sociological aging processes discussed above.

These numbers are also important for the legal profession. Certainly they foretell a need for the legal profession to become more knowledgeable about the law regarding the elderly and the options available to the elderly when, for example, they need long term care, options which may include home care by family members with or without formal home care assistance, assisted-living facilities, and independent living facilities. Not so long ago for those nearing the end of their lives there was only one option — hospitalization (which was itself a change from the period when the only significant option was to die at home). Options now include hospitalization, hospice facilities, hospice assistance at home, and dying at home with only the family. Each of these options, and payment for them, has legal ramifications.

Just as society must plan for the increased number of elderly individual, so each individual ought to plan for the increased likelihood that he or she will be among the old, from the young-old to the old-old. This means the legal professional must also be more aware of the need for estate planning; in particular more aware of the need for estate planning to anticipate extended life as a member of the "elderly." Estate planning will be discussed in depth in Chapters Six and Seven.

Client planning should include plans for the likely effects of biological, psychological, and sociological aging. Thus, estate planning is not limited to financial planning. Although many of the concerns must be thought of in terms of finances, finances are not the only factors involved. For example, while a client may have a preferred method of long-term care, each of the options for long-term care have related cost factors. Those cost factors, however, often include the necessity to draw on family psychological, physical, and emotional resources as well as monetary resources.

The legal professional ought also be aware of the options for dealing with end of life issues such whether to continue medical treatment that will prolong life even when the client himself or herself is unable to make those decisions. This will be the topic of discussion in Chapter Eight.

As this book argues, there is also a need for legal professionals to become more knowledgeable regarding the elderly client. This knowledge should include

---

6. *Id.* at 16.

being aware that demographics have changed and, in turn, will continue to change perceptions of aging, dying, and death. Some of the various cultural, ethnic, religious, and other factors influencing those perceptions are discussed in Chapter Five. The next chapter will expand upon some of the items introduced in this section—understanding and accommodating the various effects of biological, psychological, and sociological aging.

CHAPTER TWO

Understanding and Accommodating Elder Clients and Their Families

A. Accommodating the Elder Client

In some respects the word "accommodation" has taken on negative connotations, perhaps because it is perceived as being something the government requires in laws such as the Americans with Disabilities Act. However, the traditional dictionary definition of "accommodate" simply means to "give consideration to," "allow for," "provided something needed," or "make fit and suitable." This is the sense in which "accommodate" is being used here.

In fact, for our purposes "accommodate" is really used as a particular application of The Empowered Paralegal approach, i.e., gain a comprehensive understanding, identify potential problems or difficulties, determine and prioritize potential solutions for those problems *before* they occur, develop a plan for implementing the selected solution(s), and implement the plan. We began the process of understanding the elder client in Chapter One. In this chapter we will continue that process and proceed with the succeeding steps in The Empowered Paralegal approach.

As discussed in *The Empowered Paralegal: Effective, Efficient and Professional*, this process is not unique to the elder client. In addition to the factors discussed there, we should be aware that many problems that arise with clients occur because clients feel that they have been de-personalized. Frequently, this feeling arises from the legal situation in which clients find themselves. Arguments over bills, for example, or complaints about lack of communications, are often without basis in fact, and are actually complaints that arise from the fact that the client does not feel acknowledged or respected as an individual.

Clients are persons, not just cases. Even when their case is being handled quite professionally and competently, they may complain because they are not being acknowledged as persons. However, since they often are not aware of the real problem, and do not know how to express their needs in those terms, they may express their frustration in other ways.

The need to recognize and address the needs of the elder client are, thus, not unique. However, they are often much more pronounced. To an extent this is simply because the needs themselves are more pronounced. In comparison to the general population the elderly have greater needs—or at least a greater need for others to accommodate their needs, since their own capacity to meet them is diminished. More important, perhaps, though is the fact that many of the factors that attend aging tend to diminish or put into question a person's own self-identity. Indeed, as we will discuss briefly in the section on the psychological effects of aging, elder clients often struggle to preserve their sense of self.

In the end though, the empowered paralegal seeks to understand his clients and accommodate their needs because it is the professional thing to do. It helps the paralegal do his job in the most effective and efficient way possible. Working with the elderly, when done with the proper perspective, patience, and understanding can be especially gratifying. Billie Lord York, a paralegal who at the time of this writing provides freelance paralegal services through www.hirealegalassistant.com describes one of her experiences this way

> Working with elderly clients does force you to go beyond just being professional but also putting on different hats, i.e., consideration, patience, listening attentively. These things, of course, go for every client yet with those of the "golden age" it can especially apply. I have had many experiences with the elderly as a litigation paralegal for the last 13 years. There are two in particular that come to mind: I will call them Barb and Evan. They were involved as plaintiffs in the same case in which our firm represented them against a pharmaceutical company. It was my responsibility to interview them for discovery responses, keep them updated as to the status of the case, assist them with attending their required screenings, preparing them for trial, making their accommodations for the trial, keeping them updated on the defense's appeal.

> Talking to them on the telephone was the preferred communication method since neither was familiar with the computer and both lived several miles away from our office. I tried to make time for them every time they called and be patient with their questions, even if they were repetitive.

> I also had to remember they, and not their children, were our clients. As long as the client is mentally stable, we cannot divulge confidential information to someone that was not our client. Also, as with both

young and old clients, they want to ask legal advice from me almost regularly. There is a fine line between UPL and status update of the case so I had to be careful not to cross it.

Although both have passed on now, I found working with Barb and Evan taught me a great deal of patience and also allowed me to grow in my career with teaching me how to deal with the non-typical client.

In this book we will be discussing the issues raised by Billie in her vignette. We will begin by discussing some of the ways in which aging affects the capacities of persons with a goal toward identifying ways in which these diminished capacities may make it more difficult for legal professionals to perform legal services for the client. We will also discuss using that understanding to formulate solutions.

B. Changes in Physical Capacities

In this section and in the section on the psychological effects of aging we will be discussing changes that occur to some degree in all persons as they age. It is important to keep in mind, however, that these changes take place at different rates for each individual. Thus for each client we should assume that each of these changes is taking or has taken place, but we should be careful not to stereotype or assume that any individual has already undergone particular changes. Some people will assume based on their experience with their own grandparents, for example, that all elderly people cannot hear well and begin shouting whenever they talk to an older person. Worse yet, they assume the elder person cannot hear what they say around that person if they speak softly!

The physical changes that occur during aging are far too numerous and complex to be discussed in detail here. Gerontologists may write entire books covering just one aspect of the aging process such as the changes that relate to vision. For our purposes, we will focus on three aspects that are particularly significant for legal professionals—the changes to hearing, sight, and mobility.

These changes do not suddenly come upon persons when they turn sixty-five and qualify for Social Security retirement benefits. In fact, physical changes are part of our lives at every stage. For most purposes we reach a peak in physical capacities in our twenties. Generally, we seem to be at our peak capacity for only a few years. This is especially evident for athletes whose ability to continue performing after reaching this peak diminishes to the point where it is rare for an athlete to remain competitive for more than a decade.

Once it begins, the decline is usually gradual through our thirties and early forties, and then accelerates through the subsequent decades. However, remember that these are all generalities. As I previously noted, my client Louisa Mae retained an ability to climb stairs in her late seventies that exceeded many younger clients. The same can be true for changes in hearing and vision. Also, each of these changes in capacity changes at its own rate, so a person with greatly diminished hearing may continue to possess great visual acuity.

Many persons are not willing to accept or acknowledge the changing they are experiencing. At the very least they attempt either consciously or unconsciously to compensate for the changes. One person I know is experiencing changes in his ability to distinguish one speaker from another in a crowded setting such as a restaurant. The person speaking to him at his table merges with the background noise and speakers from across the restaurant, making it very difficult to hear the person at his own table. He compensates for this by making sure he takes the seat opposite from his table mate so he can watch for visual cues on his mate's face and other body language or engage in basic lip reading to compensate for this change. We are all familiar with persons who consciously or unconsciously move a paper further from or closer to their eyes in order to read what, only a few years ago, was easily seen.

While many persons do acknowledge and accept the changes associated with aging, we should keep in mind that not all do. Therefore, as we seek solutions to the problems that arise in legal practice as a result of those changes in our clients, we should seek solutions that can be implemented without emphasizing the point to the client.

As noted above, the diminution in hearing, sight and mobility are of primary concern for legal professionals. We will look at those changes one at a time, but ultimately it would be best not to think of them in purely their physical context which can tend to take on an academic tone—a detached objectivity. So once we have looked at the science, we will seek to understand that science in the context of the law office.

Hearing Loss

Changes in hearing do not occur uniformly. The physical structure of the ear, or parts of it, change as we age. These changes do not take place uniformly. Sound comes into us at different frequencies. Some sounds are at frequencies too low or too high for any human to hear. A dog whistle is audible to dogs without us hearing it because it is at a frequency too high for us to hear. At any age, we hear different frequencies differently which sometimes leads to conflicts even among persons of the same generation over the level at which the treble and bass should be set on the car radio.

When working with elderly clients, legal professionals are primarily concerned with the effects of aging on the ability of the client to hear speech. Changes in the ability to hear speech occur rather slowly up to about the age of 60 and then they accelerate. By age 70 one in three will have some loss of hearing and one in two by age 85.[1] This effect is not only one of loss of volume. There is also the possibility of distortion of sounds. Some letters of the alphabet require different sound frequencies than others, so some older people have particular difficulty hearing or understanding various letters or sounds. Obviously, this difficulty diminishes their ability to comprehend what is being said, especially when it is combined with a slowing of the ability to process information.

Hearing problems can often be lessened by hearing aids, but there is still substantial reluctance to wear hearing aids, perhaps because of the reluctance to accept the existence of the diminished capacity or the social stigma that continues to attach to the use of hearing aids. It is also possible that a client may not be using a hearing aid due to cost. Also, since hearing aids raise the volume of all sound, they may contribute to the problem of inability to distinguish speech from background noise. While some of the newer digital hearing aids are better at reducing background noise, they are much more expensive than standard hearing aids and do not reduce the other impediments to use.

In any case, raising the topic of a hearing aid with a client can be touchy. If you are going to raise it, you should keep in mind that there are a variety of reasons why the client may not be using one, so do not assume the client's reason is the one that you might have heard from other elderly persons. If the reason is cost, you may be able to help by investigating the availability of insurance or other means of payment, although hearing exams and hearing aids are not generally covered by Medicare or even private insurance plans unless they are the result of a specific injury as opposed to the aging process.

Thus, in most cases, the hearing loss must be accommodated. While it may seem that the solution to this problem is fairly simple, i.e., turn up the volume, it is not. Shouting is accompanied by body language that can contribute to communication problems with the client. That body language is, at best, distracting. In addition, it can be misinterpreted as irritation (or, perhaps, correctly interpreted as the irritation that the speaker feels at having to shout). Shouting can be exhausting. Even speaking very loudly can be difficult to sustain consistently, leading to speech that fades in and out for the listener. Shouting is distracting even for the shouting person as at least some of their attention must be focused on maintaining the volume.

---

1. Nancy R. Hooyman and H. Asuman Kiyak, *Social Gerontology: A Multidisciplinary Perspective*, 96 (7th ed., Pearson 2005).

In general, simply increasing volume is not a good answer because it increases the volume of the sounds a person can hear as well as those he or she cannot. As stated above this is one problem with the use of hearing aids. If a client is having difficulty distinguishing speech or other desired sound from background or other undesired sound, simply increasing the volume of all sound will not help, and may make the problem worse.

Finally, shouting and other means of raising volume can lead to confidentiality problems. It increases the chance that the conversation will be overheard by other persons. This is especially true when we must meet our client outside of the office—in their home, a hospital, nursing home, or other assisted living facility. If the solution implemented to accommodate the loss of hearing is increased volume, then we must also adopt some means of maintaining confidentiality. Sound-proofing rooms is quite expensive but provides the additional benefit of screening out distractions. Certainly we should consider rugs (well secured so as not to create a tripping hazard) and wall décor that deaden sound. However, we can take simpler steps such as conducting conferences in rooms detached from waiting rooms and other high traffic locations. In addition, we can follow the lead of therapists and use "white noise" machines outside of conference rooms.

Fortunately, simply raising the volume is not the only and often is not the best way to accommodate our clients' diminished hearing. Gerontologists inform us that there are ways to communicate that compensate for much loss of hearing. Many of the techniques are helpful in ensuring understanding of our communications with any client. Those methods include:

- Face the person and maintain eye contact. This minimizes distractions and provides non-verbal clues as to what is being said as well as directing the sound at the listener.
- Sit somewhat close to and at eye level with the listener. Large, fancy conference tables are nice, but it may be better to sit next to the listener rather than across the table. Placing the client at the end of the long side of the table and sitting at the closest point on the short side allows closeness without the need to turn uncomfortably to the side to maintain eye contract. Watch the client's body language for signs that you are too close for their comfort.
- Do not cover your mouth or face with your hands or objects such as papers while speaking. This muffles and deflects the sounds and creates an unnecessary distraction.
- Speak slowly and clearly but not in an exaggerated way.
- Minimize distractions, especially background noises. Again, sound proofing a room can be excessively expensive, but distractions can be minimized by holding conversations away from high-traffic areas, using "white

noise" machines, and décor that deadens sound. Sometimes it is as simple as remembering to close the door. "White noise" machines can be purchased in sizes that fit in a briefcase and brought to out-of-office meetings with the client.

- Speak in a lower tone of voice. This is not as counter-intuitive as it may seem. We are not talking about lowering volume but tone of voice, thus conveying our words in frequencies within the listener's ability to receive. Speak as you normally would in terms of cadence and modulation.
- Especially important information should be repeated often and in different ways. If the client fails to catch the point due to sound distortion, distraction, background noise or the like when it is stated one way, they may understand the same point when it stated a different way.
- Speak from a checklist or agenda so that points are made in a clear, systematic way. Provide the client with a written checklist of the topics covered and/or specific information conveyed such as items they must bring with them to the next meeting.[2]

With regard to each of the diminished capacities that we discuss in this book, I suggest you literally put yourself in the place of the client. Sit in your conference room at different times of day and listen to the background noise. Do this not from the seat you normally take, but the seat or seats normally assigned to clients. Sit outside your conference room and listen for indications that conversations can be overheard. Conduct conversations with earplugs that deaden, but do not eliminate sound. Ask the other person to try the techniques listed above in various ways and settings to see how they work from the perspective of the listener with diminished hearing capacity.

Accommodating our clients' diminished hearing capacity is generally not difficult if we make ourselves aware of it and implement reasonable steps in response to it. It helps not only the client but the entire legal team. Effective and efficient communication among the members of the team is essential in order for any member of the team to be able to perform at his or her best. Increasing the chances that the client will hear and understand your communications, regardless of the age of the client, will make the performance of the legal team easier and better.

Vision Loss

Vision loss follows a similar, although not identical, path as hearing loss. They can occur together, but frequently do not. It does appear that the effects

---

2. Modified from information contained in Hooyman and Kiyak, *supra* n.1 at 100.

of vision loss are more readily apparent at younger ages than the effects of hearing loss. This may be simply because people are more likely to wear eyeglasses than hearing aids, and glasses are more visible than hearing aids. Regardless of the reason, the easiest way to accommodate for much vision loss is to compensate with eyeglasses.

Not all vision changes are solved with eyeglasses. You should be aware that as they age, clients may have particular difficulty in low-light conditions, conditions that create glare, or in conditions where the available light changes. For example, older people may need three times more light than younger persons under the same conditions.[3] They may have more difficulty in shifting focus say from a document in their hands to an exhibit on an easel close to the jury or to the face of a speaker across the conference room table. People developing cataracts may experience cloudy or fuzzy vision, double vision, problems with glare, and problems with color discrimination.

Most of these changes affect the client's ability to see what we may need them to see during our activities with them. Others contribute to problems with mobility. In addition to the other physical restrictions we will discuss in the next section, many older people experience difficulty with depth and distance perception as well as narrowing peripheral vision. These changes in vision affect the ability of the client to navigate our offices, courthouses, and hearing rooms. We will discuss some ways to accommodate these changes in the section of decreased mobility, as the methods are often the same.

These changes in vision may also affect a client's ability to drive. This can become a legal issue in terms of their retention of a driver's license, but it is also an issue in terms of the client getting to our office or a hearing, requiring us to assist them in arriving where they need to be when they need to be there.

The most obvious solution here is large print. Even if the contract, deed, or other document that must be signed is on a required form with small print, enlarge a copy so that it can be read by the client before the original is signed. Enlarge not only the documents you need them to read, but diagrams and charts. Be particularly mindful of using large print on instructions and other written materials the client will be taking home. Place large print editions of magazines in your waiting room. But enlarging print is not the only step you can take. Use paper and lighting that reduces glare. Increase contrast on documents, charts and diagrams. Keep a magnifying glass available for review of documents that cannot be enlarged.

---

3. *Id.* at 91.

Also be mindful of the environment in which the client is doing the reading. Provide a place with sufficient, non-glare lighting. Provide indirect lighting such as reading lamps rather than relying on overhead lighting, especially florescent lighting. Reduce glare from the sun coming through windows by installation of blinds or light filtering covers.

Again, place yourself, to the extent possible in the position of the client. Check glare and lighting not from where you normally sit or the attorney normally sits, but from the seat or seats most normally occupied by clients. If you are aware a client has diminished vision, review each document, exhibit, diagram, and the like you will be showing the client to determine its ability to be seen by those with diminished vision, rather than from the perspective of a person who still has full vision.

Mobility Loss

Many aging changes make it difficult to move whether the movement is full body motion or difficulty in holding a pen or typing on a keyboard due to stiffness in the hands. Some of the changes are "normal" in that they are part of the aging process itself. Others are by-products of age-related diseases. For example, as part of the normal aging process people can lose as much as three inches of height due to curving of the spine and disc compaction that is part of the normal aging process. Bone mass loss caused by osteoporosis also contributes to reduced height, but osteoporosis is a disease rather than a part of the normal aging process. Joints become stiff due to normal thinning of the cartilage between joints and also because of diseases such as arthritis.

As legal professionals we are less concerned with the causes of these changes than we are in noting the changes, understanding the effects of the changes, and considering ways to accommodate those effects. Frequently, the effects brought on by muscle, joint, or skeletal changes are heightened by changes in vision and other problems. For example, changes to the ear can affect balance and the ability to locate oneself in space. These factors are heightened by changes in the nervous system and in vision. All of this can lead to dizziness, vertigo, and fear of falling. To compensate, many people move with more slowly, shuffle and take more deliberate steps. This can occur even if stiffness or other muscle, joint, or skeletal changes do not reinforce such actions.

The important thing to keep in mind here is that elder clients may need more time to do what younger folks do quickly and smoothly. They are *not* slow because they want to be, but because they *have* to be. The solution here is *not* to hurry them, but to *allow the time necessary* for them to move.

Here, at least as much as with vision and hearing, it is helpful to place yourself in the position of the client. Borrow a walker and attempt to navigate from the parking lot into the conference room. How difficult are the steps? Is there sufficient room between furniture for the walker? Are rugs secured so that shuffling feet and the walker do not catch on the edges? Are electrical cords out of the way and secured so they will stay that way? Is there sufficient lighting so that the client can see to navigate?

Again, gerontologists can provide useful advice. Here are some environmental modifications they suggest:

- Place contrasting color strips on stairs, especially on carpeted or slippery linoleum stairs. This aids with depth perception.
- Use color to show changes in elevation especially doorway transoms.
- Clearly mark changes in floor surfaces such as door sills.
- Increase non-glaring light sources.
- Install nonslip and non-glossy floor coverings.
- Use flat paint instead of glossy finishes to reduce glare.
- Install blinds or light filtering covers to reduce glare through windows.
- Use indirect lighting or task lighting rather than ceiling fixtures.[4]

Remember that all observations should be made from the point of view of the elder client rather than from our point of view. Perhaps the best example of this is the often noted problem of reception area seating. Law offices tend to provide seating that gives the impression of luxury—soft, cushy, well-padded, and preferably leather. One attorney I know commented after a trip to his doctor on how hard the chairs were in his doctor's office, suggesting that at the rates the doctor charged she might provide more comfortable chairs for her patients. The fact is, however, that the doctor was providing chairs comfortable for her clients. Here's how Tim, a paralegal commenting on my blog put it:

> Early on in my career an attorney astutely pointed out a basic necessity for elderly clients visiting the office is to be able to find comfortable seating. Reception areas can be filled with low, deep seating making it difficult for an older person to easily stand up. There should be straight backed chairs available in the area. Wheeled, swivel chairs

---

4. Adapted from Hooyman and Kiyak, *supra* n.1 at 395.

around conference tables may need to be held firmly while a person seats themselves, particularly if they use a cane or other walking aid.

The need to make these observations does not end at the interior of the office. The next time you come in to work, come in as if you were an elderly client. Would you travel the same route if your vision, reaction time, and mobility were that of many elderly clients? Are there alternate routes that should be provided when giving directions to clients? Is there parking from which the office can be accessed by such clients? Are pathways wide, clear, non-slippery, and well marked? If there is an elevator as well as stairs, is it well-marked? Are snow and ice removed quickly and completely? Are there handrails?

Not all deficiencies can be removed, but they most definitely will not be removed or minimized if they are not recognized and identified as deficiencies. As with all other aspects of their professional life, the empowered paralegal will (1) take stock (analyze the situation), (2) identify problems, (3) research the information necessary to understand the problems, (4) identify and prioritize possible solutions, (5) create plans for correcting or managing those aspects of the problems that they have the ability to correct or manage, and (6) implement (or approach their attorney about implementing) those plans.

Finally, keep in mind that the difficulties we have reviewed here, and those we will review in the following sections, affect the client at home as well as in the office. Many elderly clients will need you to accommodate them at home even if you never enter their home. Provide letters and documents in larger, high-contrast print on non-glare paper. Allow more lead time for items needing responses such as answers to interrogatories. Let the phone ring a few more times before assuming they are not home. Remember, the clients are part of the legal team. Accommodating them is not *just* a matter of courtesy or good public relations. It is a matter of maximizing the potential of that legal team and obtaining the best possible results. It is what professionals do.

With regard to mobility, vision loss, loss of balance, and the like, accommodating the client is even more—it is a matter of health and safety for the client. Elder clients are much more at risk for falls than other clients, and they are much more at risk for serious injury from falls.

C. Psychological Effects of Aging on the Elder Client

Physical and psychological aspects of aging are intertwined. Many of the psychological effects are linked to physical changes such as those we have already discussed. But hearing, sight, and mobility loss can also have psychological effects. As previously discussed it is often difficult to separate changes that are a normal part of aging from problems that are related to specific disorders.[5] At this point I will be discussing primarily those effects which arise from the aging process itself. In another section I will deal with the effects of a specific type of disorder—dementia.

Let us conceptualize there being two types of psychological effects from aging. One is more directly related to physical changes and the other is related to the stage of life, although they may also relate in a broader way to the need to adjust to physical changes. The former includes effects on learning, memory, attention, and understanding. The latter consists of loss of self-identity, depression, disorientation, and the like. Each of them affects the elderly *as clients* and, therefore, requires that legal professionals gain some understanding of them.

Learning, Memory, Attention, and Understanding

For most clients, each legal experience is a new experience. Certainly some clients will have reason for repeated experiences with a particular legal proceeding. Real estate agents, for example, become quite familiar and comfortable with real estate closings, corporate chief financial officers with SEC compliance procedures, and tax preparers with IRS statutes, rules, and hearings. However, each of these clients will find any legal experience outside their realm strange. Each brings with it its own set of rules and jargon, much of which can have the feel of a foreign language.

Thus, in order for the client to become a fully functional member of the legal team, we must to some degree teach them and they must learn. At the very least we, like the medical profession, have a responsibility to ensure that our clients make fully informed decisions. The general obligation to make sure our clients have the capacity to even make fully informed decisions takes on more significance with regard to elderly clients.

In *The Empowered Paralegal: Effective, Efficient and Professional* we discussed at length various learning styles and some of the more common barriers to communication. All of that discussion applies, of course, to elder clients. With elder clients, however, there are additional considerations stemming from

---

5. "For example, tinnitus is a condition in which noise is experienced in the absence of auditory stimulation—ringing, buzzing, whining, voices, or even loud music. This can lead to considerable psychological upset." D.B. Bromley, *Behavioural Gerontology: Central Issues in the Psychology of Aging* 19 (Wiley, 1990).

changes that occur in one's ability to learn resulting from changes in one's memory, ability to pay attention, and ability to understand what occurs during the normal aging process.

As with the strictly physical changes, there is not one clear path on which one travels through the aging process. When discussing the concept of capacity in my classes, there are always two or three students who can relate stories of a grandparent, great-grandparent or other aged relative who, like my client Louisa Mae, retains a remarkable quickness of mind with seemingly undiminished capacity to learn, analyze, and retain information. My own grandmother seemed to lose little of her mental agility as her eyesight and mobility decreased in the decade prior to her death at the age of 94! Yet it is a fact that the normal course is for us to experience changes, usually in the nature of diminished capacity, in our ability to learn, memorize, attend, and understand as we age.

Memory

Perhaps the most well known of these changes relates to memory. Simply put, as we age we tend to forget things. More than when we were younger, we forget, at least momentarily, the first name of a distant relative and eventually of a close friend. We misplace our keys. We go from one room to another only to realize we cannot remember why we decided to leave the one room to go to the other. Such lapses of memory are normal for everyone, and increases in such lapses are a normal part of aging. They are different than the memory difficulties associated with Alzheimer's, a disease associated with aging that we will discuss in another section.

Changes in memory, especially when taken in combination with other changes experienced as we age, affect a person's ability to learn, i.e., his ability to assimilate new information. Since a paralegal's job frequently involves the communication of new information to a client, it is important to understand and accommodate those changes.

Let us begin by taking a look at the process by which information is processed. Scientists have several theories or models for that showing how this process works. For our purposes we will use a fairly simple model. It is not intended as a scientific explication of what is happening in a person's brain, but rather as a way of looking at the process that helps us to understand it.

1. First, information is presented to and taken in by a person through one of the senses. To the extent that the information can be presented in a way that eases assimilation by the client, we improve the chances that it will ultimately be understood and learned by the client. Many of the barri-

ers to communication itself are discussed in *The Empowered Paralegal: Effective, Efficient and Professional.* In the last section we discussed methods of accommodating changes in our clients' senses that make it easier for them to take the information in. To the extent we make it easier for our clients to see and hear the information, we also ease the first step in information processing.

2. Second, the information passes through "sensory memory." It does not stay there long—only a few tenths of a second. The little research that exists indicates that there is not a significant change in this form of memory as we age,[6] so we will not spend time discussing it here.

3. Next, the information passes through another temporary memory stage known as primary or working memory. Again, the information is stored here for a very short period of time, but long enough for it to be organized and for us to "work" with it for a limited amount of time. The work consists of the information being processed for further storage. This memory has to decide what needs to be stored and where to store it. The primary danger here is distraction. If we are distracted while the information is in this stage, we tend to forget it as it is replaced by the distracting information before it can be organized and stored. We discussed earlier the need for and methods of reduction of distractions.

    There is a second difficulty at this stage. It is believed older people process information more slowly than younger people. (Because of increased experience and practice, they may process it better than younger people, especially the very young who have not yet gained the ability to apply judgment to the information they process.) This is true in two respects. First, there may be an increase in the time needed to react and respond to the information. Second, the organizational processing that takes place may be slower, allowing less information processing while the information is in this stage of memory. Finally, it may take longer for an elderly client to filter out irrelevant information, for example, noises coming from the hallway.

    There are a number of things we can do to prevent problems at this stage in addition to reducing distractions. Avoid information overload. Present information in a well-organized way. Present information in several different ways. Use imagery (demonstrative aids) and mnemonics.

4. Finally, the information is stored in secondary memory. Do not view this storage in terms of a physical location that can become overloaded.

---

6. *Id.* at 173.

There is generally not a problem with storage capacity. Rather the problems that arise are related to the ability to process and retrieve information from secondary memory where it is permanently stored. To a degree this depends on how well the information was organized and encoded while in the working memory. Retrieving information from storage requires both the ability to recall it, i.e., to search through all the information in storage to obtain the information, and recognition, the ability to match stored information with current information.

There are a number of theories about why older people have more difficulty with information retrieval. Some scientists prefer the theory that information is lost through disuse; others focus on likely interference that occurred during the processing phases. We are less concerned with the reasons for the difficulty than we are with what can be done to accommodate the increased difficulty in retrieving information.

As discussed above, many of the retrieval problems can be reduced by making accommodations at the initial stages of information processing. The use of visual aids and mnemonics while delivering information can be reinforced through the use of similar aids once the information has been processed.

Provide the client with lists and checklists. Organize the lists by topic. Provide information in a form that can easily be transferred to calendars and other records used by clients to prompt recall. This can be as simple as a card that has the date and time of their next appointment or court appearance. At the university where I teach, student calendars come with a set of stickers that say things like "test" and "paper due." Similar stickers would be helpful to any forgetful client.

Follow up with the client. Call to remind them of appointments and deadlines for tasks. During these calls check to see if they have remembered the important points of the information presented to them earlier. Reinforce that information if it is recalled; repeat it if it is not.

There are certain things we ought not to do. While we never want to speak exceptionally quickly when addressing any client, neither do we want to speak artificially slowly in a manner that appears demeaning or patronizing. Our efforts to accommodate the client in this respect should be invisible—the client should not be aware that efforts are being made. They will note, unconsciously or consciously, the results of those efforts and appreciate them, but not if it is done in a way that emphasizes the need for those efforts. As we will discuss in a later section, older individuals are frequently struggling to maintain a self-concept. Emphasizing lessening memory, especially for those who are fearful of Alzheimer's or dementia, adds significantly to this struggle.

Attention

As discussed above, a good deal of a person's ability to learn information is dependent on how well it was processed. This can often depend on the client's ability to "pay attention" to the information. Gerontologists group several abilities under the title of attention. One is the ability to select needed information from all that is presented, and ignore the rest. There are some physical aspects to this, such as the decreased ability to filter sounds as previously discussed. However, there may also be a decrease in this ability associated with age. A second ability is the ability to attend to a specific source of information over time, e.g., to pay attention to a person delivering a long set of instructions. Finally there is the ability to determine how much attention to pay to one source of information and to move attention from one source to another. Each of these abilities shows some decline as one ages, particularly in complex situations.

In addition to clarifying the means by which information is presented to the client, e.g., reducing distractions, increasing fonts, reducing glare and the like, there are ways to increase the ability of the client to attend to important information. For example:

- Break complex tasks down into specific steps, a process I recommend for everyone, especially paralegals attempting to organize their time and work.
- Avoid speaking over another person. It is difficult for anyone to attend to a source of information if another person is delivering information at the same time.
- Do not speak to the client while they are attempting to read documents or review a demonstrative aid.
- Do not carry on a conversation with other people in the room when the client is speaking to someone or attempting to read documents or review a demonstrative aid.
- Prepare the client. As with other clients, the elderly client will be better able to attend to the significant aspects of an event if they understand the significance of the event. They should know in advance who the people will be at a meeting, mediation, or hearing, and what the role of each of those people will be. They should know in advance the likely order in which events will occur. It would be helpful if they can visit the hearing

room or meeting room in advance. Familiarity will diminish distraction by the unfamiliar.

- Minimize anxiety caused by time constraints. Be aware that elder clients may take longer to complete a task than other clients. Assist them, but do not pressure them.

Understanding

The ability to learn information is not the same as the ability to understand it. Certainly understanding requires that the information be learned first. Ultimately, the attorney and you are responsible for knowing each client well enough to understand how best to not only communicate *with* the client but to communicate an understanding of the essentials *to* that client. In *The Empowered Paralegal: Effective, Efficient and Professional* we discussed many of the obstacles or barriers that can prevent understanding, so they will simply be listed here rather than fully discussed. They include differences in linguistics, culture, learning, reaction to conflict, and needs.

Each of the barriers has a particular application to the elderly. For example, each generation coins its own jargon. Sometimes a word will have a different meaning to an elderly client than it does to a young paralegal or lawyer. Many times the elderly will simply be unfamiliar with social, cultural, or technological idioms that are part of everyday communications between members of Gen X.

Often, elderly clients are first or second generation immigrants still deeply imbedded in their home culture. When representing clients in personal injury cases, it was not unusual for me to find that clients from Middle Eastern cultures had a vastly different perspective on negotiations than that of eastern Europeans, and both of these were different from the perspective of western Europeans. We will discuss some of the cultural differences relating to death, dying, and end-of-life decisions in later chapters.

To these barriers, we must add those discussed in this chapter—changes in vision, hearing, memory and the like. In the end, the obligation of an empowered paralegal is to understand those barriers and implement plans to manage them. Do not assume understanding.

The Psychology of Aging and Social Issues

The fact that our population is aging has significant social effects and raises many policy issues. We will leave policy discussion to the scientists and politicians. Our task is to take the end product, i.e., the laws that affect the elderly, and apply them to the best interest of our clients. Here, I will be discussing the social effects of the psychology of aging as they may affect our particular clients. The purpose, as always, is to gain a better understanding of our clients so that we can better manage our relationship with them, better integrate them into the legal team, and better serve their interests.

Heim's Contradictions

Understanding the psychology of growing old is made more difficult by the fact that aging appears to have contradictory effects on individuals as they age. According to Robert Slater writing in *The Psychology of Growing Old*,[7] psychologist Alice Heim noted nine such apparent contradictions:

1. Self-confidence can both grow and shrink. For example, as we age we have less confidence especially in our physical capacity which is likely to be directly related to the fact that our physical capacities are indeed decreasing or, at least, we see decreased capacity in our contemporaries. On the other hand according to Heim, social and mental confidence increases;

2. Individuals can have a sense that things matter less as they have seen so much come and go. However, the sense that there is little time left can make an elderly person feel the emotional impact of events even more;

3. Some people adopt a resigned or welcoming approach to death, while others will view it with increased apprehension;

4. Age may increase tolerance or increase irritability and rigidity. It is likely you have seen both elderly persons who seem to be able to withstand the noise and chaos of children better than the children's own parents and elderly persons who seem irritated at the slightest disturbance by the neighborhood youth like Mr. Wilson of the *Dennis the Menace* comic strip;

5. The next contradiction more specifically involves young people. Some people seem better able to understand the lack of interest young people have in hanging around with the geezers and take great delight in those instances when their advice is sought by those younger than they or when the young exhibit other signs of respect. Others, perhaps believing that their age entitles them to constant displays of respect, grow quite indignant at any less;

6. For some the generation gap widens, but other elders have better relationships with children and teenagers than they had at any other time;

---

7. Robert Slater, *The Psychology of Growing Old* (Open University Press 29–32, 1995).

7. Some express contentment at being able to fall asleep, while others express annoyance at dropping off;

8. Some accept and adapt to the need to handle declining memory. They write stuff down to help. Others deny the need and resist suggestions on how to handle it; and

9. Some look at the world as it now exists and see societal improvement, while others look back nostalgically and insist that society is not what it used to be.

Of course in most of these respects no individual is all on one extreme or the other, but will from time to time move from one end of the spectrum to the other. Perhaps, the most important point to take from this list of "contradictions" that occur as we age is the realization that the aging population, like the rest of the population, is diverse. While it is clear that aging does change our perspectives, there is no one way—and certainly no "right" way—in which this occurs. Legal professionals must keep this in mind as they deal with the elderly client and refrain from judging the client perspective or the manner in which the client copes with the changes that come with aging.

Coping

"Life is change. How it differs from the rocks."[8] And the changes that occur as we age are significant. They include the physical and psychological changes already discussed. These changes cause changes in lifestyle and social interaction which in turn cause more psychological changes. For example, as people become slower and more frail, their world, to coin a phrase, becomes smaller. They go out less to social activities. As friends and family of their generation die, their social circle may tend to constantly constrict. Thus, as a person becomes more dependent on others, there may be fewer others on whom they can depend. This makes the elderly more susceptible to abuse and neglect by those on whom they depend.

Poor vision and mobility can make even small tasks into time consuming chores. Crossing roads becomes increasingly dangerous. In general, actions that we take, and the elderly previously took for granted become enormous challenges. Daily life is simply different, and often more difficult, for the elderly. We need to be sensitive not only to this fact, but to the likely psychological impact this fact has on our clients.

---

8. I know these lyrics from *Crown of Creation* by the Jefferson Airplane, but the song's lyrics were apparently taken with permission from "The Chrysalids" by John Wyndham (1955) and set to music by the Jefferson Airplane.

The Empowered Paralegal: Effective, Efficient and Professional explored the benefits of understanding the various ways clients learn, communicate, and deal with conflict. To this list we now should add the understanding of the ways that clients cope with life changes, particularly those changes that come with advanced age. In essence the methods and manner of coping for the elderly and the young are the same. However, the utilization of those methods can depend on the physical, cognitive, and psychological resources upon which the client can draw, as well as external resources such as family and finances. As these resources decline, especially the physical, coping by doing, i.e., by "realizing there is a problem to be tackled, analyzing the problem and bringing information and ideas to bear on formulating a solution; acting on those ideas, assessing the outcome, and modifying actions accordingly,"[9] is likely to decline. As a correlation, coping by denial and avoidance is likely to increase.

Again, we should take pains not to stereotype. Individuals vary in how they cope with the changes that come with age. Slater warns against holding "a simplistic notion that most older people cope with all their problems in a similar way, a way different to that of younger people." Rather, "[T]here are situation —as well as person—specific response patterns to stress in later life."[10] Indeed, each individual may have a different way of coping with problems that relate to different areas of their life, sometimes referred to as "domains:" housing, health, income, and family. At the same time, one study found that "older people were fairly consistent over a 15-year span in their response patterns to problems within the same domain."[11]

Legal professionals need not have, and probably should not have, a comprehensive scientific understanding of coping mechanisms. We should know enough, however, to identify how our clients cope, realizing that we are not likely to change coping methods that are long engrained (and should not be involved in attempting to do so even if we could). Our goal is to assist the client in coping with the legal issues that they bring to us or become apparent to us while we work for them. This can best be done if we understand and work within the parameters of the methods used by our clients. This, at least, recognizes them as individuals. It also allows us to work with rather than against our clients in coping with the stress of dealing with legal problems.

We can support our clients where appropriate and take reasonable measures to compensate when necessary by putting into place mechanisms to deal

---

9. Slater, *supra* n.7 at 46. This is an excellent rendition of the approach I advocate for paralegal empowerment.

10. *Id.* at 47.

11. *Id.*

with, for example, a client who copes with a particular legal issue through avoidance. It makes little sense to apply the same methods to every client. Some will be capable of following up on tasks on their own with little support; some will need reminders and assistance, and some will need us to perform the tasks for them. Those that can and will actively cope may resent being treated as if they can or will not. I am reminded of the old Jack Benny comedy skits of the Boy Scout helping an elderly person across the street as that person beats the Boy Scout with his cane because he does not want the help—and may not even want to cross the street!

One's ability to cope is not just the result of psychological factors, but a cause of psychological wellness or the lack of that wellness. As mentioned above, one aspect of aging may be a loss of independence. In general, the elderly can struggle with the sense of control that comes with diminished capacities, ill-health, the loss of the social status that came with being employed, and a shrinking world. As they become more dependent on others, they feel less in control. Some psychologists who study the elderly have concluded that the lessening of the sense of control does not have a substantial effect on coping strategies. However, those studying elderly in institutions report that "In institutions, incompetence, helplessness and sick role behavior may be reinforced"[12] leading to a learned helplessness. Again, our role is not to diagnose or otherwise act in the capacity of a psychologist or other medical professional. Rather, we should be aware of what may be happening with and to our clients as we work with them as part of the legal team.

One aspect of our role is to understand that an inability to cope is likely to result in a sense of undermined autonomy and individuality, and may give rise to symptoms of anxiety or depression.[13] Anxiety and depression can seriously affect our clients' ability to cope with and respond to their role as part of the legal team. We should consider these factors as causes for client behavior, and respond accordingly. Lecturing a client who is not meeting deadlines due to anxiety or depression will only make the problem worse. Instead, without judging we must manage the client through understanding the source of the failure and addressing it, perhaps through additional assistance from our office, perhaps by arranging assistance from outside sources, or perhaps by altering the task itself. If we are to do the best that can be done for the client then we must cope with the coping methods (and the effects of those methods) utilized by our clients.

---

12. *Id.* at 49.
13. *Id.* at 50.

Attendants/Helpers

Given the discussion so far in this chapter, it is not surprising that elderly clients often arrive at the office with someone who is helping them, most often a member of their family. This, of course, should be encouraged rather than discouraged. However, it can be the source of some difficulties for the legal team.

Confidentiality

The attorney/client privilege extends to agents of the attorney and the client. This only makes sense given the purpose of the privilege which is to encourage full disclosure without fear that the information will be revealed to others, so that clients receive the best and most competent legal advice and representation. We tend to think of this extension most often in terms of the attorney's staff—paralegals, secretaries, investigators and others who assist the attorney in providing the advice and representation. However, it applies also to the agents of the client who assist in the communication. This is most obvious in the case of corporate clients since all communication with corporations must be done through one or more of their agents.

We should take care to protect the attorney/client privilege when the client is assisted by another person during communications between the attorney and the client. While we understand the workings of the privilege, many clients and the assistant will not. Like so many other aspects of the legal process, we should take the time to explain at least the basics to both the client and their agent. In this case the basics consist of the fact that for purposes of the communications that occur between the attorney and the client or the agent on the client's behalf, the third party is indeed the agent of the client. *Both the agent and client should understand and acknowledge the fact of the agency prior to the communications taking place.*

First, the client should clearly understand that there is no way to pre-screen statements made in front of the agent, so if there is any topic that the client does not want mentioned, the client should let the attorney and/or paralegal know in private. The logistics of this can be difficult, as once the two are in the room it can be difficult and embarrassing for the client to ask that the agent leave. As discussed more fully in the next sub-section, I most often handled this by making it a general rule to ask the agent to leave at the very beginning of the meeting. I explain to both the client and the agent that I do this as a matter of policy so I can document the file for the benefit of all concerned, not because of anything related to their particular circumstances.

During my experience representing attorneys against whom ethics complaints had been brought, I became aware of several instances where failure to establish such a procedure resulted in the filing of complaints. In one such instance, the client came in to discuss settlement of a personal injury claim. Of course, this required the attorney to assess both the strengths and weaknesses of the case. One weakness was certain aspects of the client's past medical history that related to alcohol and drug abuse. The client had not been aware going into the conversation that this topic would come up and was quite upset that the agent had been informed. This problem could have been avoided if the agent had been asked to leave the room long enough for the attorney to outline the upcoming discussion.

Second, the agent should be aware of his or her obligation to maintain the confidentiality that underpins the attorney-client privilege. Many people do not understand just how important the confidentiality obligation is or how deep it runs. They must be made to understand that they cannot go home and discuss what they heard at the meeting with other members of the client's family, with their own family, their drinking buddies or their co-workers—even if they change the names and other information to protect identities.

I generally handle this by having both the client and the agent sign a Confidentiality Acknowledgement. This is a simple document written in terms the client and the agent can understand. Like any form, it should be adjusted for the particular practice and circumstances.

CONFIDENTIALITY ACKNOWLEDGEMENT

_____ (Agent) agrees to act as agent for _____ (Client) for purposes of helping communication between Client and his/her attorney and that attorney's staff only.

Client agrees that Agent is authorized to act as his/her agent for purposes of helping communication between Client and his/her attorney and that attorney's staff only.

Client understands this means that Agent will hear information that would otherwise be kept confidential between Client and the attorney and the attorney's staff. Since it is not possible to identify all the topics that might be covered in advance, Client understands that this could result in Agent hearing information not expected by Client.

Agent understands that he or she must keep everything he or she hears from the attorney or Client while acting as Client's agent absolutely confidential. He or she cannot repeat it to other members of

> Client's family, Agent's family, or any other person without the express permission of Client.

While this form will provide some protection in the event the client does file a complaint for breach of confidentiality, the goal of using it is primarily educational. It will help both the client and the agent focus on the status of their relationship in terms that they can understand for purposes we understand. This helps integrate all concerned into the legal team. Such integration facilitates the purposes of the legal team while minimizing the chances of complaints.

Undue Influence Issues

A second difficulty caused when an elderly client is assisted to a law office is the possibility of undue influence being asserted by the helper on the client. The potential for undue influence is inherent in the very relationship that brings the two to the office together. This is true even if the two are not related by blood or marriage. The relationship with which we are concerned is the dependence relationship of the elderly person on the helper that is implied by the very fact that the elderly person needs the assistance provided by the helper.

The legal professional has an obligation to the client to be aware of the signs of undue influence and other elder abuse. This will be discussed more extensively in the chapters dealing with an elder client's family and elder abuse. In this context the paralegal can be especially helpful to the attorney as a "second set of eyes." Both the attorney and the paralegal should watch for signs that the helper is dominating the client, rather than assisting the client. These signs include:

- The helper speaks for the client;
- The client repeatedly asks the helper to answer a question for him or her;
- The client consistently looks to the helper before answering a question;
- The client stops or changes an answer after the helper looks at, touches, or makes a movement towards the client;
- The helper frequently corrects the client's answers;
- The helper refuses or is reluctant to allow the client to speak privately with the attorney or paralegal;
- The client appears confused or influenced by medication or alcohol.

None of these signs is definitive. Many elderly clients are confused; need help remembering, and the like. However, a legal professional should proceed with caution when these signs appear.

As stated above, it is my general practice to insist upon meeting separately with the client in any situation where there may be a conflict between my client and the person with the client. I apply this policy to parent/child and husband/wife situations as well as elder client situations. However, I do tend to emphasize it more in cases involving elderly clients, especially when a child is bringing in a parent to prepare a will, create a trust, or transfer property.

Generally, the logistics of this can be delicate as once the two are in the room it can be difficult and embarrassing for the client to ask that the agent leave. I handled this by taking the responsibility. I explain that it is my rule to ask the other person to leave at the very beginning of the meeting *before* there is any substantive discussion. I explain to both the client and the other person that I do this as a matter of policy so I can document the file for the benefit of all concerned, not because of anything related to their particular circumstances. The important thing from my perspective is (1) not to insult either the agent or the client by suggesting that the agent may be taking advantage of the client or that the client is not capable of independent thought, and (2) make it clear that I am the person responsible for this request, not the client. If an abusive relationship does exist, we do not want the abuser to blame the abused for this challenge to their dominance over the abused.

Once the other person is out of the room I look for changes in demeanor on the part of my client, ask questions intended only to determine competency, and inquire about the client's relationship with the other person. Generally, the actual answers to the questions are not important. I am more interested in the client's reactions, demeanor, and the way they respond.

D. Diseases and Disorders

Thus far we have been discussing changes that occur in the natural progression of aging—changes in vision, hearing, mobility, memory, information processing, and coping. These are normal and happen to some extent to all of us as we grow older. There are, in addition, a number of diseases and disorders which are not part of the normal aging process and, although they are not limited to the elderly, affect the elderly more often and/or more severely than they do people at other stages of life. In their early stages, many of these diseases and disorders mimic normal aging processes. This can cause anxiety as a person wonders, for example, whether forgetting where they placed their keys is an early sign of Alzheimer's or muscle weakness is a symptom of Parkinson's Disease.

Some of these diseases and disorders are physical and some psychological. It is useful for the paralegal to have a basic understanding of the more common diseases and disorders so that they better understand the lives of their clients afflicted with them, how they may affect the clients' ability to respond to legal processes and demands, and how the paralegal can adjust accommodations to best suit each client. It also helps us better understands the demands placed upon the family of our clients, particularly those involved in caring for the client.

More important, perhaps, is understanding those diseases and disorders which may affect the client's ability to exercise competent, independent judgment in the course of their financial and legal affairs. This enables the paralegal to assist the attorney in (1) documenting the file to show competency when it exists, (2) taking appropriate measures to protect clients when they are not competent, and (3) responding appropriately to instances of elder abuse and neglect.

Common Physical Diseases

Parkinson's Disease

Parkinson's disease is a chronic, degenerative nerve disease, and it is fairly common. According to the National Parkinson Foundation, about a half million people are affected each year, most commonly around the age of 60. Its symptoms, which can be treated with medication, include tremors, muscular rigidity (stiffness or inflexibility of a limb), slowness of voluntary movement and speech (bradykinesia), slowness in facial expressions, slowness in speech, and difficulty swallowing. It may be accompanied by depression, anxiety, dementia, and cognitive impairment. The tremors usually start in a hand or arm, but can occur in the legs or jaw. They occur primarily when the limb is at rest, but stop when the person is asleep.

We should be aware that these symptoms have real life effects. The slowness in voluntary movement results in a shuffled gait. The client may have a diminished sense of balance, making it all the more necessary for us to have clear travel lanes. Slow speech, especially if it is monotonous or monotonic, can be difficult to listen to attentively. The difficulty in swallowing can make the client drool. The slowness or stiffness in facial expressions, sometimes referred to as "poker face," diminishes expression; this should not be interpreted as a lack of emotion.

Additional information regarding Parkinson's disease is available through the National Parkinson Foundation's website: www.parkinson.org.

Stroke

A stroke occurs when the brain suddenly experiences an interruption in normal function as a result of a blockage or rupture of a blood vessel carrying oxygen and nutrients to the brain. The blockage may be the result of a blood clot, cholesterol, or plaque. According to the National Stroke Association, strokes are preventable but at present are the third leading cause of death and a leading cause of adult disability. Since strokes result from cardiovascular disease, they can be prevented by medications and maintaining good health through proper diet and regular exercise. Unfortunately, many elderly clients have diminished financial and physical capacity, making such steps more difficult. Of course, it appears that, overall, Americans are becoming less and less willing to maintain healthy weight, exercise, and eating habits even when they have full capacity!

The effects of a stroke depend on where in the brain the stroke occurs and how much damage is done to the brain. The damage itself is not recoverable—dead brain cells are not revived or replaced. As a result, about two-thirds of victims never recover to the point where there are no noticeable symptoms. When brain cells die during a stroke, abilities controlled by that area of the brain are lost. The most likely noticeable effects will be in the areas of speech, movement, and memory, heightening the need for the accommodations previously discussed.

Additional information regarding strokes is available through the National Stroke Association's website: www.stroke.org.

Diabetes

There are two types of diabetes. Type 1 is usually diagnosed when the patient is a child and was previously known as "juvenile diabetes." Only 5–10% of people with diabetes have this form of the disease. Type 2 diabetes is much more common. According to the American Diabetes Association, 23.6 million people in the United States, or 7.8% of the population, have diabetes. Diabetes is more common among segments of the non-Caucasian population and more common among the aged, making it a concern for us.

In type 2 diabetes, either the body does not produce enough insulin or the cells ignore the insulin. Insulin is a hormone necessary for the body to be able to use glucose for energy. Normally the body breaks down all of the sugars and starches in the food we eat into glucose, which is the basic fuel for the cells in the body. Insulin takes the sugar from the blood into the cells. Without sufficient insulin, or if the cells ignore the insulin, the glucose builds up in the blood and it can lead to diabetes complications.

Diabetes complications vary and seem to correlate with one's group, e.g., Africa-American, Asian, seniors, etc. They include heart disease, neuropathy (nerve damage which can cause, for example, numbness in feet), glaucoma, cataracts, skin infections, blindness, kidney disease, and a host of other symptoms. Obviously the eye complications add to the need to accommodate vision loss previously discussed. Diabetes is also the leading cause of lower limb amputations, which can significantly affect the mobility of the client.

The risk of developing diabetes increases with age, with as much as 50% of diagnoses occurring in those aged 55 or older. According to the American Diabetes Association, approximately 18.3% (8.6 million) of Americans age 60 and older have diabetes. Age can cause a decline in insulin production as well as increased glucose intolerance.

According to dlife.com, a website devoted to assisting those who live with diabetes, seniors face unique diabetes management challenges. This site advised that older Americans are also more likely to have complicating conditions such as retinopathy, hypertension, and kidney problems.

Like stroke, diabetes is preventable through life-style changes. It is also controllable through life-style changes combined with proper medical care. However, as dlife.com notes, older clients may face barriers in managing the disease. These include factors we have previous discussed including:

- **Economic Barriers.** Seniors on a fixed income may skimp on appropriate diabetes care, medications, and proper nutrition.
- **Transportation.** Seniors who can no longer drive may have difficulty getting to medical appointments and keeping up with appropriate diabetes preventative care.
- **Mobility.** Conditions such as arthritis that are more prevalent with age can keep older adults from regular exercise. By age 75, approximately one in three men and half of all women are physically inactive.
- **Isolation.** Seniors may lack an adequate peer or family network for emotional and social support. They may be more apt to suffer from depression.[14]

These barriers, of course, confront seniors in every aspect of their lives.

Additional information regarding diabetes can be obtained from the American Diabetes Association at their website: www.diabetes.org.

Arthritis

There are also two major forms of arthritis,[15] rheumatoid and osteoarthritis. Both of these major forms create symptoms of joint pain and stiffness.

---

14. http://www.dlife.com/diabetes/information/daily_living/seniors/index.html (Last accessed, March 16, 2010).

15. WebMD states that there are over 100 types of arthritis! http://arthritis.webmd.com/ (Last accessed, March 16, 2010).

Rheumatoid arthritis is the inflammation of the joints, a chronic condition. It can lead to joint and bone destruction. The type of arthritis more commonly associated with the elderly is osteoarthritis, a degenerative joint disease. With osteoarthritis, a breakdown of cartilage in joints occurs in almost any joint in the body. It most commonly occurs in the weight-bearing joints of the hips, knees, and spine, but it can also affect the fingers, thumb, neck, and large toe. Cartilage, the firm, rubbery material that covers the ends of bones in normal joints reduces friction in the joints and serves as a "shock absorber." Osteoarthritis causes the cartilage in a joint to become stiff and lose its elasticity. The cartilage becomes damaged or wears away altogether, allowing the bones to rub against each other. It can be extremely painful and severely affect movement, increasing the need for us to accommodate decreased mobility in our clients.

Additional information regarding diabetes can be obtained from the Arthritis Foundation at its website: www.arthritis.org.

Other Diseases

The diseases discussed here by no means comprise a comprehensive list of the physical diseases that afflict the elderly, or afflict the elderly more often or more severely than the young. There are many others, but they do not so clearly correlate with aspects of a paralegal's job on a day-to-day basis. A partial list includes:

- Hypertension (High blood pressure)
- Cancer
- Pneumonia
- Chronic Bronchitis
- Emphysema
- Heart Disease
- Shingles
- Hemorrhoids

When we know that a particular client is afflicted with one of these diseases, it is good to make a quick review of the disease through a quick internet search of *reliable* sources. This will give us a frame of reference for comments made by the client, allow us to make intelligent remarks to the client (and avoid making unintelligent remarks), and place some of the conduct and needs of the client into context.

Falls

Sure, falls are not a disease. However, the many changes we have discussed here—changes in vision, mobility, and balance—together with the disabilities created by several of the diseases we have discussed here, create a high-risk of falls for the elderly. According to *American Family Physician,*

> The mortality rate for falls increases dramatically with age in both sexes and in all racial and ethnic groups, with falls accounting for 70 percent of accidental deaths in persons 75 years of age and older. Falls can be markers of poor health and declining function, and they are often associated with significant morbidity. More than 90 percent of hip fractures occur as a result of falls, with most of these fractures occurring in persons over 70 years of age. One third of community-dwelling elderly persons and 60 percent of nursing home residents fall each year. Risk factors for falls in the elderly include increasing age, medication use, cognitive impairment and sensory deficits.[16]

Hip factures especially tend to further diminish the physical capacity of the elderly which in turn decreases their independence and their social interaction. The elder client experiences loss of vision, loss of balance, dizziness, and/or confusion, and also becomes more conscious of the risk of falling and is thus more fearful. This alone makes them less likely to venture into the outside world.

Thus, as discussed previously, in this respect accommodating the client is not *just* a matter of courtesy or good public relations. It is not even *just* a matter of maximizing the potential of that legal team and obtaining the best possible results. It is what professionals do. It is a matter of health and safety for the client.

Common Psychological Disorders

Depending on the subject population and the categories of disorders examined, from 15% to 25% of the elder population living in the community are found to have psychological disorders.[17] These include mood disorders, dementia, paranoia, anxiety disorders, phobias, panic disorders, schizophrenia, and substance abuse. We will focus in this section on depression, paranoia, and dementia.

These disorders are of particular interest to legal professionals because of the impact they have on the issue of legal competency, which arises not only in terms of whether the client is in need of a conservatorship or guardianship,

---

16. Am. Fam. Physician 2000; 61:2159–68, 2173–4, cited at the American Family Physician website, http://www.aafp.org/afp/20000401/2159.html., (Last accessed March 16, 2010).

17. Hooyman and Kiyak, 214.

but whether he or she has the requisite competency to convey property, execute a will, or grant a power of attorney.

Depression

In today's world depression not the hidden disorder it once was. It is discussed around the dinner table and water cooler, and medications are advertised on TV. However, my experience has been that elderly people, having lived a large portion of their lives when the disorder carried a heavy stigma, remain reluctant to admit in a legal setting to having a problem with depression. Yet depression is the most common psychopathology afflicting the elderly.

There are several types or categories of depression. Psychologists distinguish between unipolar and bipolar depression, the latter characterized by mood swings from a depressed state to a manic state. Unipolar is most common. Major depression may also be secondary or reactive, arising from events which overwhelm the ability of a person to cope. There is also a less severe type of depression known as dysthymic disorder.

The factors conducive to depression in the elderly are many. According to the Mayo Clinic, depression is not a normal part of growing older, and most seniors feel satisfied with their lives.[18] However, the elderly also confront a loss of their sense of identity and self-worth that accompanies the loss of their roles as workers, providers, and caregivers, and the general loss of independence that comes with diminished physical and cognitive capacities, and general ill-health. Financial stress is often a major issue for the elderly. As discussed previously, their social world shrinks as they lose mobility and friends and family contemporaries die.

Unfortunately, depression often goes undiagnosed and untreated. Diagnosis can be confusing and complex. Most of the factors listed above can cause grief and sadness which can be misdiagnosed as depression. But the real problem, insofar as it leads to depression not being treated, is that so many of the symptoms, such as inability to sleep, fatigue, loss of appetite, and loss of interest in sex may be caused by other illnesses or may be under-reported by the patient. Other symptoms of depression such as a general loss of interest in life and daily activities can, at least initially, be confused with normal aging. Many adults with depression feel reluctant to seek help when they're feeling down.

The list of symptoms of depression is long. The Mayo Clinic provides this list:

---

18. Mayo Clinic.com, http://www.mayoclinic.com/health/depression/DS00175/DSECTION =symptoms, (Last accessed March 17, 2010).

- Feelings of sadness or unhappiness
- Irritability or frustration, even over small matters
- Loss of interest or pleasure in normal activities
- Reduced sex drive
- Insomnia or excessive sleeping
- Changes in appetite—depression often causes decreased appetite and weight loss, but in some people it causes increased cravings for food and weight gain
- Agitation or restlessness—for example, pacing, hand-wringing or an inability to sit still
- Slowed thinking, speaking or body movements
- Indecisiveness, distractibility and decreased concentration
- Fatigue, tiredness and loss of energy—even small tasks may seem to require a lot of effort
- Feelings of worthlessness or guilt, fixating on past failures or blaming yourself when things aren't going right
- Trouble thinking, concentrating, making decisions and remembering things
- Frequent thoughts of death, dying or suicide
- Crying spells for no apparent reason
- Unexplained physical problems, such as back pain or headaches[19]

It only takes a quick look at the list of symptoms to see how this disorder may affect the client's ability to act effectively as a member of the legal team. Some of the symptoms, such as fatigue, trouble thinking and concentrating and inability to sit still may directly interfere with the accomplishment of even the simplest tasks requested by the attorney or paralegal. Others such as indecisiveness and feelings of worthlessness or guilt can interfere with the client's ability to make necessary decisions or cause them to make decisions they would not make but for the depression.

Depression is generally treatable, but it is not the legal professional's role to attempt therapy or provide medication. Depressed clients should be referred to the appropriate medical practitioner, but care should be applied to the approach taken with the client when making such a recommendation. Be aware that the client who is denying even to himself that he has a problem may resent your interference. Also be aware that depression by its very nature may make the client unable to take steps necessary to obtain treatment.

---

19. *Id.*

What we can do is to be aware of the potential problem. A depressed client will need more assistance and guidance than a non-depressed client. Nagging or reprimanding a depressed client will be counterproductive. Do not suggest to the client that she needs to "get over it," "snap out of it," or "plow through and get this stuff done." Empathy and understanding are more likely to be helpful. This does not mean you need to "feed" the depression. It means understanding the problem and taking measures to compensate for it that do not degrade while perhaps reinforcing the client as an individual with value in his or her own right. It may also mean, subject to our obligation of confidentiality to the client, enlisting the support and assistance of the client's family or other support group.

Paranoia

Paranoia is a difficult topic to address in this context. It is, as you likely know, a disorder in which a person is very suspicious and distrustful of others. MedlinePlus, an informational website provided as a service of the National Library of Medicine and the National Institute of Health, describes the symptoms in this way:

> People with paranoid personality disorder are highly suspicious of other people. They are usually unable to acknowledge their own negative feelings towards other people.

Other common symptoms include:

- Concern that other people have hidden motives
- Expectation that they will be exploited by others
- Inability to work together with others
- Poor self image
- Social isolation
- Detachment
- Hostility[20]

There is also a type of lesser distrustful behavior that lacks the more psychotic persecutory elements of delusional paranoia. This type is called "functional paranoia" because it serves the function of reducing the sense of vulnerability that often accompanies the loss of independence and control experienced by the elderly. In essence, functional paranoia is a coping mechanism. However,

---

20. MedlinePlus, http://www.nlm.nih.gov/medlineplus/ency/article/000938.htm (Last accessed March 17, 2010).

the "distrust, suspiciousness, and blaming of others can take on an angry quality that certainly can be aggravating for others."[21]

A paranoid client is problematic for legal professionals in at least two respects, (1) they mistrust just about everyone, including the legal professionals who are attempting to help them, and (2) it is difficult to separate out the reality from the unreality of the information they provide. To a great extent the empowered paralegal will already be prepared for dealing with the first of these problems, because the paralegal will already be communicating fully with clients. When the client's paranoia is functional, full communication can empower the client and diminish their feelings of vulnerability. However, even though functional paranoia fulfills a rational purpose, the paranoia ideation itself is not rational; the definition of paranoia is irrational suspicion. You cannot expect someone for whom paranoia is a coping mechanism to suddenly stop the ideation simply because you are in fact very trustworthy and have only the client's best interests in mind.

Paranoia is subject to treatment. Counseling in which "an individual focuses on changing negative, self-defeating beliefs or misconceptions, may be useful in treating paranoid older adults who often attribute causality to external factors (e.g., the belief that someone took their pocketbook, that they themselves did not misplace it"[22]) may enable that individual to redirect those beliefs. However, we as legal professionals cannot make it our role to counsel or treat paranoia. Rather, we best perform our role when we understand the paranoid client and use that understanding to better work with the client.

Here are some suggestions for coping with the paranoid client:

- Do not take his mistrust personally.
- Keep the client fully informed on a consistent, regular basis.
- Speak and write in short, simple, and clear sentences to minimize misunderstanding and misinterpretation.
- While you must check fairly constantly the client's thoughts and statements against reality, do not constantly confront the client with that reality. Remember, the clients delusions *are* reality for them. Chose these "battles" wisely.
- At the same time that you let client statements and ideation pass without openly questioning them, do not indicate that you are accepting or "buying into" the client's paranoia. Be firm and respectful in protecting

---

21. Sheldon S. Tobin, *Preservation of the Self in the Oldest Years* 14 (Springer Publishing Company 1999).

22. Hooyman and Kiyak, *supra* n.1 at 235.

and projecting your own reality. (We are, of course, all hopeful that our reality is *the* reality, but be mindful that each of our realities is, at least, colored by our own biases, prejudices, and suspicions.) Do not see monsters under the bed just to keep the client happy.

- Be open to the client's discussion of her mistrust and suspicions. Let her know that she is free to voice them to you. Clarify misunderstandings about your actions or motivations in a non-defensive, non-judgmental way.
- Anticipate events that are likely to give rise to mistrust and suspicions. Explain proceedings and the role of the persons in them well in advance. For example, it is useful for any client to know that a mediator may be meeting with both sides of a dispute privately and that such meetings may not be equal in length, but this is essential information for a paranoid client.
- Focus on the client as a whole and as an individual. Do not focus on his symptoms.

The empowered paralegal is also well-equipped to separate out legally relevant portions of client reports from the legally irrelevant, and is likely to have considerable practice at separating fact from fiction in the client's rendition of her side of a case. Our client's reports to us are always colored by their particular perspective, biases, prejudices, desires, and motivations. Paranoid clients are an extreme form of this. However, they are more than just an extreme form of this phenomenon. Non-paranoid clients, unless they are simply lying, color reality, but do not irrationally misjudge it.

This is a problem for the legal professional because we must make our judgments and recommendations based on the facts. If our clients are showing signs of paranoia, we need to be ever more mindful of our obligation to verify the facts before taking action. Michael Nugent Moore, a paralegal and licensed private investigator located in Boston, commented on this topic in a NFPA LinkedIn discussion thread. He gives this example,

> While working as an investigative paralegal, I had a client who was a WWII vet. He believed that someone had stolen stock from him. His mind seemed sharp, but he had bouts of paranoia. I found numerous facts that contradicted his report of the situation and I was informed that paranoia is the initial manifestation of dementia. It was a real strain constantly trying sort out reality.

However, we must also avoid swinging too far in the other direction. There is tendency to discount or even ignore *everything* a paranoid client says, especially when they are making accusations against people who appear to us to be above such accusations. As we will discuss in Chapters Four and Nine, the sad fact is that all too often an elderly client's own children, and the nursing home personnel entrusted with the care of the elderly, do steal from, neglect, and abuse those for whom they are providing care. We cannot assume these problems are not occurring simply because the client displays signs of, or even has been diagnosed with, paranoia.

Finally, as is the case with depression discussed previously and dementia discussed in the next section, paranoia provides cause for concern regarding our client's competency. We will discuss this topic at length in Chapter Three.

Dementia

Dementia is a collection of diseases that involve a marked deterioration of cognitive function. The effects of these diseases go well beyond the loss of memory and other diminished capacities associated with aging and discussed in the previous section of this chapter. In each of these diseases there is a marked diminution in the client's ability to recall recent events together with significant problems with comprehension, attention span, and judgment, and with disorientation as to time, place, and person. Dementia is non-reversible and causes permanent brain damage.

The most common and most well-known form of dementia is Alzheimer's Disease. According to Hooyman and Kiyak, the best estimate is that about 2.3 million Americans (over 7 percent of all persons 65 or over) have clinical symptoms of Alzheimer's Disease, with the percentage increasing as the age increases. Twenty-nine percent of those age 85 and older have clinical symptoms.[23]

MedlinePlus, an informational website provided as a service of the National Library of Medicine and the National Institute of Health, notes that dementia normally begins with forgetfulness. As noted previously, this can be the cause for alarm and anxiety as we develop the normal forgetfulness that comes with age. Hooyman and Kiyak provide this set of distinctions between the normal forgetfulness of aging and the problems that may be indicative of Alzheimer's Disease:[24]

MedlinePlus points out that as symptoms become progressively worse they become more obvious and interfere with one's ability to take care of oneself. Ultimately people with severe dementia can no longer understand language, recognize family members, and perform basic activities of daily living, such as

---

23. *Id.* at 223.
24. *Id.*

Figure 2-1

Normal Aging	Possible Alzheimer's Disease
• Forgetting to set the alarm clock • Forgetting someone's name and remembering it later • Forgetting where you left your keys and finding them after searching • Having to retrace steps to remember a task	• Forgetting *how* to set the alarm clock • Forgetting a name and never remembering it, even when told • Forgetting places where you might find your keys • Forgetting how you came to be at a particular location

eating, dressing, and bathing.[25] As described by MedlinePlus, there is a middle ground between normal aging, forgetfulness and dementia known as "mild cognitive impairment." They indicate, "People with MCI have mild problems with thinking and memory that do not interfere with everyday activities. They are often aware of the forgetfulness. Not everyone with MCI develops dementia."[26]

Obviously, the primary problem for the legal professional in this regard is the issue of competency. Hooyman and Kiyak report a seven stage deterioration scale ranging from no decrease in cognitive or functional ability to late dementia with loss of verbal abilities and other symptoms. In the middle is a late "confusional stage" with increased problems in planning, handling finances and the like.[27] The question for the legal professional is when, as the client passes through these stages, does the client become incompetent for purposes of transferring property, executing a will, granting a power of attorney, or simply making decisions regarding their best legal interests. This question must be asked and answered using the appropriate legal standard, and the file documented to support any action taken by the attorney. At times this means documenting what *did not* happen during a legal process. This topic will be more fully discussed in Chapter Three.

Suicide

Suicide is not itself a psychological disorder. However, it can be the result of the psychological disorders affecting the elderly. Every text I consulted on

---

25. MedlinePlus, http://www.nlm.nih.gov/medlineplus/ency/article/000739.htm, (Last accessed March 17, 2010).

26. *Id.*

27. Hooyman and Kiyak, *supra* n.1 at 227.

the psychology of aging emphasizes the risk of suicide among elderly clients. Hooyman and Kiyak note studies estimating that 17 to 25 percent of all *completed* suicides occur in persons aged 65 and older with the highest rate among older white males.[28] The legal professional should learn the risk factors for suicide in older adults and take all indications of suicidal ideation seriously. The risk factors include:

- a serious physical illness with severe pain;
- the sudden death of a loved one;
- a major loss of independence or feelings of financial inadequacy;
- statements that indicate frustration with life and a desire to end it;
- a sudden decision to give away one's most important possessions;
- a general loss of interest in one's social and physical environment.[29]

All sources report that the axiom that someone who talks about suicide will not attempt suicide is a myth. Therefore, all indication of potential suicide on the part of our clients should be taken seriously. Establish a procedure to be followed in your office if you are concerned about a client. That procedure must include voicing that concern to the attorney immediately and should also include voicing the concern to the client. In certain cases, it should also include asking the client if they have a plan and what they have done to advance the plan. Seek professional help immediately. StopSuicide.org gives the following advice to people seeking to help prevent suicide among friends:

If the person seems unwilling to accept treatment, call 1-800-273-TALK (8255) or a local emergency room for resources and advice.

If the person seems willing to accept treatment, do one of the following ...

- Bring him or her to a local emergency room or community mental health center. Your friend will be more likely to seek help if you accompany him or her.
- Contact his or her primary care physician or mental health provider.[30]

Generally we are not, and should not attempt to be, our clients' friend. Since we are legal professionals, it may not be appropriate to act in accordance with this advice because we must confront the issue of breaching attorney/client confidentiality. Under these circumstances is not clear whether disclosing a client's suicidal intentions constitutes a violation of the rules regarding attor-

---

28. *Id.* at 219.

29. *Id.*

30. StopSuicide.org, www.stopasuicide.org/help.aspx (Last accessed March 17, 2010).

ney/client confidentiality, at least according to some writers,[31] so again it is important to discuss this matter with your attorney. Your office should have a clear policy and written procedures in place *before* the need arises. However, suicidal intentions may be considered a form of self-neglect subject to mandatory reporting in states with mandatory reporting as discussed in Chapter Ten, and may also be permitted under bar rules permitting disclosure to prevent death or serious bodily injury.

E. Meeting the Elder Client Outside the Office

Before leaving the topic of accommodating the elderly client, it is important to note that frequently that accommodation must take place outside of the office. Our clients are often restricted to their residence whether that residence be their home, the home of a family member, or a nursing home. Sometimes you will accompany an attorney; other times you will be on your own. It is not unusual for paralegals to leave work early to interview clients, have papers signed, and the like. These trips can be quite pleasant and give the paralegal an opportunity to better know the client as they are often more relaxed and speak more freely in familiar surroundings. Glenda, a paralegal working in Fort Pierce, Florida, sent me this example:

> Our office currently represents an elderly Hispanic couple who are currently in foreclosure. It's difficult for them to come to the office so I take time after work and drive to their home to discuss whatever matter is at hand. I remember one night I was there for about two hours. Keep in mind I was done with their actual file in about 10 minutes. The gentleman was reminiscing his days in Cuba and how he came to the U.S.

The purpose of such meetings is to get work done, and accomplishing that work often requires preparation over and above the preparation done for an in-office meeting, as well as controlling the desire of clients to go off topic. (Some of the ways to keep a client on topic are discussed in *The Empowered Paralegal: Effective, Efficient and Professional.*)

The well-prepared legal professional will anticipate the needs and problems that are likely to arise in an out-of-office meeting, adopt a plan for meeting those needs, and implement that plan. I suggest a packaged "travel-kit" in-

---

31. See, e.g., Weiss, *Evidence of Client's Contemplating Suicide: A Lawyer's Duty Not To Disclose*, http://www.abanet.org/cpr/comments/weiss16.pdf (Last accessed March 17, 2010).

tended to meet the most likely needs. Determining those needs is a matter of creating a checklist based on the particular aspects of the elderly client that give rise for those needs, many of which have been discussed in this chapter. For example, the kit would include large, firm, easily held, broad tipped pens, a magnifying glass to assist clients with poor vision, and the like.

Perhaps the most significant and most likely problem to be anticipated is the lack of privacy and the difficulty of preserving client confidentiality. If we are meeting the client at their residence, it is usually because they are unable to come to us independently and are under the care of others. Whether those "others" are dependent living facilities staff or family members, their presence jeopardizes our ability to maintain confidentiality during our conversations with our clients. Because people are naturally inquisitive, because the caregivers frequently are genuinely concerned about the well-being of those in their care, and because the caregivers often believe they can be helpful during the conversation, the caregivers will often just assume they should be present during the meeting. The client is seldom in a position to request that they leave, so it is up to us to see that it happens at least long enough for us to consult with the client about whether or not the third-party ought to be included. As discussed above, this can be done without offending the third-party if the request is stated to be standard policy and/or required by law office procedures. The travel kit should include Confidentiality Acknowledgement forms discussed in Section D of this chapter, pre-printed in large print on non-glare paper with high contrast between the font and the background, for those occasions when it is decided the third parties are to be included.

There will be times when it is impossible to completely separate the client from all other persons. At times the client will be sharing the room with other patients and those patients may have visitors. This is a difficult situation, but I found in most instances the other patients, the visitors, and the facility's staff to be understanding and cooperative in making arrangements for privacy, if the request was made politely, the reason for the request stated clearly, and the imposition upon their time kept to a minimum. Arrangements can include the visitors temporarily leaving the room, sometimes with the other patient, or the client being moved to another location.

Of course, there will be some situations where the problem cannot be resolved. Under those circumstances you will have to make a decision about whether to proceed and do the best that can be done to preserve confidentiality or to return at another time.

Because people are naturally inquisitive and because caregivers, and even family members, *do not* always have the best interests of our clients at heart, they may attempt to, or accidently, overhear the conversation. Therefore it is important that we remain aware of their presence and take whatever steps are possible to preserve privacy. There are available, for example, "white noise" machines of a size that could easily be included in the travel kit. These machines will also help minimize the distractions of the natural background noise that occurs in assisted-living and other facilities. Recall that such distractions can be obstacles to communication with, and information processing by, the client.

While the particular preparation that needs to take place will depend on the particular client, the tasks to be accomplished, and the circumstances of the meeting, there are a few other areas that should be considered in almost every instance. For example, it may be difficult to find disinterested witnesses for document execution, so arrangements should be made in advance. You may consider bringing a witness with you, especially if that witness is also a notary public.

An accompanying witness will be useful not only in accomplishing the contemplated task, but in confirming competency and noticing signs of abuse or neglect. Competency will be discussed at length in Chapter Three, and elder abuse and neglect in Chapter Nine. At this point, I suggest that your travel kit include a small digital camera to document any signs of abuse or neglect (or the absence of such abuse and neglect).

F. Conclusion

We have covered a lot in this chapter with the focus on identifying and understanding the ways in which the changes that occur as a natural result of aging, and the less natural changes that occur as a result of diseases and disorders afflicting the elderly, can assist us in better accommodating our elder clients. The overall theme is that the empowered paralegal can best do their job by applying to the elder client the same procedures as they do to every situation that arises in their career: identify and understand the problems, seek out and prioritize solutions, create a plan for putting the chosen solution(s) into effect, and implementing that plan. The idea is to manage the circumstances rather than allowing them to control you.

Remember, the clients are part of the legal team. Accommodating them is not *just* a matter of courtesy or good public relations. It is a matter of maximizing the potential of that legal team and obtaining the best possible results. It is what professionals do.

During the course of this discussion, I have indicated several times that topics raised in the context of the changes brought on by aging would be discussed in more detail in other chapters. We are about to begin that process with an in-depth look at competency in Chapter Three. But this has been a long chapter. Take a break. Get up and stretch. When you are ready, join me on the next page.

CHAPTER THREE

Understanding and Documenting Competency

A. Louisa Mae

In Chapter One I introduced you to my client, Louisa Mae, who was able to walk right beside me as we ascended the long and steep stairs to my office while discussing the rather frustrating performance of the Boston Red Sox and of Congress as we went. When we first met, Louisa Mae was seventy-seven years old! Now for the rest of the story:

Louisa Mae's husband had died almost twenty years prior to our meeting leaving her his estate which she reported consisted almost entirely of their house which was purchased when she was 25. The house had been built in a then unpopulated area overlooking the Atlantic Ocean. Its value had increased substantially as the population in the neighborhood increased and the area experienced a tourist boom. Unfortunately, Louisa Mae was unable to keep the place in good repair as she lived only on Social Security and a small amount of dividends from stock her husband had acquired as an employee of General Electric. Much of her income went to pay the property taxes on the place that had risen dramatically with the value of the property.

The purpose of Louisa Mae's appointment with me was to create a will. She had never done one before, but had heard someone talking about them on the radio and decided she should have one. The will itself would not be difficult, except that she had no children and was uncertain as to whom to leave her estate. She did have some nieces and nephews whom she seldom saw because they did not come to visit her and she could not go to them. Louisa Mae did not have a car and had never had a driver's license. One nephew had visited her each Christmas when he lived in the area, but he now lived about 250 miles away and no longer made the trip. She did receive Christmas and birthday cards, often with a short note informing her of their whereabouts, weddings, births, and deaths.

After some deliberation, Louisa Mae determined to have her house sold on her death and the proceeds divided among her nieces, nephews, grandnieces, and grandnephews in accord with her basic sense of fairness and in a way that she felt met the needs of each as she perceived them. The will thus became quite complex because it required a testamentary trust to pay for post-secondary education for the benefit of grandnieces and grandnephews.

Matters became even more complex when we discovered that Louisa Mae had money! At our request she brought in all the paperwork she could find so we could obtain the necessary information regarding the stock her husband had left her. In that paperwork we discovered the stock had substantial value, even though it paid a relatively small dividend. More surprising, we learned of some savings bonds and two savings accounts which started out rather modestly but had been earning interest since her husband's death!

Louisa Mae came back once a week for several weeks while we worked out the details. Once the will was completed and executed (quite a task at that time as it had to be done on a typewriter and started anew each time a mistake was made in the typing, and ours being a new practice we did not yet have a secretary!), Louisa Mae's appointments did not stop. Only one month went by before she was back to discuss some possible changes in the will. She had been thinking about the distribution and decided it was not quite fair. She came back the next week to execute a codicil.

This process repeated for several months. As time went on she began to be less and less sure that she wanted to leave everything to her family as they had less and less contact with her. She had written to them several times, but had not heard back, except for one Christmas card that informed her one niece and her family had been in the area for a long weekend and had not stopped in to visit! This led to a series of codicils leaving money to a variety of charities. On more than one occasion she offered to leave money to my partner and me, because we had been so nice to her!

And, we were convinced, this was the real problem. Louisa Mae did not really want all those codicils, which grew to the point where it was necessary to totally re-write the will. She was lonely. She wanted someone with whom she could talk about the Red Sox and Congress. She wanted someone to be nice to her.

At our suggestion Louisa Mae used some of the savings to have some work done on her house, which was dreadfully drafty and leaking. The neighborhood handyman performed the work at a reasonable price, but more significantly his wife started coming with him and playing cards with Louisa Mae while her husband worked on the house. From time to time she would take Louisa Mae for rides in her car, either for errands or just to see the sights. When Thanksgiving arrived, they invited her to join them for dinner and they brought her a small Christmas tree the next week. By spring we were no longer being visited by Louisa Mae.

Louisa Mae remained both mentally and physically spry for another four years until she fell and broke her hip. She recovered to the extent one her age recovers from such an event, but she was far less mobile. Louisa Mae became more and more frail and was not able to go out much. I would stop by from time to time when I was in the neighborhood. We arranged for her to receive "Meals on Wheels" and some other services, but most of her socialization and assistance was provided by the handyman, his wife, and their son until her death at the age of 86.

About a year after Louisa Mae died I received a deposition subpoena. I was being called as a witness in a lawsuit brought by some of the nieces and nephews against the handyman and his wife! I had previously provided the eldest nephew with the original of the Will I had done for Louisa Mae since he was the named executor. There had been no other wills drawn for Louisa Mae, but about a year before her death she had conveyed her house, retaining a life estate, to the handyman and his wife. The deed had been drafted, notarized, and recorded by their attorney. There was little money left in the bank accounts and the stock had been sold by the handyman, using a power of attorney from Louisa Mae, also drafted by his attorney.

The issues were clear. Was Louisa Mae competent when she signed the deed? Had she been subjected to undue influence by the handyman and his wife, upon whom she had become increasingly dependent? Each side felt I had key information on these issues. Each had contacted me to obtain that information. Each had been told the same thing: I could not talk to them about my conversations with Louisa Mae due to the attorney-client privilege. They served me with the subpoena and at the deposition I answered their questions in the same way. Finally, they obtained a court order relieving me of the obligation and I told them what I knew.

Of course, I could not answer the key questions since the events to which they related—the execution of the deed and power of attorney—happened several years after my experience with the will, but my information was clearly relevant. It worked, I suppose, for both sides. Clearly, at the time of the Will, Louisa Mae intended to leave her house to her "family." Just as clearly, she was doing so only because she thought it was what she was supposed to do and because she had no one else. She had offered to leave it to me and my partner! This could easily suggest that she had given the deed and the power of attorney of her own free will.

However, it could just as easily suggest that she was especially susceptible to undue influence by the handyman and his wife. One nephew, who had moved back into the area about six months before her death, claimed he had attempted to visit her several times, but the handyman's wife was always there and always said Louisa Mae was not feeling well and could not see him. The wife was always polite, but clearly was not going to allow him to see his aunt. At one point she threatened to call the police and have him removed.

In my last visits to her house Louisa had demonstrated some loss of her mental faculties. She did not recognize me at first and had to be reminded who I was. When reminded she did recall our meetings and would ask how the Red Sox were doing. If I mentioned that the season was over, she might seem a bit confused at first, but then would say, "Oh yes! They don't play baseball in the snow do they!" or something of that sort. When I asked if she there was anything I could do for her, she'd consistently reply, "No, Joey and Vi take good care of me." She never mentioned that deed or the power of attorney.

Eventually, the parties settled this case. I am not privy to the details because of the confidentiality each attorney owed their clients, but the settlement generally favored the handyman and his wife.

This case was special because I remembered Louisa Mae. During the course of my practices I drafted many wills. Some attorneys do hundreds. To this we add deeds, powers of attorney, health care directives and dozens of other transactions that require our clients to have a particular legal capacity. Did they have that capacity? We cannot remember every one of them. How can we *show* that they did have the capacity if that capacity is challenged?

The answer should be—the answer *must be*—in the file. In many, if not most cases, the answer is best placed there by the paralegal. This requires that we understand both the legal concept of competency and the means of documenting that capacity.

B. Understanding Competency

Legal competency is a fairly fluid concept. It changes somewhat, but less than one might suspect from state to state depending on common law either as it establishes legal standards for competency or as it interprets statutes that set forth those standards. It also changes depending on the particular action for which we are determining competency. Thus, rather than by asking simply "What is legal competency?" we must ask first, "What are the legal standards for establishing competency to Act X in State Y?"

In addition to understanding the standards for determining whether a person is competent to do a particular act, we must also understand the standards for determining whether a person is so lacking in general competency that he or she must have someone else legally responsible for their well being, i.e., whether they need a guardian or conservator. As we will discuss below, a person may not be competent enough to perform a particular act at a particular time, yet not be so lacking in competency that they need a guardianship. At the same time a person can be so lacking in competency that they do need a guardian, yet still have the legal capacity to perform some acts.

Driver's Licenses

We tend to think of competency solely in terms of mental capacity and in terms of acts such as signing wills or deeds, but there are other areas of great concern to the elderly. Perhaps the most important is the ability to obtain and keep a driver's license. A driver's license is extremely important to elderly people. Losing it means losing yet another part of their identity and it also means that their world becomes smaller. Their inability to move around freely in our mechanized mobile society limits their ability to socialize and to obtain services. In yet another respect, they become more dependent on others.

Still the fact remains—as a person's vision, reaction time, and other physical and mental capacities decrease, they lose their competency to drive. On the other hand, the California Department of Motor Vehicles notes that

> [E]lder drivers are some of the most prudent; they are more emotionally mature, don't drink alcohol as often, speed less, and have the experience to judge traffic situations and plan routes for safety. Many, if not most, older drivers self-restrict their driving; that is, they avoid driving in certain situations as they become aware of increasing difficulty in handling them. Not driving at night or on freeways are common concessions to age-related limitations elderly drivers make as they begin to recognize problems in their own driving or their reactions to other drivers.[1]

---

1. Shara Lynn Kelsey, *Serving our Seniors*, http://www.dmv.ca.gov/about/profile/rd/ resnotes/serving_our_seniors.htm (Last accessed March 21, 2010). This report also notes, Because of their extensive experience and self-monitoring, older drivers pose the least risk to others on the road; their accident rate per driver does not begin to equal what might be expected for the size of their population until after the age of 85. However, their accident rate per mile and relative risk to *themselves* on the road, is another story. Surface streets, with cross traffic and many stop-and-go situations, parked cars blocking sight lines, and sometimes darting kids and dogs, are the most likely venue for accidents. Partly because older drivers spend more time on surface streets (as opposed to freeways, with controlled access and relatively even speed), their per-mile accident rate by age increasingly approaches (but never meets) that of teenagers.

Nonetheless, as a result of a teenager being killed by an elderly driver, California enacted legislation requiring persons reported to the Department of Motor Vehicles by doctors due to questions regarding their competency to drive to complete a road test to determine whether competency still exists.

Even here the question of what constitutes competency is complex. In 1994 California performed a literature review "covering literature on age-related disabilities, their assessment, and their effects on driving," as an initial step in developing an assessment system for identifying and evaluating the driving competency of older drivers with dementia or age-related frailty.[2] By 2003, the DMV continued to work on developing an assessment suitable for people of all ages with conditions that might render them incompetent to drive safely, but the current status in California is that drivers may be re-examined based on reports from physicians, who are required to report medical conditions or disorders that are characterized by loss of consciousness or control, along with other medical conditions that may affect the ability to safely operate a motor vehicle; from emergency technicians, who are required to report sudden loss of consciousness, awareness, or control; and from other sources including family, friends, and neighbors who may (but are not required to) report their belief that a person is not competent to drive safely.[3]

Few states impose these reporting requirements on doctors, however. Lawyers and other legal professionals are not mandatory reporters in this respect, and the ethical question of whether they ought to report or *can* report is difficult. That question will be discussed in Chapter Eleven.

When and whether the competency of an elderly driver will be tested is a matter of state law and varies widely by state. According to Lawyers.com, as of 2007, seventeen states required more frequent driver's license reexamination for the elderly.[4] Some states specify that competency challenges cannot be based solely on age. The Insurance Institute for Highway Safety provides a chart showing special provisions regarding the elderly in state driver licensing laws on its website.[5] It is interesting to note that Tennessee, far from requiring more

---

2. *Age-Related Disabilities That May Impair Driving and Their Assessment*, State of California Department of Motor Vehicles, http://www.dmv.ca.gov/about/profile/rd/r_d_report/Section%206/156-Age-Related%20Disability.pdf (Last accessed March 21, 2010).

3. *Senior Driver Information*, State of California Department of Motor Vehicles, http://www.dmv.ca.gov/about/senior/driverlicense/reexam.htm (Last accessed March 21, 2010).

4. *Driver's Licenses and the Elderly*, Lawyers.com, http://elder-law.lawyers.com/Drivers-Licenses-and-the-Elderly.html (Last accessed March 21, 2010).

5. Insurance Institute for Highway Safety, http://www.iihs.org/laws/olderdrivers.aspx (Last accessed March 21, 2010).

frequent renewal of a license for the elderly, provides that persons over the age of 65 need not renew their licenses!

So, you can see the question of legal competency for the act of driving is complex and varies significantly from state to state even though it is, or ought to be, determinable based on science, i.e., objectively set standards regarding vision, reaction time, judgment, and the like as assessed by the person's ability to perform certain physical maneuvers while driving. The question of legal competency, as you might expect, does not get any easier as we move into the mental acuity necessary to write a will.

Wills

Sound Mind Required

It would be great if we could look up a statute or case that told us exactly what the requirements were for legal competency to execute a will. And, of course, we have been trained to research, locate, and interpret those statutes and cases. The problem is that they do not tell us what we need to know. Instead, they speak of legal competency in terms that are as vague and difficult to understand as the term "legal competency" itself.

The Uniform Probate Code, as is the case with all of the proposed uniform laws drafted by the National Conference of Commissioners on Uniform State Laws, attempts to provide a uniform enactment of law in the various states. Uniform Codes or Uniform Laws are not codes or laws at all. They are simply proposals from the commission that the states can adopt in hopes that eventually all states will be applying the same law. This has been more or less successful depending on the uniform law. Some, including some we will discuss in other sections have been adopted almost entirely in almost every state. Others, like the Uniform Probate Code, have been adopted in their entirety (with some changes in each state) by only sixteen states. The other thirty-four states have enacted parts of, or versions of parts of, the act. In short, there is little uniformity at this time.

That being said, most state laws do mimic the basic wording of the Uniform Probate Code, which provides in section 2-501 the classic statement of who can execute a will: "An individual 18 or more years of age who is of sound mind may make a will." This is quite similar to the language used in states that have not enacted the UPC, such as Mississippi. The Mississippi statute states,

> Every person eighteen (18) years of age or older, *being of sound and disposing mind,* shall have power, by last will and testament, or codicil in writing, to devise all the estate, right, title and interest in pos-

session, reversion, or remainder, which he or she hath, or at the time of his or her death shall have, of, in, or to lands, tenements, hereditaments, or annuities, or rents charged upon or issuing out of them, or goods and chattels, and personal estate of any description whatever, provided such last will and testament, or codicil, be signed by the testator or testatrix, or by some other person in his or her presence and by his or her express direction. Moreover, if not wholly written and subscribed by himself or herself, it shall be attested by two (2) or more credible witnesses in the presence of the testator or testatrix.[6] (Emphasis added.)

A bit old-fashioned by UPC standards, but in the end it uses the same terms —"sound mind." The problem is that neither the UPC nor the other state statutes define or otherwise give much context to that term.

Four Part Test

Courts, however, have developed tests for whether or not a person has a sound mind at the time he or she executes a will. The test parts are often referred to as "elements" and usually number three or four. Here is an example of a four part test:

Soundness of mind sufficient to execute a will is present if the person:
- Has the ability to understand the nature of the act, i.e., that he is making a will.
- Has the ability to understand the beneficiaries of his bounty and his relationship to him.
- Has the ability to determine how he desires to make disposition of his property.
- Is free from delusions that would affect the disposition of his property.

The courts seem to take these tests quite literally. Let's assume that our client is subject to functional paranoia as described in the last chapter. She tends to be mistrustful of everyone and believes that the employees of the nursing home in which she is residing are plotting to kill her in order to give her place to someone who can pay more for the room. Let us further suppose that there is no basis in fact for this thought. She makes an urgent request for us to come to the nursing home to prepare a will for her because she wants to make sure her wishes for her property are carried out. She has three sons and has specific bequests she wants to make to each of them.

---

6. Miss. Code §91-5-1 (LexisNexis current through 2009 3rd Extraordinary Session).

When we arrive she is quite anxious and explains to us the reason for the urgency, i.e., the plot to kill her. We know there is little likelihood that the plot is real because she is already paying the nursing home's top rate as most of the home's patients are on Medicare and she is private-pay patient. She proceeds to tell us the names, dates of birth, and addresses of her three sons. She provides us with a list of all her assets and tells us which assets she wants to go to each of the sons. All the time she is speaking to us, she is looking over her shoulder, pacing back and forth, and asking us how quickly we can get the will done because she is not going to take any medication until it is signed in case the nursing home staff has poisoned the medication. At times she claims to see some of the staff sneaking into the bathroom attached to her room, but we see no one.

In short, our client appears, on the topic of this plot, to be delusional. It is likely, however, that she would be found competent to make a will because:

- She clearly understood what a will was and expressed a desire to execute one for precisely the purpose one normally executes a will, i.e., to dispose of her assets after her death.
- She was able to list the names of the normal beneficiaries of her bounty, i.e., her sons.
- She was able to state the nature of her property and her determination of how she wanted it to be distributed upon her death.
- She appeared to be free from delusions *that would affect the disposition of her property.*

The last one seems odd since she is *not* free from delusions. However, the delusion with which she is afflicted affects her desire to have a will, not the disposition of her property under the will.

Let's change the facts a bit and see if we get a different result. Let's assume all of the above but that instead of leaving anything to any of her sons, she wants to leave everything she has to charity. She names the charity, describes the work it does, and why she thinks it is important. She notes that each of her sons is grown and has a good job providing income sufficient to satisfy all normal needs.

While it may seem odd to us that she would leave nothing to her sons, that is not a judgment we get to make. As we will discuss later, Leona Helmsley left an estate worth billions of dollars primarily to her dog and charities that help animals. The issue is not whether our client is making a wise disposition or a disposition of which either we or the court might approve. The issue is whether she passes the test. The second element of the test requires that she be able to identify the natural recipients of her bounty, not that she actually give any of that bounty to each or any of those persons.[7] Making an odd disposition may be relevant to the determination of competency,[8] but it is not determinative or even a primary determinative factor if the person otherwise meets the four prongs of the test.

Let's try another change to these facts. Assume that we know from previous experience that this client also has a daughter. When we ask about the daughter she (1) tells use that daughter died in a motor vehicle accident many years ago, a statement we know to be false, (2) tells us the daughter has joined with the nursing home staff in the conspiracy to kill her, (3) tells us the daughter has offended her, so the client disowned the daughter and does not even want to talk about her.

In scenario (1) the client appears to have failed the second prong of the test. She does not know that she still has a living daughter. She has also failed the fourth prong of the test in that she is suffering from a delusion, i.e., that her daughter was killed in an accident. Unlike the first delusion, this delusion *may* have affected disposition of her estate. While it may also not have influenced the disposition, i.e., she may have left everything to the charity even if she knew the daughter was alive, the client's competency to execute the will is called into doubt.

In scenario (2) the client also appears to have failed the fourth prong of the test. While the delusion is the same, i.e., that people are trying to kill her, the fact that her daughter is one of the conspirators *may* affect the disposition of the estate. As in (1), she may have made the same distribution even if the daughter was not part of the delusional conspiracy, but the client's competency is nevertheless called into doubt.

In scenario (3) further inquiry may be justified as to why she did not previously at least mention the daughter. However, the mere fact that she has been offended by something the daughter did and treats the daughter as if she was

---

7. See, e.g., *Lewis v. McCullough*, 413 S.W.2d 499, 505 (Mo. 1967). "In Missouri, a testator is found to have a sound and disposing mind and memory when he has mind enough to understand the ordinary affairs of life, the nature and extent of his property, the persons who are the natural objects of his bounty, and *to weigh* and appreciate his natural obligations to those persons." (Emphasis added.)

8. E.g., "While the unnaturalness, unjustness, or unreasonableness of the provisions of the instrument offered for probate as a will may, as stated above, constitute evidence of testamentary incapacity, such circumstance should not be given undue importance in the instructions to the jury, since it is recognized that jurors are likely to seize upon any pretext to invalidate by their verdict a will which seemingly makes an unequal or inequitable disposition of the testator's property." *Matter of Last Will and Testament of R.V. Dickey*, 542 So.2d 903, 905 (Miss. 1989)

not her daughter is not a failure of the test, as we shall see, this is true even if the daughter has not done anything that would be considered offensive by other people.

Let's take a look at a real-life example. R.V. Dickey left his entire estate to his daughter, ignoring his son. The son challenged the will. According to the appellate court's opinion, the son "presented evidence that the testator: drank; used profanity; cursed his son on many occasions; struck his son without apparent provocation; stated on numerous occasions before and after making his will that he planned to disinherit his son; once attempted to take his son to a house of prostitution; was strong-willed; and was a hard worker who worked from sun-up to sun-down six days a week in the management of a 504 acre farm."[9] Witnesses testified that the father's hostility to the son appeared to be unfounded. The court's opinion notes, "Neither witness could identify a reason for this attitude, and expressed his or her belief that the son tried untiringly to please his father and obey him."

Yet all of this, given the presumption of competency when a will is duly executed, was not enough. The court, quoting precedent, stated,

> It is laid down in the authorities that an unfounded prejudice, or antipathy, or even hatred towards a near relative is not of itself enough to destroy testamentary capacity. A testator may entertain his animosities, cherish his prejudices, and nurse his wrath against those who would be the heirs at law of his estate, and may be guided by those feelings in the disposition of his property and still have testamentary capacity, unless the sentiments harbored by him amount to an insane delusion....

Thus, the test is truly whether or not a delusion exists. But it is not enough to show that the testatrix suffers from delusions, even delusions that may affect the distribution of the estate. Rather, one must show that the delusions were in play at the time the will was executed.

Intermittent Factors: Delusions, Alzheimer's, Alcohol, and Medication

The opportunities to question the competency of the elderly abound. Their physical and mental capacities are, in many if not most cases, noticeably diminished, as discussed in the previous chapter. It is not at all unusual for attorneys to be consulted by relatives who assure the attorney a will cannot be

---

9. *Matter of Last Will and Testament of R.V. Dickey*, 542 So.2d 903, 904 (Miss. 1989)

valid because the testator or testatrix had Alzheimer's, was an alcoholic, was taking heavy medications, and the like. However, the determination is not at all that simple. Simply having Alzheimer's, simply being an alcoholic, and simply being medicated (even heavily) does not alone establish a lack of competency.

The determination of competency is made based on the status of the testator at the time the will was executed. As discussed below, evidence of the testator's status before or after that moment may be relevant to the question, but what we are trying to determine is the testator's status at the time the will is made. A person with Alzheimer's may be lucid at the time of execution; an alcoholic may be sober at the time of execution; and a medicated patient may be between medications at the time of execution. Thus, courts have stated, "Mere proof that the decedent suffered from old age, physical infirmity and chronic, progressive senile dementia when the will was executed is not necessarily inconsistent with testamentary capacity and does not alone preclude a finding thereof as the appropriate inquiry is whether the decedent was lucid and rational at the time the will was made."[10]

The same reasoning applies to alcohol consumption. For example, Leo Stanton executed a will in 1974. According to witnesses, Leo had a "drinking problem between 1970 and 1976," and "Leo admitted 'he was and had been for several years suffering from blackouts and delusions.' "[11] Yet, the court upheld summary judgment as to his testamentary capacity, stating such evidence did not "establish that Leo lacked testamentary capacity at the very time he signed the will."[12] The court also noted, "Frequent drinking is not proof of a lack of testamentary capacity absent evidence of alcohol consumption at the time of the signing."[13]

In general, then the issue of capacity will focus on the moment the will is executed. Evidence of the delusions, dementia, alcoholism and the like will be relevant to that determination. However, they will not necessarily be determinative if the testator demonstrates capacity at the time the will is executed. In fact, even the fact that a person requires a guardian or conservatorship because of mental incapacity does not necessarily mean that person lacks testamentary capacity, although statutes regarding guardianships and conservatorships may establish a presumption in that regard.[14]

---

10. *In the Matter of The Estate of Jane B. Buchanan*, 665 N.Y.S.2d 245, A.D.2d 642, 644 (1997).

11. Matter of Estate of Stanton, 472 N.W.2d 741, 746 (N.D. 1991).

12. *Id.*

13. *Id.*

14. *Hugenel v Estate of Keller*, 867 S.W.2d 298 (Mo. 1993).

Other Instruments

As discussed later in Chapter 5, wills are a basic tool, but not the only one, used in planning for distribution of estate assets. Indeed, the lawyer's task will frequently be to establish a plan that avoids passing on as much of a client's assets as possible through use of a will. The elder, as is the case for any other person, may also need or want to execute contracts, deeds, trusts, and powers of attorney. While the standards for the capacity required for each of these instruments is often quite similar to that required for a will, the standards can vary for each instrument within a particular state and often vary from state to state. Thus, it is often difficult to make general statements about those standards. However, we can gain insight from looking at examples of the statements of those standards in various courts.

Trusts

Trusts can be established within wills in which case they are known as testamentary trusts. They come into being at the time of death. Since they are established in wills, the legal capacity for a will is required, even if the will makes no other dispositions.

Trusts can also be established as *inter vivos* trusts, that is, trusts that are established and come into being during the life of the person creating the trust. These *inter vivos* trusts are often viewed in the same light as a contract. They are thus subject to the standards for contracts. For example, in *Girsh Trust* the issue for the Pennsylvania court was whether Girsh possessed "sufficient mental capacity to understand and appreciate the meaning and nature of the agreements which she executed discussed in the next section."[15]

The important moment for trusts, as for wills and other instruments, is the moment of execution. *Girsh* provides a clear statement in this regard

> A review of this record clearly indicates, as found by the court below, that shortly before and after June 29 appellant was mentally incompetent. Our task is to ascertain from this record whether the evidence clearly demonstrates that in the interim period appellant was in such a state of remission and was experiencing such a lucid interval that she was then mentally competent. In this connection it must be noted that there is no evidence of record that the type of mental illness which afflicted appellant precluded the occurrence of states of remission and

---

15. *Girsh Trust*, 410 Pa. 455, 473 (1963).

lucid intervals; in fact, the record indicates that prior to June 29 appellant had one definite period of remission.[16]

Despite the extensive confinement of Girsh to mental institutions both before and after the execution of the trust and the fact that she was under the care of a psychiatrist in the months immediately before and after the execution even when not so confined, the court upheld a finding that she was competent on June 29th and thus the trust was valid.

Contracts

The Michigan Court of Appeals in *Star Realty, Inc. v. Bower* set forth a fairly simple statement of the standard for capacity to contract: whether the person in question possesses sufficient mind to understand, in a reasonable manner, the nature and effect of the act in which he is engaged.[17] As with wills, if one alleges that the person was of unsound mind or insane when the contract was made, one must show the unsoundness or insanity was of such a character that he had no reasonable perception of the nature or terms of the contract.

Star Realty is an interesting case because the court also deals with the relationship of intelligence, emotional stability, and weakness of mind to the existence of capacity. The court states that while weakness of mind is an important element for the consideration of the court in determining the nature of such transactions, weakness of mind alone is not sufficient to warrant the setting aside of a contract. On the other hand, mere intelligence is not sufficient to uphold a contract. Rather, "What is significant from a legal standpoint is capacity, i.e., how defendant is able to utilize his intelligence."[18] Finally, "[J]ust as intelli-

---

16. *Id.* at 473. Elsewhere the opinion notes, "It is to be noted that during the period from October 14, 1947 until June 28, 1950—approximately 32 1/2 months—appellant was confined in mental institutions approximately 21 1/2 months; that only one definite period of remission occurred, i.e., from March to August, 1948 when she was at home under the care of a nurse; that of the time thereafter when she was not in mental institutions, i.e., April to August 1949 (5 months) and from April 23, 1950 to June 28, 1950 (2 months), she was not only under the care of a psychiatrist but also experienced nurses. *Id.* at 461.

17. *Star Realty, Inc. v. Bower*, 17 Mich. App. 248, 250, 169 N.W.2d 194 (1969).

18. *Id.* at 257. The court noted further, "Dr. Dupler's unrefuted testimony is that it is quite possible for a person to be intelligent and still lack the capacity to understand in a reasonable manner the nature and consequences of his act. He described defendant as one who could easily understand individual facts but because of impaired judgment could not relate the facts or put them together. Defendant, therefore, might know the acreage of the property, its value in his parents' estate and the terms of the sale, but still not be able to comprehend all these facts in combination. Thus defendant's intelligence alone does not necessarily equip him with the understanding requisite to a valid contract."

gence alone will not validate a contract, neither will emotional disorders alone invalidate a contract. But if a person is unable to understand in a reasonable manner the nature and consequences of his act, he lacks capacity and there ends our inquiry. We are not concerned with what impairs capacity. There is considerable testimony of emotional instability on the part of defendant."[19]

Olsen v. Hawkins, an Idaho case, provides other indications of what will and will not result in a determination that a person lacked the capacity to contract. The court notes,

> In this connection it should be noted that where a person possesses sufficient mental capacity to understand the nature of the transaction and is left to exercise his own free will, his contract will not be invalidated because he was of a less degree of intelligence than his co-contractor; because he was fearful or worried; because he was eccentric or entertained peculiar beliefs; or because he was aged or both aged and mentally weak.[20]

Thus, while the standard for legal capacity to contract may vary from the statement of the standard for legal capacity to execute a will, the process by which the determination is made and the factors to be considered are quite similar.

As is the case with wills, the determination will be made based on the capacity of the person at the time the will is executed. Take, for example, the *Olsen* court's statement regarding habitual drunkards:

> Accordingly, the rule is that in the absence of an adjudication finding a habitual drunkard to be incompetent, in order to avoid his contract or deed on the ground of his incompetency, it must be shown that his mental condition was such, at the time the contract or deed was made, that he lacked the power of reason and was unable to comprehend the nature and consequences of his act in entering into the contract or executing the deed. A deed executed in a sober interval by one who is addicted to the excessive use of liquor, but who has not been adjudicated incompetent and has not suffered a permanent impairment of mind as a result of his excessive indulgence, will stand, at least in the absence of undue influence or fraud.[21]

As with wills, evidence of the contractor's capacity before and after the time of execution of the contract is relevant to the determination, the real issue is whether the person was competent at the time of execution.

---

19. *Id.* at 258.
20. *Olsen v. Hawkins*, 408 P.2d 462 (Idaho 1965).
21. *Id.* at 465.

Powers of Attorney

Powers of attorney are basically contracts that create an agency relationship between the person giving the power (principal) and the person receiving it (agent). Thus, in *Golleher v. Horton*[22] Arizona has applied the law of agency to determine the standard for legal capacity to execute a power of attorney. In general, agency laws require that we apply to the power of attorney the same standard as that established for the act delegated in the power of attorney. However, the court rejected a test for the capacity to execute a general power of attorney that would require inquiry into each potential transaction which it authorizes. Therefore, the court applied the general contract standard, i.e., whether the principal is capable of understanding in a reasonable manner, the nature and effect of his act. The Michigan Court of Appeals states the test as whether "the principal [has] the ability to engage in thoughtful deliberation and use reasonable judgment with regard to its formation."[23] Other states such as New Mexico apply the standard for executing a deed to a power of attorney used for that purpose.[24]

Deeds

Deeds, too, are often categorized with contracts for purposes of the mental competency determination or use language suggesting the standard is quite similar to that used to determine competency for purposes of a contract. For example, Tennessee courts say, "In order for a deed to be valid, it must be the conscious, voluntary act of the grantor, and a deed executed when the grantor is mentally unbalanced, has no intelligent comprehension of the performance of the act, and is incapable of transacting is void."[25] In *Citizens Nat'l Bk of Paris v. Pearson*, the Illinois court asserted a distinction between standard deeds and deeds reserving a life estate, stating, "Greater mental capacity is required to make a deed than is required to execute a will. However, no greater mental capacity is required to make a deed of voluntary settlement reserving a life estate than is required to make a will."[26] Maryland courts state their state's rule quite simply and confirm that, as is the case with all instruments, the proper focus is on the time when the deed was executed: "The necessary mental capacity of

---

22. *Golleher v. Horton*, 148 Ariz. 537, 715 P.2d 1225 (1985).
23. *Persinger v. Holst*, 248 Mich. App. 499, 639 N.W.2d 594 (2001).
24. *Roybal v. Morris*, 100 N.M. 305, 669 P.2d 1100 (1983).
25. *Bright v. Bright*, 729 S.W.2d 106, 109 (Tenn. 1986).
26. *Citizen Nat'l Bk of Paris v. Pearson*, 384 N.E.2d 548 (Ill. 1978). (Internal citations omitted.)

the grantor in a deed is that he be able to understand and comprehend its nature and natural consequences, the property with which it deals, and to act with judgment and understanding in respect to it. And the crucial time concerning such capacity is the time of the execution of the deed."[27]

Burdens and Presumptions

Generally the person promoting a document has the burden of proving the validity of the document, including an instrument such as a will, deed, trust, or power of attorney. However, in many jurisdictions the general rule is that the law presumes every man to be sane until the contrary is proved, and the burden of proof rests upon the party who asserts the lack of testamentary capacity.[28]

The burden and presumptions can change when the issue of undue influence arises. Undue influence will be discussed more fully in the next section. For now it is sufficient to be aware that a presumption of undue influence arises from the existence of a confidential relationship between a testator and the beneficiary under a will and stated those to be as follows. However,

> [T]he presumption is not raised and the burden of proof is not shifted by the mere fact that a beneficiary occupies, with respect to the testator, a confidential or fiduciary relation, ... although the existence of such a relationship may demand a close judicial scrutiny. On the other hand, it is the general rule in practically all jurisdictions that undue influence is presumed and the burden of proof shifted so as to require the beneficiary to produce evidence which at least balances that of the contestant, when, in addition to the confidential relation, there exist suspicious circumstances, such as the fact that the beneficiary or person who benefits by the will took part or participated in the preparation or procuring of the will, or actually drafted it or assisted in its execution.[29]

While it is good to know what presumptions exist and how they apply, our task is to provide documentation of the facts that support our position rather than relying on presumptions. In many cases proper documentation will avoid litigation on the issue and avoid the necessity of relying on presumptions. Therefore, after we examine more fully the issue of undue influence, we will

---

27. *Cromwell v. Sharon Bldg. Assoc.*, 220 Md. 317, 322, 152 A.2d 548 (1959).
28. See, e.g., *Shevlin v. Jackson*, 5 Ill.2d 43, 124 N.E.2d 895 (1955).
29. *Barber v. McClure*, 165 So.2d 156, 250 Miss. 396, 405 (1964).

discuss steps that can be taken to document the competency of our clients when they execute a document or their incompetency when we are refusing to allow them to sign.

C. Undue Influence

Even when a person has the competency to execute a document, there are times when the document will be found invalid on other grounds such as duress, fraud, or undue influence. Here we will focus on undue influence because it is so often co-joined with claims of incompetency, and it is such a common claim. Indeed, several courts have noted that "undue influence has also been a much litigated question."[30] Also, duress and fraud are seldom committed in our presence and are thus not in our control, while undue influence can sometimes be detected by a legal professional in the course of performing legal services for an elder client.

Undue influence occurs when one person exercises enough dominion or control over another person to coerce that person into performing an act they would not otherwise perform. We often think of coercion in terms of "putting a gun to his head" which is more properly categorized as duress than undue influence. Undue influence does not require a gun or any other formal act of coercion. There are many instances in which the relationship between the person executing a document and another person is such that the person executing the document is no longer free to act. This can occur when one person is heavily dependent on another, a situation in which elder clients often find themselves.

The courts have several ways of characterizing this phenomenon, but they all amount to the same thing: something about the relationship allows one person to deprive another of their free will. Consider this language from a Maryland court:

> [T]estator was under the domination of an influence which prevented the exercise of his own judgment" and that "[t]he influence which the law condemns as undue is that which is operative to such a degree as to amount in effect to coercion." To warrant a finding that it invalidates a will, it must be shown that there existed "that degree of importunity which deprives a testator of his free agency, which is such as he is too weak to resist, and will render the instrument not his free and unconstrained act."[31]

---

30. See, e.g., *Sellers v. Qualls*, 206 Md. 58, 70, 11 A.2d 73 (1954).
31. *Arbogast, Exec. v. MacMillan*, 221 Md. 516, 521, 158 A.2d 97 (1960).

There are certain "suspect" situations which give rise to a presumption of undue influence. A primary factor is the existence of a confidential relationship. These relationships include "doctor or a physician, guardian, religious and spiritual adviser, employer, landlord, or a close business relation, such as that of partner, principal, or confidential business manager,"[32] but can also exist in situations such as that described in the story of Louisa Mae in the first section of this chapter.

The Oregon Supreme Court explains the theory behind undue influence in this way:

> The theory which underlies the doctrine of undue influence is that the testator is induced by various means to execute an instrument which, although his, in outward form, is in reality not his will, but the will of another person which is substituted for that of testator. Such an instrument, in legal effect, is not a will at all. Although executed by the testator, his intention to make a will is so defective that the instrument is invalid.[33]

As discussed in the next chapter, most care for the elderly is given by a member of the family. Whenever the elder client becomes substantially dependent upon one particular person or small group of people, there is a potential for undue influence. Here is how the Maine Supreme Court put it:

> Thus, the relations and duties involved need not be legal but may be moral, social, domestic, or, merely personal. Id. In a legal sense, confidential relations are deemed to arise whenever two persons have come into such a relation that confidence is necessarily reposed by one and the influence which naturally grows out of that confidence is possessed by the other and this confidence is abused or the influence is exerted to obtain an advantage at the expense of the confiding party.[34]

As mentioned in the last section, the simple existence of such a relationship itself does not give rise to a presumption of undue influence, although it will call for close scrutiny by the court. However, whenever such a relationship exists *and* the beneficiary of a will or other instrument is involved in procuring the instrument, a presumption does arise. As stated by the Mississippi Supreme Court:

---

32. *Barber v. McClure*, 165 So.2d 156, 250 Miss. 396, 405 (1964).
33. *In re Reddaway's Estate*, 214 Or. 410, 329 P.2d 886 (1958).
34. *Ruebsamen v. Maddox*, 340 A.2d 31 (Me. 1975).

> [I]t is the general rule in practically all jurisdictions that undue influence is presumed and the burden of proof shifted so as to require the beneficiary to produce evidence which at least balances that of the contestant, when, in addition to the confidential relation, there exist suspicious circumstances, such as the fact that the beneficiary or person who benefits by the will took part or participated in the preparation or procuring of the will, or actually drafted it or assisted in its execution.[35]

This would clearly apply to situations in which a client leaves a bequest to the attorney drafting a will or to her paralegal![36] However, more to the point, it *could* apply in just about any situation where the elder client is brought into our office by another person, including members of their own family. While no one is advocating indicting a person based solely on the fact that they are assisting our client, the legal professional should take steps to ensure that the client is acting freely, not only in executing the documents, but in coming to our office in the first place.

D. Documenting Competency in the File

The Need for Documentation

It is not enough that our client be competent to execute a document. We must be able to show, if challenged, that the client was sufficiently competent to justify our conclusions regarding competency. As will be discussed in Chapter Four, we cannot assume that because a family is getting along when the document is executed they will still be getting along in the future, especially after our client dies. A quick run of any legal search engine with the words "will and testament undue influence" or "deed undue influence" will demonstrate this point all too well.

While paralegals can go through their entire careers without becoming a witness in a legal proceeding, it is not unusual and every paralegal should be aware that each event of their day could lead to their being called to testify.[37]

---

35. *Barber v. McClure*, 165 So.2d 156, 250 Miss. 396, 405 (1964).

36. The person exerting the undue influence need not be the direct beneficiary. See, for example, *Sellers v. Qualls*, 206 Md. 58, 70–71, 11 A.2d 73 (1954) where the court noted, "It is true that under the will Mr. Qualls is named as executor and not as a beneficiary, but the church of which he is pastor is apparently the principal beneficiary; and the fact that he himself is not a beneficiary is not controlling if the will was the result of undue influence exercised by him."

37. Some of these occasions can be quite striking. For example, here is part of an August 2009 entry on *The Empowered Paralegal* blog:

Paralegals called as witnesses in court proceedings seem to be cropping up in the news

This means keeping good, comprehensive records of those events in each client file.

One difficulty is that on occasion what must be recorded is what *did not* happen, as in the story "Silver Blaze," in which Sherlock Holmes informs Inspector Gregory:

> Gregory: "Is there any other point to which you would wish to draw my attention?"
> Holmes: "To the curious incident of the dog in the night-time."
> Gregory: "The dog did nothing in the night-time."
> Holmes: "That was the curious incident."

Paralegals are not expected to record directly what did not happen. However, if one can show that records are regularly and comprehensively kept, the absence of a record becomes significant. For example, if a law office keeps a telephone log of every call that comes into the office, the absence of a call is evidence that none came in. This can be important when a client has filed a complaint or is claiming that you did not return a call. If you keep good records of your conversations with clients, the fact that you did not record a statement can be evidence that you did not give the client the legal advice she now claims you gave.

There are some times, though, when you should actually be recording the absence of problems through records of what was present. For example, in a will contest claiming either incompetency or undue influence, you may be called regarding the testator's demeanor, state of mind or clarity, but the absence of certain factors can also be important, e.g., the fact that the client arrived alone under her own power rather than with the primary beneficiary of the will as her attendant. Further, you may be called upon to testify many years

---

this week. In one case a witness has denied meeting with a police detective. That witness will be testifying at a search warrant hearing as will "a paralegal who brought her to speak to police and another lawyer that was involved in the case." In another the paralegal has been called as a defense witness in a murder trial to testify regarding an incident involving the murder victim. The report states:

[She] said on the stand that while she was analyzing jewelry at the couples' Mocksville home as part of a court-ordered appraisal of the Turners' belongings, Jennifer Turner shoved her after becoming upset that jewelry purchased before the couples' marriage was also to be appraised. "Mrs. Turner was standing about 6 or 8 feet away and said, 'I want you to leave now.' And Mrs. Turner charged at me. She put her hands on my shoulders and shoved me back and said, 'Get out!' I was stunned," McMullan said, adding that she was especially frightened since she was 18 weeks pregnant at the time.

Fortunately, most occasions on which a paralegal is called to testify are less dramatic.

after your actual interactions with the client. Or you may be unavailable and the record you make will have to speak for itself. Thus, the file should, at least, reflect the absence of abnormalities. Better yet, it will reflect that you asked questions or engaged in discussions specifically intended to elicit signs of incompetency or undue influence.

It will also reflect that the attorney asked any attendants to leave the room so that the client and the attorney could speak freely. If there are any concerns about possible incompetency or undue influence, those concerns and how they were dealt with will be part of the file. For example, if it appears the client is heavily dependent on an attendant to answer questions, those questions asked again and the client's ability in general should be investigated outside the presence of the attendant. In some cases it may be appropriate to require the client to undergo a medical evaluation before proceeding.

If you have concerns, report them to the attorney. The attorney will decide what steps to take after consulting with you. Your responsibilities will include noticing the areas of concern, reporting them to the attorney and recording both the concerns and the steps taken to address them in a clear fashion that will be understandable to persons who may be reviewing the file without you or your knowledge of the background and context to assist them.

There is a tendency to rely on the mere fact that a will was made self-proving (see Chapter 5) or that a notary notarized a deed, together with the presumption of capacity. This reliance is justified in the vast majority of cases. It will, indeed, be quite difficult for anyone to challenge the validity of a will when two witnesses sign the self-proving affidavits of a will attesting that they found the testatrix to be of sound mind at the time and place of signing the will. After all, any challenger will have to rely on evidence from before or after the signing while, as discussed previously in this chapter, the degree of lucidity at the time of signing is what counts. However, we do not know which cases will be challenged or what evidence the challenger might have available. Our responsibility is to prepare every case as if it was the challenged case and the challenger has significant evidence, because every case *might be* that case. In addition, a properly documented the file may be instrumental in *preventing* a challenge from taking place, saving all parties to the dispute a great deal of stress, frustration, and money.

The How and What of Documentation

As our client executes a document we will have an opinion as to the client's capacity to sign the document, but like Sergeant Friday of *Dragnet* our primary concern is "just the facts." Rule 701 of the Federal Rules of Evidence does provide for opinion testimony by lay (non-expert) witnesses when "limited to those opinions or inferences which are (a) *rationally based on the perception of the witness* and (b) helpful to a clear understanding of the witness' testimony or the determination of a fact in issue, and (c) not based on scientific, technical, or other specialized knowledge within the scope of Rule 702." (Emphasis added) This means we need to record *our perceptions* rather than (or as well as) the opinion we have drawn from those perceptions.[38] This principle is well stated in an opinion by the Pennsylvania Supreme Court:

> We have said that a person's "mental capacity is best determined by his spoken words, his acts and conduct." These witnesses did outline and describe the words, acts and conduct of the appellant and, from their observation of such words, acts and conduct, they all concluded that the appellant *on those dates* did possess sufficient mental capacity to understand and appreciate the meaning and nature of the agreements which she executed. This conclusion, in a sense, was an *opinion* but "an opinion arrived at after an observation of facts, i.e., their sensory impression of [appellant's] words and actions," and "Their testimony was neither entirely factual nor entirely opinion but mixed opinion and factual." These three witnesses were not only the best but the sole living witnesses of how appellant spoke and how she acted on the critical days when these agreements were executed.[39] (Emphasis in original.)

---

38. In some instances the court will not allow the opinion itself to be expressed, but only the facts themselves. Rule 701(b) requires that the opinion be "helpful to a clear understanding of the witness' testimony or the determination of a fact in issue." If the fact-finder can assess the facts without help from the witness' opinion, then the opinion is not admissible under the rule. See, e.g., this case (which was not decided under Rule 701):

> The testimony of two lay witnesses on the mental capacity, or lack thereof, of the testatrix was excluded. Each of them was a sister of the testatrix, and each of them happens to be one of the caveators. The rule is well established ... that: "A witness who is not an expert, an attending physician, nor a subscribing witness to the will, is not competent to express his opinion as to the capacity of the testator, without first stating facts upon which his opinion may be adequately founded." If such facts are not sufficient to support an opinion of the testator's lack of mental capacity, the witness should not be permitted to express such an opinion. All of the facts upon which these two witnesses would have based their opinions are among those enumerated upon which the caveators rest their claim of the testatrix' lack of mental capacity. We agree with the learned trial judge that they are not sufficient to warrant the expression of their opinion. *Sellers v. Qualls*, 110 A. 2d 73 (Md, 1954) (Internal citations omitted.)

39. *Girsh Trust*, 410 Pa. 455, 472 (1963). (Internal citations omitted.)

It would be best for your office to have a form upon which relevant information can be recorded and placed in each file with the document to which it refers. That form would provide places to record not only who was present, but *why*, i.e., what the connection is between those who are present and the person executing the document. We do not need the life story of the witnesses or the client in the file, but a brief notation of how the witnesses knew the client, whether they are interested (in the legal sense) in the document being executed, and the like can be helpful.

Such a form would also record the client's "spoken words, his acts and conduct." This need not be a transcript of the proceedings. Rather it is a short record of information pertinent to the task at hand. The *Girsh Trust* matter again provides us with an example of the types of information which are helpful to the court:

> Mr. Goldstein's arrival at the hotel apartment with the agreements, the discussion, sometimes in loud tones, between appellant and Mr. Goldstein of the contents of the agreements, the reading at length of the agreements by appellant, the execution of the separation agreement, the deletion by appellant from the trust agreement of references therein to a certain law firm and her refusal to execute the trust agreement until such references were deleted in a redrafted agreement, the execution on June 29 of the trust agreement redrafted to suit appellant's wishes, appellant's actions on both dates subsequent to Mr. Goldstein's departure, etc.[40]

Our task is often not just to record what happens but to ensure a *proper* record is made. That means designing the process and the discussion that occurs during that process to elicit the information you need. For example, we often see in movies or TV shows persons being asked who the president is or other such information to determine whether they are functioning mentally. When I spoke of Louisa Mae, I recounted her interest in and current knowledge of the Boston Red Sox. This information is indeed relevant and helpful, but not really designed to the task. Consider this comment from a Tennessee Court of Appeals case:

> It should be noted that the physician did not examine deceased for competency to execute the papers in question. His examination sought to determine slowness or impairment of mental function as a measure of the toxic effect of a nosebleed which had caused blood to enter

---

40. *Id.* at 472–473.

the digestive system and overload the capacity of the liver to remove toxic matter from the blood which nourished the brain. His questions to the deceased included, "who is the president"; "count down from 100 by 7's." *There was no effort to ascertain whether deceased was aware of the identity of his relatives or estate or other facts relating to the competency to execute the instruments in question.*[41]

Thus, our form should be designed to prompt questions that will elicit information specifically addressed to the test for capacity related to the instrument the client will be executing. For a will, we will want to be able to elicit statements or affirmations from the client that he:

- Clearly understood what a will was and expressed a desire to execute one for precisely the purpose one normally executes a will, i.e., to dispose of assets after death
- Was able to list the names of the normal beneficiaries of bounty, i.e., his sons
- Was able to state the nature of his property and his determination of how he wanted it to be distributed upon his death
- He appeared to be free from delusions that would affect the disposition of his property

This should not amount to a formulaic test for the client to pass before they are allowed to execute the document. Rather, discussion of these topics can and should be worked into the normal preliminary chit-chat that takes place before and during the process of executing the document.

Witnesses can actually pose somewhat of a problem during this process in at least two respects. First, they may be asked to attest to the soundness of the client's mind without really knowing on what grounds a court will ultimately make that decision. I often make a short statement in this regard before the document is executed. This both informs the witness and highlights this part of the process for purposes of their later recollection. Second, the information necessary to show mental capacity must be elicited without putting or drawing forth information that might be subject to attorney/client confidentiality, or might be embarrassing to the client. Sometimes there are things about the natural beneficiaries of our bounty that we do not want others to know. While the confidentiality issue is lessened if the witnesses are all members of the attorney's staff and thus subject to the rules of confidentiality, these people are likely to be viewed as strangers by the client and thus not persons who should be privy to "family secrets."

---

41. *Roberts v. Roberts*, 827 S.W.2d 788 (Tenn. 1991).

Video Recordings

It has become increasing easy and inexpensive to record and store information electronically. There is some value to making a video recording of the execution of documents, especially wills. However, there are also dangers and concerns that should be kept in mind:

- Many elderly clients are not as familiar with or comfortable with new electronic technologies as are clients of younger generations. This unfamiliarity and discomfort can be misinterpreted by those viewing the record at a later date.
- Having a video record of the document being executed will not substitute for proper execution of the document and may actually record improprieties in the execution. For example, most statutes require that wills be executed in the presence of the witnesses and that each witness also is present when the other(s) sign. A recording may show what appears to be one witness who slipped out to take a call on their cell phone at a crucial moment. Or a recording may show that the notary never actually asked if the client was executing the deed as "her free act and deed." If a recording is being done, it is especially important that there be an agenda (script) and that it be followed exactly by all participants.[42]
- Video recordings tend to emphasize certain features more than others. This is not helpful if those features make the client appear more ill, tired, or confused than they actually are.
- Unless your office makes it a general policy to record all such events the fact that *this one* was recorded can lead to questions about why it was chosen for recording, e.g., whether the attorney herself have doubts about capacity. In most instances, the attorney anticipates a challenge, so it makes sense to have a recording, but this will not stop efforts to put a different "spin" on the decision to record.

Admissibility of such a recording in a proceeding to contest the validity of the executed document is governed by Article X of the Federal Rules of Evidence and comparable state rules.

In any case, just as we ought not to depend on the presumption of competence in lieu of other documentation, we ought not to depend on video record-

---

42. I once represented buyers at a real estate closing where one of the sellers responded to the notary's "free act and deed" inquiry by joking, "I've got to sign or my wife will be all over my ass!" The notary refused to notarize the deed. The closing was rescheduled for the next day before another notary and with a seller who stuck to the "script."

ing as a substitute for traditional file documentation. Video recording, if used at all, should be used *in addition to* traditional file documentation, not *in lieu of* it.

E. Guardianships and Conservatorships

Guardianships and conservatorships are imposed by courts upon people who do not have the competency to act for themselves. The public often thinks of guardians only in relationship to minor children or adults who have lacked capacity since childhood. However, while exact data is scarce, a generally accepted estimate is that in the early 1990s about 1.5 million people were subject to either public or private guardianships, about one for every 1,750 people in the country.

Guardians are appointed to make decisions regarding the welfare of a person for people who cannot, or who can no longer, make such decisions for themselves. The person for whom the guardian is appointed is referred to as the "ward." In a full guardianship, the guardian will make decisions regarding most aspects of the ward's life, but guardians can also be appointed for limited purposes (and are then referred to as "limited guardians"). Limited guardianships are generally preferred as only so much interference with a person's right to make their own decisions can be justified as relates to the type and extent of their incompetency.

Generally, while a guardian may decide where the ward will live and make a number of non-financial decisions, including decisions about medical care and finances, a conservator is appointed to handle the financial affairs of the ward. However, statutes and terminology can vary widely from state to state. As discussed below, the extent of disability necessary for a conservator can be less than that required for a guardian.

Guardianship Abuses

While guardianships and conservatorships are imposed on people by the courts, they are imposed *for the benefit* of the person. Unfortunately, this does not always turn out to be the case. A variety of studies by groups such as the ABA Commission on Legal Problems of the Elderly have determined that both the process of appointing guardians and guardianship itself has been subject to widespread abuse. As we will discuss in Chapter Four, family members are the primary caregivers for the elderly, but the fact that the caregiver is a family member does not, by any means, assure that the elderly person under care will be provided with proper care. All too often, as discussed in Chapter Nine, the elderly are subjected to neglect, physical abuse, emotional abuse, or financial abuse, even when the caregiver is a spouse, child, or other member of the family.

There are fairly public examples of both private and public guardianships in which the guardian has taken advantage of his or her ward. Often such abuse is not noted for quite some time, if at all, because the guardian has the ability to isolate the ward from those who might likely report the abuse. However, there are instances when another relative or a friend of the ward is willing to take some action on behalf of the ward.

Perhaps the most famous example involves multi-millionaire heiress and philanthropist Brooke Astor. In 2006, when she was 103 years old, her grandson filed a petition asking the court to remove his 83-year-old father as Astor's guardian. The petition alleged that the son, Anthony Marshall, was misusing $14 million of her money and that she was forced to sleep in a cold bedroom in a "torn nightgown" that "smells probably from dog urine." She was not allowed to see her own beloved dogs, was denied medicines and forced to eat "pureed peas, carrots and oatmeal."[43] The case was settled out of court, but Anthony Marshal was ultimately convicted of defrauding his mother and sentenced to one to three years in prison.[44]

Even public guardians are not free from taint in this regard. The National Association of Attorney Generals' *NAAGazette* noted the 2009 sentencing of a former Buchanan County, Mo., public administrator to three years' imprisonment for embezzling over $119,000 from Social Security payments intended for clients served by her office.[45]

The UGPPA

As a result of the exposure of abuses in the system for determining the need for guardianships and the deficiencies in monitoring guardians, most states

---

43. "Obituary: Brooke Aster," *Guardian*, August 16, 2007, http://www.guardian.co.uk/news/2007/aug/16/guardianobituaries.usa (Last accessed April 3, 2010).

44. *The New York Times,* December 21, 2009, http://topics.nytimes.com/top/reference/timestopics/people/m/anthony_d_marshall/index.html (Last accessed April 3, 2010).

45. "Protecting the Protected: Overseeing Adult Guardianship," *NAAGazette,* National Association of Attorney Generals, http://www.naag.org/protecting-the-protected-overseeing-adult-guardianship.php (Last accessed April 3, 2010).

have taken steps to revise their guardianship laws over the last two decades. However, much more needs to be done, although the exact extent of the problem is difficult to ascertain due to the lack of statistical data.[46]

One significant step towards providing protection in the process for appointing guardians is the approval by the National Conference of Commissioners on Uniform Laws of the Uniform Guardianship and Protective Proceedings Act (UGPPA). Now in a revised form, the UGPPA has been adopted by Alabama, Colorado, Hawaii, Massachusetts, Minnesota, Montana, and U.S. Virgin Islands. Those states adopting this act who had also adopted the Uniform Probate Code may integrate the UGPPA into the UPA replacing UPA Article 5. The remaining 14 states adopting the Uniform Probate Code rely on the provisions of that act's Article 5, "PROTECTION OF PERSONS UNDER DISABILITY AND THEIR PROPERTY."

These acts provide due process and other protections for the person for whom guardians or conservators are sought. Under UGPPA those protections include:

- A hearing with the alleged incapacitated person present if at all possible;
- The right to be represented by counsel;
- The right to present evidence and cross-examine witnesses;
- The court has broad discretion to appoint counsel for the person;
- There must be a visitor to report to the court.

In essence the Act seeks to provide the person claimed to be incompetent with a fair and impartial proceeding.

The UGPPA attempts to minimize the extent to which the personal freedom and integrity of the protected person is limited. To this end it provides for limited guardianships and conservatorships. The intent is to invoke the "least restrictive alternative," often referred to as LRA. With a limited guardianship or conservatorship, a guardian or conservator obtains only the powers that are the least restrictive to the protected person possible.

---

46. A 2006 study included among its conclusions, "There is no state-level guardianship data for the majority of the reporting states. For states that do receive such data, comparison may be limited by differing definitions and coding. Data reported to state court administrative offices is limited to filings and dispositions. There is no data on a range of elements that would be critical for guardianship research and reform efforts. Whether, and to what extent, such data is maintained at the local court level is not known." Erica F. Wood, "State-Level Adult Guardianship Data: An Exploratory Survey," American Bar Association Commission on Law and Aging for the National Center on Elder Abuse 7 (August, 2006).

Evaluating Competency for Guardianship and Conservatorship Purposes

There is no one uniform standard for determining competency for guardianship purposes. Article 5 of the Uniform Probate Act defines an "Incapacitated Persons" as "any person who is impaired by reason of mental illness, mental deficiency, physical illness or disability, chronic use of drugs, chronic intoxication, or other cause except minority to the extent that he lacks sufficient understanding or capacity to make or communicate responsible decisions concerning his person."[47] The UGPPA's definition is similar, but not the same: "an individual who, for reasons other than being a minor, is unable to receive and evaluate information or make or communicate decisions to such an extent that the individual lacks the ability to meet essential requirements for physical health, safety, or self-care, even with appropriate technological assistance."[48]

For states that have not adopted either the UPA or the UGPPA, the situation is more complicated. Consider this statement from a 2002 Mississippi Supreme Court opinion:

> Guardians may be appointed for ... incompetent adults, Miss.Code Ann. § 93-13-121 (Supp.1983); a person of unsound mind, Miss.Code Ann. § 93-13-123, 125 (1972); alcoholics or drug addicts, Miss.Code Ann. § 93-13-131 (1972); convicts in the penitentiary, Miss.Code Ann. § 93-13-135 (1972); ... The guardian is the legally recognized custodian of the person or property of another with prescribed fiduciary duties and responsibilities under court authority and direction. A ward under guardianship is under a legal disability or is adjudged incompetent.
>
> In recent decades there has been an increased number of older adults in our society who possess assets in need of protective services provided through a guardianships. But modification of laws have broadened the definition of persons for whom assistance can be afforded by the courts, and such statutes do not restrict such protection only to the adult incompetent or insane.
>
> Noting that trend in our society, the Mississippi Legislature incorporated into law in 1962 the conservatorship procedure for persons who, by reason of advanced age, physical incapacity, or mental weakness, were incapable of managing their own estates. Miss.Code Ann. § 93-13-251, et seq. (1972).

---

47. See, e.g., Maine Revised Statutes, 18-A M.R.S.A § 5-501.
48. UGPPA, Article 1, Section 102 (5).

Thus, the Legislature provided a new procedure through conservatorships for supervision of estates of older adults with physical incapacity or mental weakness, without the stigma of legally declaring the person non compos mentis....

Therefore, the distinguishing feature of conservatorship from a guardianship lies in part in the lack of necessity of an incompetency determination of the existence of a legal disability for its initiation. After establishment of such protective procedures, the duties, responsibilities and powers of a guardian or conservator are the same. Miss.Code Ann. §93-13-259 (1972). See also 51 Miss.L.J. 239, 266 (1980).[49]

Thus, Mississippi appears to have three standards: incompetency, unsound mind, and inability to manage one's own estate depending on which statute is called into play. However, the standards tend to merge upon further examination. The reference to incompetent adults refers to a person for whom a guardian has been appointed in another jurisdiction. The statute (93-13-121) requires the chancery judge to examine the applicant in person and find after the examination that the applicant is *incompetent to manage his or her estate*, but "infirmities of old age shall not be considered elements of infirmities." As noted by the court, a conservatorship can be obtained by showing the *inability to manage one's own estate* through those very infirmities of old age.

The bottom line here is that an attorney working for a client seeking formal protection or contesting a petition for protection must be intimately familiar with both the procedural and substantive law of the state in which the procedure is to take place. There is a lack of uniformity in the standard to be applied, in the burden of proof required, and even in the court having jurisdiction over the procedure.

As a paralegal you should also have an awareness of the laws applicable in your jurisdiction in order to best assist the attorney. Perhaps more important because of the contact you have with the clients and with guardians, you should be prepared to notice, report to your attorney, and document in the file, indications that your client may need protection on the one hand or that the protector appointed for the protected person is abusing the trust placed in him.

---

49. *USF&G CO. v. Conservatorship of Melson*, 809 So. 2d 647 (Miss. 2002). In addition to the list set forth by the court in this opinion, Miss. Code. Ann. §93-13-111 provides for guardians for persons "in need of mental treatment."

Avoiding Guardianships and Conservatorships

In addition to the dangers of abuse cited above, proceedings for appointment of a guardian or conservator can be time-consuming (although there are procedures for appointment of a temporary guardian) and expensive, especially when they are contested. Assuming incompetency, decisions regarding who should be appointed as guardian and what constitutes the best interest of the protected person are made with little, if any, input from that person. This can be especially stressful when members of the protected person's family cannot agree.

While there are times when a guardianship is the only alternative, we can often avoid the need for a formal guardianship by planning for incapacity before it occurs rather than dealing with it after it occurs. As we will discuss in Chapter Six, estate planning ought to go well beyond simply making provisions for one's assets after one's death. One aspect of this enlarged concept of estate planning is the use of devices such as durable powers of attorney. Powers of attorney allow a client to give another person the authority to make decisions for the client. Powers of attorney can be general or limited. General powers of attorney give that person the authority to make most decisions the client can make. Durable powers of attorney allow that authority to continue in effect even after the client herself is found "impaired by reason of mental illness, mental deficiency, physical illness or disability, chronic use of drugs, chronic intoxication, or other cause except minority to the extent that he lacks sufficient understanding or capacity to make or communicate responsible decisions concerning his person."[50]

In addition to general durable powers of attorney which give vast authority to the agent granted the power, there are a number of devices that can be used which allow the grantor to specify the way in which his finances or other issues will be handled even after he is unable to make decisions. These devices include limited powers of attorney and trusts. In order for these instruments to be truly effective, they must be well-crafted. In Chapter Five we will look at one case involving millions of dollars in which the trust as drafted has led to extensive litigation. While the final drafting of these documents is the responsibility of the attorney, paralegals frequently are charged with or participate in initial drafts. However, the most important function of paralegals in this regard may lie in their ability to interview and communicate with the

---

50. UGPPA, Article 1, Section 102 (5). While the UGPPA language is used here the principle applies to all standards for incapacity.

client, for it is only when we really understand the desires of the client that we can draft a document designed to effectuate those desires when the client is no longer able to do so herself.

Our ability to provide for incapacity by planning ahead is not limited to financial matters. In fact, I would argue that the financial decisions that must be made for a person not competent to make their own decisions are the least important. In Chapter Eight we will discuss the availability of healthcare powers of attorney and other advanced healthcare directives which allow a person to decide in advance what medical treatment they will receive in situations where they are unable to make those decisions at the time the decision is necessary.

This advanced planning not only provides that the decisions made for the client will likely more closely mimic the decisions the client would make if she were able to make them, but also minimizes stress and conflict among the client's family if they are properly crafted. In order to understand what is necessary to consider when assisting a client in making these decisions we must have an understanding of the family dynamics and related factors that arise when confronted with the reality of aging, death and dying. That is the subject of the next chapter.

CHAPTER FOUR

UNDERSTANDING AND DEALING WITH FAMILY

More so than most other areas of law, elder law involves the client's family. While there is no doubt that care of the elderly is an ever-increasing policy concern for society, nearly 94% of elders have living family members who serve as their primary source of social support.[1] About 66% of older adults live in a family setting.[2] This number is likely to be even higher if "non-traditional" families are considered, including lesbian and gay couples.

Family's involvement extends beyond social support, however. The family is the primary source of long-term care assistance for older Americans.[3] "Nursing home" care remains a focal point of discussion both socially and within families, including both societal and individual estate planning for the costs of such care. However, most of the assistance provided to the elderly comes from families, although it may be more appropriate to say that the care is provided by *a member* of the elderly person's family. Most studies have confirmed that "the family" does not provide the care—at least not directly. Rather, 80% of the unmarried "frail" elderly, i.e., elderly who are limited in normal activities of daily living (ADL) are cared for by women, most often a spouse and next, a daughter.[4]

While family involvement with the elder members of the family is, in general, to be encouraged, it creates several issues for the legal professional. As discussed in Chapter Two, it can raise issues of confidentiality and undue influence. While family involvement can relieve many stresses in the lives of our clients, it can also create stress. Family members often do not agree with one another about to the best way to care for the elder client. Some will disagree

---

1. Nancy R. Hooyman and H. Asuman Kiyak, *Social Gerontology: A Multidisciplinary Perspective*, 307 (7th ed., Pearson 2005).

2. *Id.*

3. Jeffrey W. Dwyer and Raymond T. Coward, *Gender, Families, and Elder Care*, 5 (Sage Publications, 1992).

4. *Id.* at 12.

with advice given by the attorney. Some family members may be waiting, jock-
eying for position for the favor of the client—to be "remembered" in their
wills. Some may not be waiting.

It is important that the legal professional have a sound basic understanding
of how the elder client's family interacts with the client and with each other.
Perhaps the biggest danger legal professionals face is that of assuming that our
clients' families function in a manner similar to our own. It is a mistake to assume that the client's nephew will provide transportation for the client because your nephew would provide it for you, or that your client wants to leave
her estate in equal shares to her children because that is what you would do.
This mistake becomes particularly harmful when we judge our clients or their
families based on our own views of how a family should act or interact, especially when our disapproval can be sensed by the clients or their families.

In this chapter we will take a look at families as caregivers and examine some
of the issues that can arise as a result of family dynamics.

A. Family as Caregivers

Costs and Benefits of Family Caregiving

The statistics[5] on family care-giving for the elderly are impressive. Over 65%
of the elders in the community receive care solely from their family and friends.

---

5. The National Long-term Care Survey, a joint project of Duke University and the National Institute on Aging, has comprehensive data collected from the elderly in the community and in institutions. The survey has been conducted six times beginning in 1982 and
ending in 2004, allowing researchers to discern trends. According to the project's website,
The NLTCS is a very data-rich resource with many components, including disability
measures, medical conditions, attained education levels, and income. Numerous papers
have used it as a source of data addressing a wide variety of topics related to aging and disability. The NLTCS website currently categorizes the varied types of publications under the
headings of Active Life Expectancy, Activities of Daily Living, Aging, Assistive Devices,
Caregiver Income, Cognitive Functioning, Disability Trends, Disease, Ethnicity, Family
Support, Gender, Institutionalization, Instrumental Activities of Daily Living, Insurance,
Mathematical Modeling, Medical Providers, Medicare and Medicaid, Military Service, Mortality, Paid Caregiver, and Unpaid Caregiver.
NLTCS data have been used by researchers to examine health and behavioral factors associated with changes in chronic disability and mortality.
Ancillary surveys have been added to measure other characteristics of the 65 and older
population, to include a Caregiver Survey to acquire data on informal caregivers themselves
(done in 1982, 1989, 1999, and 2004) and Next-of-Kin (NOK) surveys administered to the
survivors of sample persons who had died between 1982 and 1984 and again between 1994

Only 5% rely exclusively on paid care. The benefits of this to society and the health care system are enormous. The benefits to the client and the family are fairly obvious. The financial costs of long-term care are substantial. The Georgetown University Long-term Care Financing Project reports that the national average cost of a private room in a nursing home is about $70,900 a year.[6]

Although much of this cost is covered by Medicare, Medicaid, or private insurance, on a national level 18.1% is paid for out-of-pocket by the patients and their families.[7] These costs can impoverish a family. The *New York Times* reported in 2009 on research by the Pew Research Center, showing that about 30% of adult children contribute financially to their parents' care and that, on average, those children contribute $2,400 a year for items ranging from uncovered medical costs to food. Even those not impoverished neglect their own retirement accounts or go into debt to meet these costs.[8]

Other, perhaps more important, benefits are the emotional support, feeling of belonging, and intimacy that comes when care is provided by a member of the family. The frail elder will likely be more comfortable accepting help from a family member than a stranger.

These benefits do not come without costs, however. These costs fall into two categories which gerontologists label "objective burden" and "subjective burden." The objective burden includes the on-going physical demands on the caregiver. Often, this balancing requires the caregiver to reduce hours at work and thus reduce income. Caregivers must often balance their employment, care of other members of the family, and care to the family elder. The subjective burden relates to the feelings and emotions attendant upon the role of caregiving. According to Hooyman and Kiyak, these feelings and emotions include "grief, anger, guilt, worry, tension, loneliness, sadness, depression, difficulty sleeping, withdrawal, and empathic suffering."[9]

In his wonderful story, "Letting Go of My Father,"[10] Jonathan Rauch talks about the toll caregiving can take. He was the caregiver for his father who was initially diagnosed with Parkinson's, a disease in which there is gradual loss of

---

and 1999. "Overview of the NLTCS," *The National Long-term Care Survey,* http://www.nltcs. aas.duke.edu/overview.htm (Last accessed May 17, 2010).

6. "National Spending for Long-Term Care," *Georgetown University Long-Term Care Financing Project,* http://ltc.georgetown.edu/pdfs/natspendfeb07.pdf (Last accessed May 17, 2010).

7. *Id.*

8. Walecia Konrad, "Taking Care of Parents Without Going Broke," *The New York Times,* September 19, 2009, http://www.nytimes.com/2009/09/19/health/19patient.html (Last accessed September 19, 2009).

9. Hooyman and Kiyak, *supra* n.1 at 351.

10. Jonathan Rauch, "Letting Go of My Father," *The Atlantic,* 54–58 (April 2010).

functioning. However, he was later re-diagnosed with multiple system atrophy, a much faster developing disease. The greatest burden on Jonathan was not the aid his father needed, but the emotional toll his caregiving placed on both him and his father. There was shame and embarrassment on both sides as his father lost his independence and Jonathan eventually had to admit he could no longer provide the necessary care. Jonathan noted that the Rosalynn Carter Institute for Caregiving has determined that family caregivers face elevated risks to their physical health, mental health, finances, employment, and retirement.[11]

Given these costs, one may wonder what motivates family members to make and keep the commitment to giving that care. Some researchers suggest there are three primary motivators, "love and affection, a desire to reciprocate for past assistance, and 'a more generalized societal norm of spousal or filial responsibility.'"[12] Others point out that there are benefits to the caregiver. Most of the caregivers are women and some writers argue that the role of caregiver is part of their identity. Providing care for their elderly family members thus confirms and supports that identity.[13] Among the benefits to the caregiver Hooyman and Kiyak list "efficacy, confidence, self-affirmation, pride, partial satisfaction, and greater closeness with the care recipient and other family members."[14]

Sadly, the legal professional must also be aware that in some instances the caregiver's motivation may be entirely selfish. Some caregivers seek to exclude and gain an advantage over other potential heirs of the person needing the care. Some seek to take advantage of the person needing the care sometimes leading to abuse and neglect. Indeed, regardless of the motivation the burdens of caregiving can lead to abuse and neglect of the elderly by their caregivers. We will look more closely at this issue and the legal professional's obligations with regard to it in a later chapter.

It is a fact that women provide most of family based elder care. Most care is provided by spouses, then by an adult child, then by siblings. Since men have shorter life expectancies than women, care by spouses is primarily care by a wife of the husband. However, this does not explain why most elder care provided by adult children is provided by daughters rather than sons.

Certainly there is a case to be made that the prevalence of care by daughters over sons is related to societal factors and perceptions of who "ought" to

---

11. *Id.* at 57
12. Dwyer and Coward, *supra* n.3 at 11.
13. *Id.* at 36.
14. Hooyman and Kiyak, *supra* n.1 at 353.

or who "is better at" providing that care. Interestingly, Dwyer and Coward report that data from the National Survey of Informal Caregivers show that husbands report providing more hours of care and helping with more caregiving tasks than do wives. This could be, however, simply because they define caregiving differently. Women may looks at many of the caregiving tasks as part of what they do normally, while men look at those same tasks as extraordinary. Sons and daughters make similar distinctions.[15]

While women provide most of the care when care is defined as assistance with activities of daily living such as bathing, feeding, dressing, providing transportation, men do assist elderly family members in other ways. Dwyer and Coward note, "there is evidence, for example, that men help with different tasks, fulfill different roles, and define the context of caregiving differently than women and that these dissimilarities have not been addressed adequately in family caregiving research."[16] Men are more likely to assist by repairing the home, mowing the lawn, and performing other tasks more associated with the male role in the typical American family.

In my experience, it is not uncommon for the primary caregiver to be determined by geography—one of the children remains in the same town or city as the elder parent while the others move (generally long before the parent joins the ranks of the frail elderly). The one remaining behind falls into the role of primary caregiver by default. Those who have moved away may provide other support for the elder parent. This support can take the form of financial assistance, financial or other business advice, financial management, or giving instructions for stopping the VCR from flashing "12:00."

Caregiving Relief

The legal professional should be aware of the limited help available to caregivers. The Family and Medical Leave Act of 1993[17] provides that employers with over 50 employees must grant up to 12 weeks of unpaid leave annually when an immediate family member with a serious health condition needs care. While the reach of the act is limited and the fact that the leave is unpaid is a barrier to its use by many employees, clients and their families should be informed of it.

Under the Older Americans Act, state and area agencies are required to serve older adults and their family caregivers. The Administration on Aging states,

---

15. *Id.* at 11–12.
16. *Id.* at 14.
17. 29 U.S.C. 2601.

Congress passed the Older Americans Act (OAA) in 1965 in response to concern by policymakers about a lack of community social services for older persons. The original legislation established authority for grants to States for community planning and social services, research and development projects, and personnel training in the field of aging. The law also established the Administration on Aging (AoA) to administer the newly created grant programs and to serve as the Federal focal point on matters concerning older persons.

Although older individuals may receive services under many other Federal programs, today the OAA is considered to be the major vehicle for the organization and delivery of social and nutrition services to this group and their caregivers. It authorizes a wide array of service programs through a national network of 56 State agencies on aging, 629 area agencies on aging, nearly 20,000 service providers, 244 Tribal organizations, and 2 Native Hawaiian organizations representing 400 Tribes. The OAA also includes community service employment for low-income older Americans; training, research, and demonstration activities in the field of aging; and vulnerable elder rights protection activities.[18]

As a legal professional serving elder clients, you should become familiar with the services, including respite care and support groups, available in your area and be prepared to direct your clients and their caregivers to those agencies as needed. In some instances it is necessary and appropriate to assist the client in contacting the appropriate agency for assistance.[19]

Caregiving Disparity

Disparity among children in caregiving is often more perceived by the primary caregiver than the other children or the parent. From the standpoint of the parent, each child may be perceived as doing the same in the sense that they are "doing what they can." This can create a feeling of resentment and en-

---

18. Older Americans Act, *Administration on Aging,* Department of Health and Human Services, http://www.aoa.gov/aoaroot/aoa_programs/oaa/index.aspx (Last accessed on May 19, 2010).

19. One helpful resource is the National Caregivers Library which describes itself in this way: "The National Caregivers Library is one of the most extensive libraries for caregivers that exist today. Hundreds of articles, forms, checklists and links to topic-specific external resources are organized into logical categories on the side of each page." Here is the URL: http://www.caregiverslibrary.org/Default.aspx?tabid=1.

titlement on the part of the primary caregiver. This, in turn, can lead to conscious or unconscious efforts on the part of the primary caregiver to influence or take advantage of the parent.

At the very least, the primary caregiver can feel they have or ought to have a greater say in important decisions regarding the elder parent. When it is necessary to decide whether or not to continue medical care, the primary caregiver will often feel they know best what the parent would have wanted because of the intimacy of the caregiving relationship. Meanwhile another child will claim that the parent had given contrary instructions during the last conversation between the parent and that child. Often elderly parents, especially frail elderly, will avoid confrontation with a child by appearing to agree with whatever position the child advances. Equally often the child will be so invested in a position that they will hear only what they want to hear. This is especially true if the decision has religious implications, such as a "Do Not Resuscitate" order or cremation of a body. These problems can best be avoided by sound estate and end-of-life planning as discussed in later chapters.

At times the role of primary caregiver may be taken on out of possessiveness. Even when this begins as possessiveness regarding the person needing the care, that possessiveness can translate into a desire for that person's "things." Julie Hall from *The Estate Lady Speaks* recounts a typical story of a family with three children, all of whom seemed to get along nicely with each other and the parents until the father was diagnosed with cancer. One of the daughters became uncharacteristically possessive of her father. This may have been the result of realizing she was going to "lose" him soon. She stayed with her father every day and night until his death, often snapping at others and accusing her siblings of not caring about their father. When he died she did not join her family while the body was taken away. Instead, she took the opportunity to take the father's personal items that she had stashed away during her vigil. The father's will also disappeared![20]

A much more sophisticated example may be that of multi-millionaire heiress and philanthropist, Brooke Astor discussed in the last chapter. As noted there, her son and guardian was ultimately convicted of defrauding his mother and sentenced to one to three years in prison.[21]

---

20. Julie Hall, "The Death Bed Thief," *The Estate Lady Speaks*, http://ezinearticles.com/?Death-Bed-Thief&id=3598708. (Last accessed May 18, 2010).

21. *The New York Times*, December 21, 2009, http://topics.nytimes.com/top/reference/timestopics/people/m/anthony_d_marshall/index.html (Last accessed April 3, 2010).

Examples of caregivers taking advantage of their role are not limited to children of the elder care recipient. Claims of undue influence are frequently made against stepparents by stepchildren, especially when the stepparent is much younger than the stepparent. Other cases involve caregivers who are not family. Recall also the story of Louisa Mae I related in Chapter Three involving a "handyman" and his wife who received the primary asset in Louisa Mae's estate.

One currently pending case illustrates the step-child/step-parent issue. The *Wall Street Journal* reported in January of 2010 that months before he died of cancer the previous September, billionaire mall magnate Mel Simon made some big changes to his will. Under the new will his wife's share rose from a third to a half. Melvin's children from his first marriage were cut out of the will. The estate is worth from $1 billion to $2 billion. Not surprisingly, the changes to the will have resulted in a court challenge with Mr. Simon's daughter Deborah suing her stepmom alleging the stepmom persuaded Mel Simon to change his will to reduce the children's inheritances while he was suffering from dementia at the time. "It had become apparent to Melvin Simon that the children might not be fair or equitable to Bren Simon if the children were left with the ability to impact Bren's financial situation or business interests," Bren Simon's court filing states.[22]

B. Family Fairness

This concept of "fairness" is the cause of a great deal of stress and distress for our elderly clients. Many clients will express a desire to "be fair to the children," yet be quite indecisive regarding what they consider to be fair. This can be a sign that they are being unfairly influenced by one member of the family. However, it can also reflect a genuine perplexity about what is fair in a particular situation.

At times, the client may be "floating a trial balloon," trying to gauge the legal professional's reaction to a proposed action because, while he wants to take that action, he is fearful of being perceived as unfair. It is important that we not react to the client's statements of intent based on our own subjective feelings regarding fairness. In fact, I avoid expressing my opinion on what would be fair, instead asking questions of the client to ascertain what her basic concept of fairness is and how she thinks it applies to her present situation.

---

22. "Billionaire's Will Sparks Family Feud," *Wall Street Journal,* January 25, 2010, http://blogs.wsj.com/wealth/2010/01/25/billionaires-will-sparks-family-feud/ (Last accessed May 18, 2010).

The very concept of fairness can vary depending on a person's cultural or religious background. Let's take this situation as an example:

> Our client, Mr. Johns, is a very wealthy man and has three children. One is a neurosurgeon with a husband and three children of her own. In addition to her income from her medical practice, she has additional income from a patent on a medical device she helped develop. Her husband is also a doctor.
>
> The second child is attempting to make his living as a poet and playwright. While several of his poems have been bought by magazines such as *The New Yorker* and one of his plays is now under consideration by a producer for an off-Broadway production, he has not yet achieved anything Mr. Johns considers "success." He lives with several other aspiring artists in a three-room apartment in New York City. Surprisingly, he is probably the happiest of Mr. Johns's children.
>
> The third child is severely disabled. He has little awareness of his surroundings and is likely to need a paid attendant for the rest of his life. Fortunately, Social Security Disability and Medicare are available to assist, but there is no doubt that his life will be much better if he does not have to depend on SSD and Medicare to meet his needs.

Johns wants to be "fair" in the distribution of his estate to his children, but is quite uncertain what "fair" means under these circumstances. What are his options in terms of fairness?

One concept of fairness would have Mr. Johns divide his estate equally between the three children. They are, after all, each his children and equally deserving in their own ways. If Mr. Johns applies this concept of fairness, each child will receive one-third of the estate, even if it means the disabled child will ultimately be impoverished and have to live on government benefits.

Another concept would distribute the estate based on need. In this case, the disabled child is clearly the neediest. In fact he is so needy it may be fair to leave the entire estate to that child. The neurosurgeon does not appear to have any financial needs. While the poet is not as well-off financially, he is apparently happy and not "in need" of additional finances.

Still another concept would give the estate to the person or persons who could do the most with it, i.e., make the estate produce the most benefit for society. Under this concept, the disabled son would receive nothing as he can produce nothing while the neurosurgeon and the poet produce healthcare and art for the benefit of all society.

As if these three basic concepts of fairness do not make the issue of fairness difficult enough, if one is to give the issue full consideration there are a seemingly infinite number of other factors that might be considered. How has each of the children treated Mr. Johns over the years? Has one of the children already received more from him than others, for example, perhaps the neurosurgeon's medical school costs were paid by Mr. Johns? Are there gambling, drug, alcohol, or other issues that might make it unwise to leave one of the children large amounts of money? Are there grandchildren that survive a deceased child?

Once we have advised the client of the options, it is for the client to decide what is fair. For our purposes, whatever he or she decides is right. Our task is to use the correct legal tools and to use them correctly to effectuate the client's desires. Failure to do so is a disservice to our client and to the family. In the next section we will consider some of the ways in which the legal professional can, and in some instances must, deal with the elder client's family. We will also take a look at some of the problems that can arise when we fail to articulate clearly the desires of our clients, keeping in mind that it is our responsibility to ask the questions necessary to gain a clear understanding of those desires.

C. Dealing with the Elder Client's Family

The elder client's family is likely to play a significant role in any legal process involving that client. The client may be physically dependent on one or more members of the family and is likely to be emotionally tied to the family. The family members may be very helpful in working to obtain and maintain Social Security, Medicare, and other benefits for the client. One goal of the client and the legal professional is likely to be to minimize the stress, trauma, confusion, frustration of and *conflict between* members of the client's family. At the same time, the client's family can pose special problems for the legal team.

The Client is Our Client

Despite the often intense involvement of the family with our elder client, we must keep in mind exactly who our client is *and* communicate that fact clearly to everyone else. The paralegal should discuss exactly how and when this is to be done with the attorney. Even the most genuinely concerned members of the client's family are likely to have difficulty separating their own needs and concerns from that of the client. The bare fact of their connection to the client interferes with them maintaining the objectivity that the legal professional must maintain. This lack of objectivity is intensified by the stress brought on by the very age-related changes affecting our client that make legal assistance necessary.

Even if the client has a primary caregiver, each member of the family is likely to have an opinion about what should be done for the client and by the client. Each member of the family also has an interest in the work being done for the client by the legal team. Each member of the family will have expectations regarding how the client should be treated, how that member of the family should be treated, and how other members of the family should be treated by the legal professional. Each is likely to be voicing their opinion on the job the legal professional is doing.

Thus, it is important to establish and communicate ground rules at the initial interview. The client and each involved family member should clearly understand that she and only she is our client. As discussed in the next section, there are special considerations that must be given to confidentiality when dealing with an assisted elder client. The rules regarding confidentiality should also be explained clearly to the client and to the family.

Confusion regarding who the client is often arises when a caregiver makes the initial call to an attorney or arranges for the initial meeting. It is not at all unusual for an existing client to bring a parent to the "family attorney" and declare "My father wants to make a will." While this is a perfectly acceptable situation, it must be made clear at once—in a cordial and diplomatic way—that it is the father, not the child who is the client for purposes of making the will. The same is true when we are contacted to act on behalf of an elder client by a conservator or guardian.

Further, the legal professional must be careful to avoid a conflict of interest. The ethical rules in all jurisdictions have provisions covering representation of multiple clients when those clients *may* have conflicting interests. If a child who is already our client brings in a parent for legal services, that child may have an expectation that we will protect her interest in the course of providing those legal services. A conflict may arise, for example, if the parent wants to favor another child over that child or a stepparent over all of the children. The legal professionals have an obligation to reject matters in which they cannot maintain objectivity because of conflicts. There is also an obligation to disclose potential conflicts and obtain an informed, knowing waiver from the clients. That waiver should be in writing.

This point can be particularly difficult to maintain and explain when our client wishes to, or we are advising the client to, delegate authority through powers of attorney, advanced directives, trusts, or similar documents. Once the authority has been delegated, the agent will often act for the client. Their authority may extend to making legal decisions for the client and giving the legal professional direction with regard to those decisions. It is especially necessary in this situation for legal professionals to keep in mind who the client is.

While the agent speaks for the client, she is not the client. The elder person who delegated the authority must remain our primary concern and we have an obligation not to partake in decisions that are clearly not in the client's best interest. The agent owes certain fiduciary duties to the principal granting them authority. It may be necessary for the attorney to remind the agent of those duties. It is ethically required that the legal professionals not participate in acts that violate those duties.

My approach has been to make it clear to the agent that the principal is my client. To the extent that the agent works on behalf of the client, the attorney/client privilege extends to the agent. If, however, it is my determination that the agent is violating his fiduciary duties—especially if the violation amounts to a crime or abuse of their authority—then the attorney/client privilege does not protect them. If a paralegal suspects that an agent is not acting in the best interest of the client, this fact should be discussed with the attorney immediately.

Confidentiality[23]

The attorney/client privilege extends to agents of the attorney and the client. This only makes sense given the purpose of the privilege, which is to encourage full disclosure without fear that the information will be revealed to others, so that clients receive the best and most competent legal advice and representation. We tend to think of this extension most often in terms of the attorney's staff—paralegals, secretaries, investigators and others who assist the attorney in providing the advice and representation. However, it applies also to the agents of the client who assist in the communication. This is most obvious in the case of corporate clients since all communication with corporations must be done through one or more of their agents.

We should take care to protect the attorney-client privilege when the client is assisted by another person during communications between the attorney and the client. While we understand the workings of the privilege, many clients and the assistant will not. Like so many other aspects of the legal process, we should take the time to explain at least the basics to both the client and their

---

23. Confidentiality and undue influence were discussed in Chapter Two. Those discussions are repeated here. The issues are important enough to bear repeating. However, the primary reason is structural, i.e., a desire to ensure that the materials are covered for those readers who read only selected chapters.

agent. In this case the basics consist of the fact that for purposes of the communications that occur between the attorney and the client or the agent on the client's behalf, the third party is indeed the agent of the client. *Both the agent and client should understand and acknowledge the fact of the agency prior to the communications taking place.*

First, the client should clearly understand that there is no way to pre-screen statements made in front of the agent, so if there is any topic that the client does not want mentioned, the client should let the attorney and/or paralegal know in private. The logistics of this can be difficult, as once the two are in the room it can be difficult and embarrassing for the client to ask that the agent leave. As discussed more fully in the next sub-section, I most often handled this by making it a general rule to ask the agent to leave at the very beginning of the meeting. I explain to both the client and the agent that I do this as a matter of policy so I can document the file for the benefit of all concerned, not because of anything related to their particular circumstances.

During my experience representing attorneys against whom ethics complaints had been brought, I became aware of several instances where failure to establish such a procedure resulted in the filing of complaints. In one such instance, the client came in to discuss settlement of a personal injury claim. Of course, this required the attorney to assess both the strengths and weaknesses of the case. One weakness was certain aspects of the client's past medical history that related to alcohol and drug abuse. The client had not been aware going into the conversation that this topic would come up and was quite upset that the agent had been informed. This problem could have been avoided if the agent had been asked to leave the room long enough for the attorney to outline the upcoming discussion.

Second, the agent should be aware of his or her obligation to maintain the confidentiality that underpins the attorney/client privilege. Many people do not understand just how important the confidentiality obligation is or how deep it runs. They must be made to understand that they cannot go home and discuss what they heard at the meeting with other members of the client's family, with their own family, their drinking buddies or their co-workers—even if they change the names and other information to protect identities.

I generally handle this by having both the client and the agent sign a Confidentiality Acknowledgement. This is a simple document written in terms the client and the agent can understand. Like any form, it should be adjusted for the particular practice and circumstances.

CONFIDENTIALITY ACKNOWLEDGMENT

_____ (Agent) agrees to act as agent for _____ (Client) for purposes of helping communication between Client and his/her attorney and that attorney's staff only.

Client agrees that Agent is authorized to act as his/her agent for purposes of helping communication between Client and his/her attorney and that attorney's staff only.

Client understands this means that Agent will hear information that would otherwise be kept confidential between Client and the attorney and the attorney's staff. Since it is not possible to identify all the topics that might be covered in advance, Client understands that this could result in Agent hearing information not expected by Client.

Agent understands that he or she must keep everything he or she hears from the attorney or Client while acting as Client's agent absolutely confidential. He or she cannot repeat it to other members of Client's family, Agent's family, or any other person without the express permission of Client.

While this form will provide some protection in the event the client does file a complaint for breach of confidentiality, the goal of using it is primarily educational. It will help both the client and the agent focus on the status of their relationship in terms that they can understand for purposes we understand. This helps integrate all concerned into the legal team. Such integration facilitates the purposes of the legal team while minimizing the chances of complaints.

Undue Influence Issues

A second difficulty caused when an elderly client is assisted to a law office is the possibility of undue influence being asserted on the client by the helper. The potential for undue influence is inherent in the very relationship that brings the two to the office together. This is true even if the two are not related by blood or marriage. The relationship with which we are concerned is the dependence relationship of the elderly person on the helper that is implied by the very fact that the elderly person needs the assistance provided by the helper.

The legal professional has an obligation to the client to be aware of the signs of undue influence and other elder abuse. This will be discussed more extensively in the chapters dealing with an elder client's family and elder abuse. In this context the paralegal can be especially helpful to the attorney as a "second set of eyes." Both the attorney and the paralegal should watch for signs that the helper is dominating the client, rather than assisting the client. These signs include:

- The helper speaks for the client;
- The client repeatedly asks the helper to answer a question for him or her;
- The client consistently looks to the helper before answering a question;
- The client stops or changes an answer after the helper looks at, touches, or makes a movement towards the client;
- The helper frequently corrects the client's answers;
- The helper refuses or is reluctant to allow the client to speak privately with the attorney or paralegal;
- The client appears confused or influenced by medication or alcohol.

None of these signs is definitive. Many elderly clients are confused, need help remembering, and the like. However, a legal professional should proceed with caution when these signs appear.

As stated above, it is my general practice to insist upon meeting separately with the client in any situation where there may be a conflict between my client and the person with the client. I apply this policy to parent/child and husband/wife situations as well as elder client situations. However, I do tend to emphasize it more in cases involving elderly clients, especially when a child is bringing in a parent to prepare a will, create a trust, or transfer property.

Generally, the logistics of this can be delicate as once the two are in the room it can be difficult and embarrassing for the client to ask that the agent leave. I handled this by taking the responsibility. I explain that it is my rule to ask the other person to leave at the very beginning of the meeting *before* there is any substantive discussion. I explain to both the client and the other person that I do this as a matter of policy so I can document the file for the benefit of all concerned, not because of anything related to their particular circumstances. The important thing from my perspective is (1) not to insult either the agent or the client by suggesting that the agent may be taking advantage of the client or that the client is not capable of independent thought, and (2) to make it clear that I am the person responsible for this request, not the client. If an abusive relationship does exist, we do not want the abuser to blame the abused for this challenge to their dominance over the abused.

Once the other person is out of the room I look for changes in demeanor on the part of my client, ask questions intended only to determine competency, and inquire about the client's relationship with the other person. Generally, the actual answers to the questions are not important. I am more interested in the clients' reactions, demeanor, and any changes in their behavior that might indicate a problem.

All of the law office staff should be given a clear understanding of to whom they can speak regarding the client. If the agency is established for one member of the family, it does not extend to other members of the family or members of the agent's family. For example, if a son is the agent, the staff should speak only to the son and not to the son's wife. This is not an unusual situation. The son brings the parent into the office for the legal services, but depends on the daughter-in-law to carry on the dialogue with the law office because the son works during the day and the daughter-in-law does not. If it is necessary, formally establish the daughter-in-law as an agent, but do not begin "stretching" the agency beyond that which is formally established.

This procedure provides practical benefits to the legal team while preserving the attorney/client privilege. It is important to limit the number of persons calling the office regarding the client. Even when the number of children or other interested parties is small, the number of phone calls or "drop-ins" can become overwhelming for the legal staff. Further, each of the callers is likely to have their own perspective on what is being done and what should be done. Even if they are all told the same things, they may each hear it differently or put their own gloss on what is said. The legal team then has three or four often conflicting versions of what was said circulating among the family. As noted previously many client, and especially frail elder clients, will "feed" these conflicting versions in individual conversations in order to avoid upsetting the person with whom they are talking.

There is one danger to this focused approach to communication: a freer flow of information may better assist the legal professional in ascertaining abuse by the agent. In this respect it is good to keep in mind that there is nothing preventing that professional from *listening* to and using information from any source. Complaints by a person interested in our client's estate or the outcome of decisions being made by or for our client are somewhat suspect. Many attorneys discount such complaints when they come from someone with "an axe to grind." However, they should be considered and investigated.

One goal of the elder client's legal team is to minimize the stress, trauma, confusion, and frustration of and *conflict between* members of the client's family. The better we do at keeping communications clear, the more likely it is that we will have accomplished this goal.

D. Obtaining and Effectuating Clarity

Minimizing stress, trauma, confusion, frustration of and conflict between members of the client's family is often crucial to the well-being of the client.

When assisting clients with obtaining Social Security benefits or other rights granted by law, this can often be accomplished simply by being effective, efficient, and professional in completing the necessary legal process. When dealing with effectuating the client's desires regarding their property and end-of-life decisions, more is required. The legal professional must (1) gain a clear understanding of the client's desires, and (2) provide the documentation necessary to clearly effectuate those desires. Even when the family members do not like and do not agree with the wishes of the client, stress, confusion, frustration and especially conflict are reduced when the client's wishes are clear, clearly expressed, and legally binding.

Gaining the necessary clarity can often be difficult. On the whole, Americans are not very adept at contemplating their own death, much less talking about and planning for it. They have not—and are reluctant to—consider all the "what ifs" attendant upon the planning process, whether they are financial or estate planning or end-of-life decisions. We will discuss those issues extensively in Chapters Six, Seven, and Eight. For now, it is enough to acknowledge that the obligation for considering the "what ifs" rests on the legal professional. Even those clients who are willing participants of the legal team in addressing these issues are unlikely to be aware of which "what ifs" ought to be considered.

The legal professional must know what questions to ask and how to ask them in a way that enables real understanding between the client and rest of the legal team. *The Empowered Paralegal: Effective, Efficient and Professional* deals extensively with understanding and overcoming many of the obstacles to that understanding. Other obstacles are considered in Chapter Two of this book. Further, obstacles arising from the various stressors and motivations of family members have been discussed in this chapter. In addition, we will consider some of the obstacles arising from differing perspectives on death, dying, and end-of-life care in Chapter Five.

At this point we will focus on the second prong of the legal professional's role in obtaining and providing clarity. We will do this by examining a few examples of situations in which that clarity was not provided either because the "what ifs" were not considered, the client's desires were not understood, or the documents used to effectuate those desires were not sufficiently clear.

The first such situation formed the basis for my first brief and oral argument before the Maine Supreme Court. In that matter, property had been left to a brother and sister by an aunt. The property consisted of a house and a "cottage" on a single parcel of ocean front land. The problem was that no one had considered, or had not adequately planned for, the possibility that the brother and sister would not be able to agree on how the property was to be used. Ultimately, one party petitioned the court to divide the property between them. However, as the court noted:

> The evidence disclosed that the property concerned was residential-recreational type property consisting of a very old farmhouse with a newer two-story ell addition, a very old barn, a storage building which had been converted into a small apartment (referred to as "the garage house") and a cottage, all located on a lot containing 2.15 acres. It is immediately apparent that a division into two identical units cannot be made.[24]

The commissioners nonetheless divided it, granting the farmhouse and a part of the land to the brother and the cottage with its land to the sister. The sister appealed asking that the commissioner's division be rejected because, among other grounds, "The Report does not show the Commissioners' basis for division or that they considered the money value in the market or its productive value or that of its respective parts."[25] However, the real controversy arose because the commissioners could not ascertain or even consider the value of the property in terms of what it meant to the parties and their relationships to the aunt and to each other.

Each of the parties "knew" what the aunt would have wanted to happen, but each of them "knew" something different. Each of them attached a value to the property that had little to do with money and much to do with their own memories of the property and the aunt. Further, their relationship with each other was such that each of them placed a value on "winning."

The dispute did not end there. The lot on which these buildings were located lay between a road and the ocean. All of the living quarters were serviced by a water line that ran under that road to the property. All of the living quarters were accessed by a driveway off of that road.

The difficulty was that the description of the real property given to the brother did not contain language creating an easement over his property on the driveway for the sister to access her property; and the sister's property description did not have the necessary language giving it rights of access over the brother's parcel. Nor were there provisions for the use of the water line by the sister's parcel. You may have already guessed the result—the brother blocked the driveway and cut off the water. For two years while this issue was being resolved, the sister could only access the property by parking a mile away and walking along the public beach, carrying her water with her.

---

24. *Eaton v Hackett*, 352 A2d 748, 749–50 (Me. 1976).
25. *Id.* at 749.

Figure 4-1

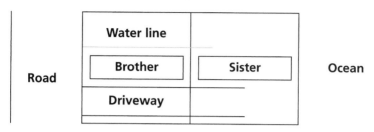

Now, it could be argued, as it was in this case, that the intent of the commissioners' was clear. No "reasonable" person would contend that the commissioners did not intend to give the sister the right to access her property or to receive water through the water line. Yet, such arguments are made by family members in our courts every day. Those arguments relate to the division of property, the intent of the person giving the property, the desires of the person regarding end-of-life medical care, disposal of the person's body, funeral rites, and countless others.

Most, but probably not all, of these arguments could be avoided if the legal professionals involved clearly articulate the intent of the client in the documents prepared for the client. While not all families go to this extent to resolve their differences, even the most cordial of families can find themselves engaging in a conflict engendered by unsettled issues from their youth, the stress of the current circumstances, or strong but differing perspectives on what is right. These conflicts are especially likely to happen when there is a disparity, real or perceived, among the family members in terms of caregiving responsibility. Our next example illustrates this point.

Henry died owning a house sitting on a large tract of land just outside the main part of town in a growing area. Henry had two children, a son, Henry Jr. and a daughter, Maria, by his first wife, and a daughter, Ava, by his second wife. All were adults when he died. The son was a successful professional living across the country from his father with his family. The first daughter was married and also lived many miles away.

But Ava still lived in the house and had taken care of Henry during his decline, final illness, and death. They had spent many hours together discussing the property. Ava had heard many times every story Henry had to tell about the land, which had been in Henry's family for generations, and the people who lived there. She felt she knew intimately Henry's thoughts about the land.

Henry left his entire estate to his children: one half to the son, and one quarter each to the daughters. Some may question whether it was fair to favor the son simply because of his gender, especially given the care that Ava had rendered during the final years, but that was never an issue. However, there was significant dissent regarding what to do with the property. It could be sold immediately, but the market value of the undeveloped land was small compared to what could be gained if it was developed into a subdivision.

Henry, Jr., quickly developed a plan for a gated community, one that would maximize the property's value. Ava did not, however, feel that this is what Henry, Sr. would have wanted done with the land. She felt it was important to preserve the portion with the house and keep it in the family. She was willing to accept that portion as part of her overall share. Further, she felt Henry, Sr. would have wanted the rest of the property developed in a way that preserved its character and served persons of more modest income. Her plan would not have yielded as much profit as Henry, Jr.'s, but she felt it was more in keeping with Henry, Sr.'s wishes. Maria, perhaps simply because Henry, Jr. and she had the same mother, sided with him.

The result, of course, was years of conflict and court action. All three were named as co-executors of the will, but Henry and Maria were in a position to out-vote Ava at every turn. Her recourse would be to file a partition action similar to the one discussed in the last example.

Here we see not only the general family dynamic, but the added dynamic of the caregiver role creating a feeling on the part of one of the parties that she knew better than the others what Henry, Sr. would have wanted. Much of this conflict could have been avoided if more thought had gone into articulating Henry, Sr.'s desires and more consideration had been given to what should be done if the children did not agree on the use of the property.

Our final example is a more celebrated case that illustrates a different point. Leona Helmsley was a hotel owner and investor who left an estate of over four billion dollars. Initial news reports focused on the distribution of the estate, but asserted she "left no uncertainty about the future of her fortune."[26] And certainly it appeared at first that Ms. Helmsley and her legal professionals had avoided all of the pitfalls these examples are meant to illustrate. Her will was unusual, but quite specific. In fourteen pages Helmsley laid out her wishes sometimes with great clarity. Most of her estate was left to the Leona M. and Harry B. Helmsley Charitable Trust, but she set aside $12 million to a trust for the care of her 8-year-old dog, trusts of $10 million to benefit her brother and trusts of $5 million each to benefit two of her grandsons, David and Wal-

---

26. Sewell Chan, "Leona Helmsley's Unusual Last Will," *The New York Times*, August 29, 2007, http://cityroom.blogs.nytimes.com/2007/08/29/leona-helmsleys-unusual-last-will/ (Last accessed May 19, 2010).

ter Panzirer, $5 million to each of those grandsons outright, and $100,000 to her chauffeur. She also specifically left nothing to another two of her grandchildren "for reasons which are known to them." She further specified that to receive money from the trusts, the two grandsons must visit the grave of their father each year.

Yet, even this specificity did not prevent problems from arising. The will was clear but the charitable trust was not! The trust itself gave a significant amount of discretion in how to spend the money, but Ms. Helmsley left a two page "mission statement" for the trust specifying exactly how the money was to be used—to promote canine well-being. However, the mission statement was never incorporated into the trust or her will. The trustees petitioned a court for a declaration that the mission statement had no legal validity and did not limit their discretion in the use of the money for any charitable purpose. The court ruled that the trustees may apply trust funds for such charitable purposes and in such amounts as they may, in their sole discretion, determine.[27]

The problem here was not that Helmsley's wishes were not sufficiently or clearly ascertained. Nor were they inarticulately stated. However, the legal documents she executed were not properly drawn to effectuate that intent. Of course, it may be that Helmsley always intended the mission statement simply as a guiding, rather than binding, document. Yet, if this is the case, why does not one of the documents—the will, the trust, or the mission statement—say so?

The use of documents to effectuate the wishes of clients will be discussed extensively in Chapters Six, Seven, and Eight. Before engaging in that topic, we will examine some of the various perspectives that our clients and their families may have on death, dying, aging, and end-of-life decision making.

27. Stephanie Strom, "Not All of Helmsley's Trust Has to Go to Dogs," *The New York Times*, February 25, 2009, http://www.nytimes.com/2009/02/26/nyregion/26helmsley.html (Last accessed May 19, 2010).

CHAPTER FIVE

Perspectives on Death, Dying, and End-of-Life Planning

As I progressed through my research and reading for this book, I found that there were many areas of disagreement among gerontologists and other specialists who deal with the elderly. For example, as noted in the last chapter, there are several theories as to why most of the informal care given to elder clients is provided by women. There is, however, one point on which there is uniform agreement: In general, people in the United States are reluctant—at best—to contemplate and talk about their death. There is a similar reluctance with regard to aging and illness. This, obviously, interferes with the legal team's ability to engage in effective planning for old age, disability, dying, end-of-life care, death, and postmortem.

This reluctance to face the reality of our own death is just one of many ways in which our culture differs from other cultures. Understanding and over-coming the reluctance to speak about death, understanding the stages that our clients and their families go through as they confront death, and understanding the different perspectives on issues surrounding death are essential to effective and professional paralegals working with the elder client and their families. It is the goal of this chapter to begin the process of that understanding.

A. On Death and Dying

"Good Death"

The reluctance to contemplate and plan for death weighs heavily on our society. It has not always been so. In her book, *This Republic of Suffering*, Drew

Gilpin Faust speaks of the "Good Death."[1] Prior to the Civil War, which is the topic of her book, Faust describes dying and grieving as processes that were a normal and expected part of family life. A person died "well" when at peace with God, conscious of the significance of the event to come, and among one's family members, who were present to hear the significant last words of the decedent.

Elizabeth Kubler-Ross puts a similar gloss on the change in the way our society copes with death, dying, and dying patients. She recounted the story from her own childhood of a man who fell from a tree and was not expected to live:

> He asked simply to die at home, a wish that was granted without questioning. He called his daughters into the bedroom and spoke with each one of them alone for a few minutes. He arranged his affairs quietly, though he was in great pain, and distributed his belongings and his land, none of which was to be split until his wife should follow him in death. He also asked each of his children to share in the work, duties, and tasks that he had carried on until the time of the accident. He asked his friends to visit him once more, to bid good-bye to them."[2]

For Kubler-Ross, these "old-fashioned" customs were an indication of acceptance of death and helped the dying person and his family accept the loss. She noted that while in all societies and at all times death has been "distasteful," many societies at many times had been able to accept death and ended their lives in a "familiar and beloved environment," requiring less adjustment for the dying and their families.

Kubler-Ross notes the difference between that perception of death and dying and that of society existing at the time she did the research for *On Death and Dying*, a "society in which death is viewed as taboo, discussion of it is regarded as morbid."[3] She went on to declare, "Dying nowadays is more gruesome in many ways, namely, more lonely, mechanical, and dehumanized; at times it is even difficult to determine technically when the time of death has occurred."[4]

Faust traces the beginning of this change in the perception of death to the Civil War. Over 620,000 soldiers died during the war, most without the Good Death ritual. Faust notes, "the sudden and all but unnoticed end of the soldier slain in the disorder of battle, the unattended deaths of unidentified diseased and wounded

---

1. Drew Gilpin Faust, *This Republic of Suffering: Death and the American Civil War* (Alfred A. Knopf, 2008).

2. Kubler-Ross, *On Death and Dying* 5 (MacMillan Publishing Co., Inc. 1969).

3. *Id.* at 6.

4. *Id.* at 7.

men denied these consolations."[5] Death became impersonal partly because of its prevalence. Even in hospitals there was no record of the names of those who died, because, "death had become too commonplace even to take note of."[6] However, it was the fact that the dying took place far from home and away from family that dehumanized it for the family as well as the dying person.

In Kubler-Ross' book, dying had become lonely and impersonal because it occurred in impersonal hospitals with patients connected to machines that were intended only to stave off death, rather than heal. Worse, "When a patient is severely ill, he is often treated like a person with no right to an opinion. It is often someone else who makes the decision if and when and where a patient should be hospitalized. It would take so little to remember that the sick person too has feelings, has wishes and opinions, and has—most important of all—the right to be heard."[7]

Hooyman and Kiyak note that death has come to be viewed as the "province of the old" and, for many, an unnatural event that is to be delayed as long as medically possible. They state, "achieving a peaceful death is difficult because of the complexity in drawing a clear line between living and dying—which is partially a result of technology and of societal and professional ambivalence about whether to fight or accept death."[8] They go on to note that, "The majority of dying patients, regardless of age, experience severe, undertreated pain, and nearly 40 percent spend at least 10 days in an intensive care unit. This is the case even though most people express a preference to die at home, without pain, surrounded by friends and family."[9]

On Death and Dying began the long process of changing the perception of the "right" way to care for dying patients, a perception seemingly at the same time shared by the medical and legal professions, policy makers and general society, but not shared by large numbers of individuals who comprised those same groups. While much progress has been made, society as well as the medical and legal professions has much work to do in dealing with the issues raised by death and dying, as suggested by the above quote from Hooyman and Kiyak.

There are several trends in healthcare that attempt to reinstitute the concept of a "good death." The Institute of Medicine Committee on Care at End of Life sets three criteria for a good death in our present society. A good death is:

---

5. Faust, *supra* n.2 at 9.

6. *Id.* at 145.

7. Kubler-Ross, *supra* n.2 at 7–8.

8. Nancy R. Hooyman and H. Asuman Kiyak, *Social Gerontology: A Multidisciplinary Perspective*, 481 (7th ed., Pearson 2005).

9. *Id.*

- Free from avoidable distress and suffering for patients, families, and care-givers
- In general accord with patients' and families' wishes
- Reasonably consistent with clinical, cultural, and ethical standards.[10]

There are practical difficulties with attaining a good death under these criteria. For example, it is not unusual for clinical and cultural standards to conflict. In addition, there are legal hurdles that must be overcome.

Within the medical profession there is much discussion of the medical provider's ethical obligations regarding a good death. However, there has been an increasing use of palliative care—care that focuses on relief of pain and physical symptoms rather than on life-preserving measures. There are three approaches to palliative care as defined by the American Hospital Association: pain management, hospice, and palliative care programs.[11] Pain management is a formal program of education for staff about managing chronic and acute pain. Hospice is a program providing palliative care and supportive services that address the emotional, social, financial, and legal needs of terminally ill patients and their families. Palliative care programs are programs providing specialized medical care, drugs, or therapies run by specially trained medical providers. These programs also provide services such as counseling about advance directives, spiritual care, and social services.

Hospice is a particularly popular approach to palliative care, with 20% of dying Americans participating.[12] According to the Hospice Foundation of America:

- Hospice is a special concept of care designed to provide comfort and support to patients and their families when a life-limiting illness no longer responds to cure-oriented treatments.
- Hospice care neither prolongs life nor hastens death. Hospice staff and volunteers offer a specialized knowledge of medical care, including pain management.
- The goal of hospice care is to improve the quality of a patient's last days by offering comfort and dignity.
- Hospice care is provided by a team-oriented group of specially trained professionals, volunteers and family members.
- Hospice addresses all symptoms of a disease, with a special emphasis on controlling a patient's pain and discomfort.

---

10. *Id.* at 486.
11. *Id.* at 486–487.
12. *Id.* at 491.

- Hospice deals with the emotional, social and spiritual impact of the disease on the patient and the patient's family and friends.
- Hospice offers a variety of bereavement and counseling services to families before and after a patient's death.[13]

Most studies indicate that African Americans and Latinos use hospices significantly less often than whites. This is likely due to cultural differences such as those discussed in the last section of this chapter.

Communicating with Clients about Death

In Chapter Eight we will discuss some of the ways in which laws have progressed in this regard and the options available for clients who wish to plan for end-of-life decisions. Here we can only note that attitudes toward aging, illness, dying, and death as they presently exist can be obstacles to the legal professional who serves the elderly. The reluctance to talk about death leads to the use of euphemisms such as "she passed away," "he went to meet Jesus," and "we lost our father last night." Legal professionals must be cautious and understanding in overcoming these obstacles, but ultimately our clients must accept (even if they do not express that acceptance) for so long as it takes to confront the legal issues surrounding aging, illness, dying and death, the fact that they are aged, they are dying and they will die.

In order to overcome these obstacles we must ourselves become comfortable with talking about these issues. There is no one secret to doing this. Each of us must assess our comfort level and ask ourselves how we can best increase that level. When discussing wills and estates in class, I make a point of using terms like "death" and "dying" rather than the euphemisms in order to push against the comfort levels of my students, but we must be careful not to cross our client's comfort line. Our goal is to decrease their denial rather than increase it by being too blunt and forceful.

It is especially important in this process to utilize every communication tool available to us. Remember that communication requires attention from both parties. You must "read" the client to determine the extent to which the client is truly engaged in the conversation. If the client has "closed down" on the topic, try another approach. As we will discuss in the last section of this chapter, people have different perspectives on death. An approach that works well

---

13. "What is Hospice," *Hospice Foundation of America*, http://www.hospicefoundation.org/pages/page.asp?page_id=47055 (Last accessed May 21, 2010).

with one person may not work with another. Also, as we will discuss in the next section, people tend to go through stages when confronting the reality of death. We should attempt to gain insight into which stage our client is at as an approach that works well at one stage will not work well at others.

In the rest of this chapter we will take *The Empowered Paralegal* approach to assisting our clients with discussing death. We have identified the problem in this section. The next step is to gain an understanding of the issues surrounding the problem. This should assist you in applying the remainder of the approach — identifying solutions with which you are comfortable, planning for implementation of those solutions in the context of your practice, and implementing those solutions with the client.

We will begin in the next section by discussing what Kubler-Ross called the stages of dying. In the final section, we will briefly examine some of the various perspectives of aging, dying, and death held by different cultures. It has been my experience that increasing our own understanding of death also increases our comfort level in discussing death as a natural process. This increased level of comfort in turn assists us in overcoming the obstacles inherent in discussing this process with our clients in the quite unnatural setting of the legal environment.

B. Stages of Dying

There are several "models" that describe the stages of dying. None of them can be considered "roadmaps" for the psychological and emotional processes that accompany one's own death or that of a loved one. Rather, they are helpful guides or frameworks that describe the general processes that are individualized by each person based on that person's cultural, religious, and ethnic backgrounds, and the person's own personality, the illness afflicting the person, the person's family circumstances, and other factors. Even to the extent that these models are valid frameworks for understanding the dying process, we must recognize that few people work their way through these stages in a linear fashion. Especially when transitioning from one stage to another, people are likely to fluctuate between stages.

Nonetheless, these models *are* good frameworks for understanding the dying process. While the stages may not be as clear-cut and linear as the models suggest, it is helpful to understand the stages and how they affect the person as that person experiences each stage. Do keep in mind however that each of those experiences is unique. Avoid stereotyping a client as being in a particular stage and thus subject to some requirements imposed by that stage. Keep in mind that there is no "right" way to experience death or any of the stages. Do not be judgmental or suggest to a client that it is time for them to move from one stage to another.

Be mindful that as a person experiences each stage they will have a particular view of "the facts" and that view will color their willingness to make decisions as well as the decisions they make. A decision made in one stage may appear to be quite unsatisfactory in another. The client may appear fickle to the legal professional, but there is—in the client's mind—a sound basis for her changes of mind. We must resist the temptation to complain about the client or persuade the client they do not want to make the changes they are asking for. Rather we should provide an objective forum for discussion of available options that rests in the realization of the process through which they are moving.

With all that in mind, in this section we will review the stages of dying first proposed by Kubler-Ross in *On Death and Dying* in 1969. These stages have been "refined" by other researchers and by Kubler-Ross herself in later works. However, it is not our goal here to become experts in this topic. Rather we want to achieve a basic understanding of the dying and grieving processes.

Shock and Denial

"It was so sudden" is a phrase we hear and say about almost every death. We leave aside the fact that the deceased was 94, a ten-year survivor of AIDS, or in the sixth month of killing the pain of cancer with constantly increasing morphine doses. It is no surprise then that the first reaction of a person and his family to the fact that they are facing imminent death[14] is likely to be a state of shock. After gradual recuperation from that shock, according to Kubler-Ross' studies, "[M]an's usual response is 'No, it cannot be me.'" Since in our unconscious mind we are all immortal, it is almost inconceivable for us to acknowledge that we to have to face death.[15]

This denial is, of course, consistent with our general denial of our own mortality. We tend to think of death in terms of "they" and "them," rather than "I" or "me." Clients who bring in their ill siblings for a will or advanced health care directive may scoff at the idea that they too should have one. Even legal

---

14. I use the phrase "imminent death" loosely here. We all realize, despite our efforts to avoid or deny the fact, that we face death. There comes a moment for many of us when we realize that "it's really going to happen." The time lapse and the course of the dying process from that realization to death may be quite short or may be last for an extended time.

15. Kubler-Ross, *supra* n.3 at 37.

professionals who generally tend to take a more objective and reality-based approach to any fact situations are subject to this state of mind.

When dealing with the general denial of the death process it is often appropriate to remind a client of reality and guide them towards estate planning and making advanced end-of-life decisions. Kubler-Ross' conclusions in *On Death and Dying* suggest a different approach when a client is in this stage of the dying process:

> We attempt to elicit the patients' needs first, try to become aware of their strengths and weakness, and look for overt or hidden communications to determine how much a patient wants to face reality at a given moment.[16]

The roles of the legal professional and medical professions are, of course, not the same. However, the principles stated here by Kubler-Ross are applicable to our working with our clients. It is especially important not to be judgmental, or to insist that the client "snap out of it" and face reality. We are not therapists. It is not our role to attempt to change the client or guide them through the dying process. We need to work with our client's *as they are* to serve their legal needs.

Anger

The next stage noted by Kubler-Ross is that of anger, rage, envy, and resentment. She notes that it is more difficult for family and others to cope with the client in this stage. They often displace their anger, directing it at those with whom they have contact, including those working with them to see that their legal needs are met. In the medical context, Kubler-Ross notes that "Wherever the patient looks at this time, he will find grievances."[17]

Obviously, the legal professional dealing with a person in this stage must avoid taking these grievances personally. Again, we should avoid being judgmental. Indeed, Kubler-Ross suggests respect and understanding. To paraphrase her, "A client who is respected and understood, who is given attention and a little time, will soon lower his voice and reduce his angry demands. He will know he is a valuable human being, cared for, allowed to function at the highest possible level as long as he can."[18]

---

16. *Id.* at 41.
17. *Id.* at 45.
18. *Id.* at 46.

Bargaining

The third stage is likely to be that of "bargaining," usually with God for a cure, for a postponement, for relief from pain and suffering, or for one more chance to do those things not attended to often enough. The dying will often promise God that if they have just one more chance they will do "x." Usually these bargains are negotiated with God and not disclosed to others. However, Kubler-Ross points out that when voiced these bargains are often revealing. Perhaps, for example, if a client wants one more chance to visit his daughter, it reveals guilt at not having attended to that daughter in the past. Such feelings of guilt or remorse can affect a client's decisions during and regarding the end of his life. Such comments should, at least, be noted by the legal professional and noted in the file as a record of the client's state of mind. Awareness and understanding of these concerns by the rest of the legal team can assist them in providing proper guidance to the client.

Depression

Loss triggers depression. Once clients have moved away from denial, anger, and bargaining, once they have admitted to themselves that death is inevitable, they experience a great sense of loss. Our death, of course, is a loss to ourselves and others, but even the approach of death can involve loss. We may lose our jobs and our roles as providers for our families. This will likely cause a loss of self-esteem and sense of self. We will likely undergo a long period of increasing loss of bodily and mental functioning.

Kubler-Ross notes two types of depression. One is a reactive depression developed in reaction to a past loss. Often "an understanding person will have no difficulty in eliciting the cause of the depression and in alleviating some of the unrealistic guilt or shame which often accompanies the depression."[19] However, when the depression is preparatory, that is, "when the depression is a tool to prepare for the impending loss of all the love objects, in order to facilitate the state of acceptance, then encouragements and reassurances are not as meaningful."[20]

In either case, we must keep in mind that we are legal professionals, not therapists. Attempting to act as therapists, especially with depressed clients can lead to unwanted results and may be malpractice. Thus, we should not at-

---

19. *Id,* at 76.
20. *Id.* at 77.

tempt to make the client better. There are certain things which we should *not* do. Again paraphrasing Kubler-Ross, "The client should not be encouraged to look at the sunny side of things, as this would mean he should not contemplate his impending death. It would be contraindicated to tell him not to be sad, since all of us are tremendously sad when we lose one beloved person."[21]

As legal professionals we need to work with our clients as they are. However, with the seriously depressed client we should be mindful of signs indicating the client is considering suicide, an issue discussed in Chapter Two. Also, serious depression may affect the client's competency to make decisions.

Acceptance

Many persons facing death are fortunate enough to move into the stage of acceptance. Others will fight to the end. Kubler-Ross distinguishes acceptance from "a resigned and hopeless 'giving up,' a sense of 'what's the use'" or "I just cannot fight it any longer." Rather, acceptance is a sense that the struggle is over. She describes it as being "almost void of feelings." "[I]t is as if the pain had gone, the struggle is over, and there comes a time for 'the final rest before the long journey' as one patient phrased it."[22]

During this stage the family often needs more understanding and support than the client herself. The client is likely to have diminished interest in legal concerns, wishing to be left alone. If proper planning has not been done, it may be necessary to proceed with execution of important documents at this time despite the lack of interest and the expression of desire not to be bothered. Understanding is again called for. Do not be judgmental. Lack of interest at this stage does not indicate the client does not understand the importance of what must be done or a lack of recognition of the work that has been and is being done for her.

Stages and Family

As the family comes to grips with the reality of their loved one's death, they too will likely experience stages similar to those discussed in this section. While they will experience their loved one's death together, they will each do so in their own way and on their own "schedule." This can lead to conflict within the family. This conflict, especially, during the anger stage, can be displaced, that is,

---

21. *Id.*
22. *Id.* at 100.

brought to bear against those providing services to the dying person. This can especially be the case for legal professionals when there are no clearly established ground rules regarding who the client is, confidentiality, and other issues discussed in Chapter Four.

Again, it is important not to take this personally. If it gets out of hand, it may be necessary to gently but firmly let the family member know it is time to stop the discussion. Let them know you have heard their grievance and understand it. You also understand their circumstances and look forward (if appropriate) to resuming the discussion another time. All such incidents should be reported to the attorney and recorded in the file.

C. Differing Approaches to the End of Life

The United States and thus our clientele is becoming increasingly multicultural and multiethnic. According to the U.S. Census Bureau projections, by 2050, minorities (any race other than non-Hispanic, single-race whites) will be the majority in America and the number of residents older than 65 will constitute about 20% of the population.[23] While the greatest increase as a percentage of the population will consist of Hispanics, our clients are likely to be drawn from a large mix of countries, cultures, ethnicities, and religions, each with their own perspectives on the issues under discussion in this chapter. Overall, the population of foreign-born persons in the United States in 2002 was around 33.1 million or 11.5% of the total population.[24]

It is not possible for us to examine every possible existing perspective or to examine any one of them in depth. Instead, we will take an overview sample of some of the approaches we are likely to find among our clientele. The goal is to gain an understanding of differing perspectives so that we can better identify them in our clients and thus better assist the clients in meeting their legal needs.

We must be careful not to carry this process of identification and understanding too far. We do not want to engage in stereotyping and "cultural profiling." Respect and sensitivity regarding our client's cultural background will

---

23. "Minorities expected to be majority in 2050," CNN.com/US, August 13, 2008, http://www.cnn.com/2008/US/08/13/census.minorities/index.html (Last accessed May 20, 2010).

24. Penelope J. Moore, "The New Black Migration: Dying and Grief in African and Caribbean Migrants," *Diversity and End-of-Life Care* 94 (Kenneth J. Doka and Amy S. Tucci eds., Hospice Foundation of America 2009).

improve our ability to serve our clients. Pigeonholing our clients based on characteristics of a particular culture will not. Each client will be a unique combination of characteristics combining their race, background culture, ethnicity, religion, and the like, blended with their own personality and perspective on the end of life.

Personal Autonomy and End-of-Life Decisions

I am a firm advocate of personal autonomy when decisions are to be made regarding estate planning and end-of-life issues. You may detect my enthusiasm for the rights confirmed by court decisions and the Patient Self-Determination Act when you read Chapter Eight. Personal autonomy is a fundamental concept underlying American heritage, politics, and laws. It is often seen politically and legally as a way to show respect for people as individuals. We have an obligation to see that our clients are advised of all of their rights and options under the law.

We should also recognize, however, that not all cultures see autonomy in the same way. Some researchers describe a perspective on the norm of respect for persons that is more relational, i.e., that focuses on the person's relationship to family and society rather than on the individual. One writer notes that these differing perspectives can result in a number of conflicts relating to end-of-life care:

1. Conflicts between cultural values on the one hand and professional values and institutional interests on the other. This conflict is reflected in our initial discussion in the first section of this chapter when we noted that the majority of dying patients, regardless of age, experience severe, undertreated pain, and nearly 40% spend at least 10 days in an intensive care unit even though most people express a preference to die at home, without pain, surrounded by friends and family.

2. Conflicts between cultural values and individual rights exemplified when a member of the family insists that an individual's rights be subjugated to cultural values. This is not a matter of persons disagreeing over what the person of concern would have wanted, such as happened in the Terry Schiavo case.[25] Rather, it occurs when a family member insists that the known and expressed wishes of a client not be honored because they conflict with that member's understanding of what is culturally or religiously right.

---

25. See Chapter Eight, pages 226.

3. Conflicts between autonomy and what is in the client's objective best interest. This issue arises when the client elects an option based on cultural, religious, or other belief that—using objective standards—is not in the client's best interest, for example, a Christian Scientist's refusal of a life-saving blood transfusion
4. Finally, conflicts can arise between autonomy and rationality. For example, a client may want to spend large amounts of money on a "miracle cure" that by any objective standard is a sham.[26]

These potential conflicts should be kept in mind as we continue this review.

Generalities and Diversity

Making general statements regarding racial, ethnic, religious, or cultural groups is always difficult and often dangerous. A major problem is the great amount of diversity within such groups. Every researcher must confront this difficulty. One author notes, "It is hard to speak in general terms about the Native American population. Although there are large concentrations of certain tribes throughout the southwestern and western parts of the country, there are also many smaller tribes in Florida, North Carolina, and other parts of the country. And Alaska has its own native population."[27] Another researcher states, "Generalizations about Asian elderly are difficult, not only because of their cultural diversity, but also because of the different patterns of immigration among these groups. The heyday of Japanese immigration to the United States was before the immigration restrictions of 1924 and after World War II. In contrast, Koreans entered the country primarily during the 1970s and 1980s, and Korean immigration began to decline dramatically in 1989." This means that the aged of each Asian group are of different generations.[28]

Nevertheless, certain generalizations can be made. Statistical data, for example, shows African Americans have a higher overall incidence of death from cancer, but they use hospice less than whites.[29] In general, African Americans and Latinos are less likely than other groups to engage in the end-of-life plan-

---

26. Bruce Jennings, "Ethical Aspects of Cultural Diversity," *Diversity and End-of-Life Care* 35–45 (Kenneth J. Doka and Amy S. Tucci eds., Hospice Foundation of America 2009).

27. Richard B. Fife, "Diversity and Access to Hospice Care," *Diversity and End-of-Life Care* 57 (Kenneth J. Doka and Amy S. Tucci eds., Hospice Foundation of America 2009).

28. Donald E. Gelfand, *Aging and Ethnicity: Knowledge and Services* at 72. (Springer Publishing Company 2003).

29. Hooyman and Kiyak, *supra* n.8 at 491.

ning such as living wills and in utilization of palliative care. Many of these differences can be traced to cultural, ethnic, or religious traits of a group. For example, African Americans may use hospices less than whites because of:

- Mistrust of the medical establishment
- Cultural perception of nobility in suffering
- Belief that life is sacred and must be preserved no matter what
- Long-standing traditions of the family and community taking care of those who suffer from serious illness[30]
- Perception of advance directives and palliative care as "giving up hope"
- Fear that palliative care or hospice is being prescribed as a way to limit expense or "get rid of them"[31]

Similarly, Hispanics or Latinos

- Experience discrimination in healthcare
- Fear the medical establishment
- Face language barriers
- Lack awareness of resources such as Medicare to pay for hospice care
- Know they are dying but choose not to speak about it
- Believe in the responsibility of family to care for their own rather than bring in outsiders.
- Believe that sacredness of life demands life support
- Confront lack of culturally sensitive care[32]

Several cultures including many Native American tribes and Asian cultures, such as many in Korea, China and India, include a belief that speaking openly and truthfully about death and dying hastens death.[33]

There are obvious implications here for the legal professional. Keeping in mind that no individual client can be presumed to hold the beliefs of their background culture, the legal professional must be mindful of these differences. Failure to recognize and acknowledge them in our efforts to communicate regarding legal options can lead to mistrust and a complete breakdown in communications. Sensitivity, empathy, and understanding are essential for the empowered paralegal. With this in mind we will review some of the general information available regarding some of the major groups.

---

30. For these four factors see Fife, *supra* n.27 at 52–53.
31. For these two factors see Hooyman and Kiyak, *supra* n.8 at 491.
32. Fife, *supra* n.27 at 55.
33. *Id.* at 59.

African Americans

African Americans have a long history in the United States, much of which has added to a general mistrust of the medical establishment.[34] The struggle for equality, interaction with the larger culture, and vestiges of older African culture all influence the African American perspective on death, dying, and end-of-life care. As with any group, there are significant subgroups among African Americans, and the perspectives of those subgroups can differ significantly. However, there are also common experiences for all African Americans.

Blacks, regardless of their particular cultural ancestry are poorer than whites overall. Although they comprise only 13% of the population, about 33% of blacks fall below the federal poverty level.[35] This results in less access to healthcare and less access to healthcare information. This, together with the historical factors already mentioned, tends to preserve mistrust of the medical establishment and alienation of African Americans from health care providers.

There are distinct identities and traditions among blacks, but certain general traits or inclination can be delineated. Researcher Ronald Barrett lists these characteristics:

- To be "death accepting"—that is, perceiving death as part of the natural rhythm of life;
- To oppose active euthanasia;
- To regard death, dying, and the dead with great reverence and respect;
- To regard funerals as primary rituals;
- To believe that attendance at and participation in funeral services is an important social obligation;
- To prefer ground burial;
- To believe in life after death and the notion that a person transitions to the spiritual world;
- To acknowledge the presence of dead ancestors' spirits in the community;
- To engage in rituals and traditions to honor the dead, such as naming a baby after a deceased person.[36]

---

34. *Id.* at 50–54.

35. Ronald Barrett, "Sociocultural Considerations: African Americans, Grief, and Loss," *Diversity and End-of-Life Care* 81 (Kenneth J. Doka and Amy S. Tucci eds., Hospice Foundation of America 2009).

36. *Id.* at 83–4.

Barrett also notes the significant influence an individual African American's religion can have on that individual's perspective on death and dying. These religious influences range from liberal to conservative and will override other influence. He gives the example of Jehovah's Witnesses refusing blood transfusions.[37]

African Americans view a funeral as a time to honor the worth of the deceased as an individual. It is an opportunity to show the deceased dignity and "a final triumph and one last attempt to be regarded as somebody."[38] Funerals may be delayed to allow time for the family and others to gather and fulfill the social obligation of participating in the funeral. The legal professional should be mindful of this importance as well as the importance of sincere expression of condolences. This importance to maintaining the relationships with clients and their families cannot be overstated. As Ronald Barrett, professor of psychology at Loyola Marymount University states, "Unsolicited expressions of condolence and support are expected and greatly valued. It is generally believed that the greater and more personal one's investment in expressing condolence, the greater the value and regard for the survivors."[39]

Recent African and Caribbean Migrants

While there is a tendency to group all black people under the term African American, the term is not really applicable to recent immigrants from Africa and the Caribbean. While all blacks are commonly grouped together for census and healthcare data purposes, they are culturally distinct.

Certainly there are some commonalities based on traditional African influences. For example, death is viewed as another phase of life involving a transition from the material world to the spiritual world.[40] However, recent immigrants are more closely associated with traditional religious and medical practices linked to the region from which they immigrated. Often they have a perspective formed by a blend of those traditions with the religions of the former colonial rulers of their region.[41]

---

37. *Id.* at 85.
38. *Id.* at 86.
39. *Id.* at 86.
40. Penelope J. Moore, *supra* n.24 at 93.
41. *Id.* at 96.

The legal professional should be aware that the experience of immigration, especially among the poor, predisposes the immigrants to "complicated grief," the intensification of the pain of loss to the point of being overwhelmed and resorting to maladaptive behavior. Complicated grief can result in the griever being unable to move beyond the state of grief.[42] The legal professional should be particularly sensitive and understanding in situations of complicated grief.

Because formal healthcare services are designed for (and generally delivered by) the majority, recent immigrants can be especially mistrustful of the healthcare establishment. Language differences can also be an obstacle to understanding the system. This can lead to a great deal of anger and resentment, especially if the medical establishment's use of non-traditional medicine is viewed as having denied the family "the opportunity to openly and honestly embrace the certainty of death."[43]

Much of what has been said regarding the immigrant's experience with the medical establishment can be applied to the legal establishment as we deal with the legal issues confronting our elderly clients. This advice to medical and hospice providers should also be taken to heart by the legal profession, "Assessment of a client's religious history, background, and worldview can provide valuable insights about both the client and the client's legal problem."[44]

Native Americans

Native Americans, like the other groups we have discussed, are extremely diverse, with wide variances in tribal cultures and traditions. There is no single American Indian religion, however, there does appear to be a common thread of spirituality. "For the American Indian, the life power comes from ritual, sharing with family and community, and living according to the group's model of spirituality ... [S]uffering and pain may lead patients and families to call for ceremonies to allow them to return to the sacred way. Healthcare [and legal] professionals should be sensitive to this need and encourage traditional rituals."[45]

Most Native American traditions include reverence and respect for death as a part of the total life process. It is as natural as birth. However, discussions

---

42. *Id.* at 98.
43. *Id.* at 101.
44. *Id.* at 103.
45. Gerry R. Cos, "Death, Dying, and End of Life in American Indian Communities," *Diversity and End-of-Life Care* 109 (Kenneth J. Doka and Amy S. Tucci eds., Hospice Foundation of America 2009).

about death and legal issues with the legal establishment can be difficult for American Indians. They may communicate differently with people in mainstream American society, using more nonverbal behavior and silence. Many do not look another person in the eye until a bond has been established.[46] Further, because of mistrust of mainstream institutions, they may view discussions of end-of-life issues as attempts to pressure them to assimilate into the mainstream culture.[47]

However, many of the American Indian beliefs comport with the goals of palliative care and achieving the "good death." "The naturalistic philosophy of tribes generally means that when it is one's time to die, one should die naturally, without tubes or machines. American Indians are unlikely to use medically futile interventions, and they do not believe in showing love by trying to keep a person alive as along as possible. An important belief is that one does not allow a loved one to die with strangers."[48]

Elders play an interesting role. They are respected and treated in a special way:

> Children are taught to respect them and listen to them. Elders may or may not be tribal leaders, but they help make decisions in all things that are important to the group, including education, jobs, health and health care, … They … teach children to respect their culture and themselves. They teach the three Rs: respect, reciprocity, and relationships. A fourth R might be responsibility … Elders try to live in a way that earns the respect of other and to be models so that others can learn to respect themselves.[49]

The legal professional should become familiar with protocols for interacting with elders, such as allowing them to talk first.[50] Further, the professional should be prepared to interact with the elders on behalf of the client. Like legal professionals, elders do not make choices for others, interfere with the decisions of others, or judge them. However, they do give guidance, suggestions and advice. At times it may be necessary and appropriate (with the client's permission) to obtain the assistance of elders in steering a client in the right direction.

---

46. *Id.* at 110.
47. *Id.* at 112.
48. *Id.* at 113.
49. *Id.* at 112–13.
50. *Id.* at 113.

Hispanics/Latinos

Carlos Sandoval-Cros, a psychiatrist and Episcopal priest, lists several cultural themes that have implications for working with Hispanics as members of the legal team:

- Emphasis on the well-being of the family over that of the individual with the implication that family members be included in discussions
- Trust-building over time based on the display of mutual respect. The implication here is the need to demonstrate respect for the client and his family
- Respect for authority and hierarchy. Sandoval-Cros suggests this may undermine communications between medical and legal personnel and the patient/client
- Emphasis on the present rather than the past and future with obvious implications for end-of-life planning since end-of-life occurs in the future
- Belief in good and evil spirits that can affect health and well-being
- Belief that fate determines life outcomes and is predestined.[51]

For Hispanics, the conflict between autonomy and culture is often resolved in favor of culture, i.e., the family. Researchers have found that Mexican Americans are less likely than European Americans to believe a patient should be told about a terminal diagnosis, are more likely to believe that family members should make the decisions for them, and are less likely to utilize advanced directives. They are far more likely to want life-prolonging treatments over palliative care than European Americans.

Jews

Judaism is more than a religion, it is a culture. Members of that culture may be quite religious or they be quite secularized. Those who are religious are not monolithically so. There are many Jewish sects generally grouped as Orthodox, Conservative, or Reform. Regardless of a Jew's religiousness or lack thereof, a Jew may hold to Jewish customs and honor Jewish holidays. The legal professional with Jewish client should be familiar with these holidays and

---

51. Carlos Sandoval-Cros, "Hispanic Cultural Issues in End-of-Life Care," *Diversity and End-of-Life Care* 120 (Kenneth J. Doka and Amy S. Tucci eds., Hospice Foundation of America 2009).

the events they recognize or celebrate. The fact that the Jewish Sabbath is on Saturday should also be respected.

Many Jews, especially Orthodox Jews, also live according to Jewish law, a legal system based on the Torah (the first five books of the Bible). Decisions made by these Jews must be consistent with both secular law and the Torah, as interpreted by a rabbi. For example, there is a general prohibition under Jewish law, subject to some exceptions, against autopsy. Living will forms that deal with the requirements of Jewish law are available.[52] Most Jewish law is based on legal opinions from earlier times, but many modern end-of-life medical care decisions were not considered in those eras and must be interpreted by modern rabbis. These Rabbinical opinions can differ sharply. Rabbi Barry M. Kinzbrunner reports, for example, that many rabbis have ruled that one may withhold medical interventions, while others have ruled that one may not.[53] There is, however, almost universal agreement among Orthodox rabbis that artificial hydration and nutrition may not be withdrawn.[54]

Interpreting the Torah can be a complex undertaking. Doctor Daniel Eisenberg's reasoning regarding Do Not Resuscitate orders is illustrative:

> The question of "do not resuscitate" orders is complex, yet fascinating. The Torah commandment of "do not stand by idly while your neighbor's blood is being spilled" (a mitzvah that is commonly understood to mean that everyone has a personal obligation to prevent his friend from being harmed) would seem to mandate compulsory resuscitation of everyone, since cardiac arrest and apnea certainly represent the ultimate in dangerous situations. Why then was it not always the custom to attempt CPR on every Jew who died?
> The reason is because Judaism recognizes the inevitability of death. When someone dies, we are proscribed from desecrating the body, which includes invasion of the corpse. Moreover, the Code of Jewish Law (Shulchan Aruch) explains that there is a prohibition of touching a moribund patient (goses) who is estimated to have less than three days to live. Resuscitation of a goses is not required, and in fact may

---

52. See, e.g., the United Synagogue for Conservative Judaism's website, http://www.uscj.org/Jewish_Medical_Direc5334.html (Last accessed May 20, 2010) and The Rabbinical Council of America Halachic Health Care Proxy, http://www.rabbis.org/pdfs/hcp.pdf (Last accessed May 21, 2010).

53. Barry M. Kinzbrunner, "Orthodox and Hasidic Perspectives," *Diversity and End-of-Life Care* 142 (Kenneth J. Doka and Amy S. Tucci eds., Hospice Foundation of America 2009).

54. *Id.* at 146.

be prohibited, as a forbidden intrusion on the natural dying process. Therefore, the underlying assumption in Judaism is that one should NOT resuscitate a gravely ill patient, but only a patient for whom there is a reasonable expectation of reversing the underlying cause of physiologic collapse.[55]

Dr. Eisenberg notes the proscription against desecration of the body including invasion of the corpse that necessitates provisions in living wills regarding autopsies. Despite this prohibition, the United Synagogue of Conservative Judaism, affirming the life-giving benefits of organ and tissue donation, has adopted a resolution encouraging all Jews to become enrolled as organ and tissue donors. According to the United Synagogue's website:

> The resolution further urges that potential donors sign and carry cards or drivers licenses attesting to their commitment of such organs and tissues, upon their death, to those in need.
> ... [T]he resolution—adopted at the organization's 1997 Biennial Convention—is based on the premise that consideration for the health and welfare of others is at the heart of Jewish ethics. Organ and tissue donation is recognized as a life-giving act, since "the transplantation of organs and tissues is scientifically proven as a way to save the lives of persons with terminal diseases or to improve the quality of life for the blind, the deaf and others with life-threatening diseases."[56]

The bottom line here is that we as legal professionals must understand and respect a Jewish client's relationship with his rabbi.

The mourning ritual has special significance in Judaism. Generally, the dead must be buried within 24 hours. Up to the time of burial, the mourners mourn the person who died. "As soon as the burial is over, the mourners turn away from the fresh grave. Now it is *they* who are death's victims and the center of concern, receiving the compassion that until now has been focused on the dying person. The transformation happens in a precise ritual."[57] That ritual, known as shiva, lasts for seven days. During this time we should make ourselves available to support and comfort the families, but not interfere or make demands.

---

55. Daniel Eisenberg, MD, "End of Life Choices in Halacha," *Jewish Law Articles*, http://www.jlaw.com/Articles/EndofLife.html (Last accessed May 21, 2010).

56. "Organ Donation," *United Synagogue for Conservative Judaism*, http://www.uscj.org/Organ_Donation5335.html (Last accessed May 21, 2010).

57. Maurice Lamm, Jewish Perspectives on Loss, Grief, and End-of-Life Care," *Diversity and End-of-Life Care* 134 (Kenneth J. Doka and Amy S. Tucci eds., Hospice Foundation of America 2009).

Respect the process and be aware that it will be seven days before the family will attend to any legal matter. Advance planning should minimize the necessity for action during this period.

Muslims

Religion is a comprehensive way of life for practicing Muslims. Like Jews, Muslims in the United States abide by religious law as well as secular law. The Islamic law, based on the Koran, was, like the Torah, subject to reasoning by Islamic scholars in pervious eras. However, for Muslims there can be no additions to Islamic law since the tenth century. The law and its application is, however, subject to interpretation. Most Muslims recognize no central authority, so the interpretation of Islamic law is far from uniform. There is thus a great deal of diversity within the Islamic religion.

One point on which Muslims generally agree is that Islam gives people great autonomy in determining the course of action in end of life matters.[58] However, this autonomy is coupled with a sense of responsibility for family, neighbors, and community, and Islamic law makes adults legally responsible for the economic support of their parents.[59]

Other general factors about which the legal professional should be aware include:

- Immigrant Muslims rely on their families for support and avoid institutionalized care
- As long as they are conscious, even the bedridden are expected to perform the five daily ritual prayers
- As long as ill adults are lucid, they are deemed essentially competent, which may conflict with the determination of competency under secular law
- The Koran stresses respect for parents and the duty of children to care for them in the frailty of old age
- Modesty is highly valued in Islam and dress is considered by many to be an expression of modesty
- The Islamic year follows a lunar calendar with no leap year, so the holidays (of which there are three primary) rotate throughout the calendar year

---

58. Hasan Shanawani and Syed Zafar, "Dying and Grief in the Islamic Community," *Diversity and End-of-Life Care* 155 (Kenneth J. Doka and Amy S. Tucci eds., Hospice Foundation of America 2009).

59. *Id.* at 154.

- During Ramadan, a month-long holiday, Muslims fast from sun up to sun down
- Medications are considered to break the Ramadan fast, so there may be a reluctance to take medications during the day
- Men are required to attend Friday prayer and many women do attend also.[60]

Muslim dead must usually be buried before the next sunrise or sundown after death. Mourning is usually three to seven days, but a woman who has lost her husband may mourn for several months, especially if she is pregnant. While bereaved families are distressed, the mourning process can be viewed as an opportunity for the family and friends to reflect as well as grieve.[61]

Muslims do not cremate or embalm their dead and engage in few rituals other than a ritual washing of the body by members of the family, Muslim community, or funeral home personnel, after which the body is wrapped in a shroud for a short funeral ceremony.[62]

There is no central authority to establish a formal position on end-of-life issues and thus there is a great deal of controversy on each of those issues.

Buddhists

Buddhism is based on the Four Noble Truths or insights of Buddha. First, all life is suffering, including those things which give us pleasure as they cause us to crave more. Second, we crave for that which makes us happy, but all happiness is fleeting, the cravings are endless. This turns us into slave of our desires. Buddhists seek to become free of this slavery.

Third, the way out of suffering and desire is nirvana, the state of non-being. We build up good and bad Karma through our actions in our lives. If karma has not worked itself out in a person's life, the person is reborn and repeats the cycle of suffering and desire, unless and until they reach nirvana.

When one reaches nirvana, there is no self. "Just as all pleasures are fleeting, so is the self. Part of the basic Buddhist worldview is that nothing lasts ... In Buddhism, the impermanence of all things is applied to one's ego as well. And here is the joy of Buddhism: If there is no self, why worry about oneself? The freedom gained from a realization of no-self is bliss."[63] There are many

---

60. *Id.* at 154–8.

61. *Id.* at 159.

62. *Id.* at 161–2.

63. Eve Mullen, "Buddhist Perspectives on Death, Grief, and Loss," *Diversity and End-of-Life Care* 167 (Kenneth J. Doka and Amy S. Tucci eds., Hospice Foundation of America 2009).

forms of Buddhism, but the Four Noble Truths, karma, nirvana, and the concept of no-self are common to them all. This worldview, of course, has a significant effect on the Buddhist perspective of death and dying.

For Buddhists, only death is certain and there is no certainty about the time of our death, and we should live accordingly. Other than this basic truth, there is no one Buddhist view of death. Commonality is based on the concept of rebirth and no-self. Thus, "A dying person is not a permanent self that will be lost. After one short lifetime of constant change, death and rebirth only mark more change and another transformation in a universe of almost unending movement."[64]

Since Buddhism is not a theistic religion, words like "soul," "afterlife," "God," and "creator" are not meaningful.[65] "Karma," "rebirth," and other words associated with Buddhism are, but should not be used lightly. Have a sound understanding of what they mean before you use them.

Buddhist rituals reflect Buddhist diversity, but non-attachment to the body is a tenet of all forms of Buddhism. Both burial and cremation are appropriate.

Buddhists do not deal with the "rightness" or "wrongness" of acts associated with end of life issues, but with intentions associated with the acts. Eve Mullen gives this example to illustrate this point:

> If a person trips and falls down while walking past us, we might rush to help, but think, "This person will reward me" or "Maybe this person will like me more." These are attached actions, motivated by selfish desires. In Buddhism, these are incorrect actions. The correct action would be a natural, compassionate effort with no thought of what we might gain from it.[66]

Determination of what is right and wrong in a particular end-of-life situation thus will depend on the intentions of the person making the decisions and, "Even within one religious family, individuals may come to different conclusions on end-of-life decisions."[67]

Buddhists do have a concept of a good death. It is one of "calm awareness of potential ... not an end to an individual person, but an opportunity for selfless compassion, as well as for liberation from samsara [the endless cycle of suffering and desire] in the light of the Buddha's Four Noble Truths."[68]

---

64. *Id.* at 169.
65. *Id.* at 170.
66. *Id.* at 173.
67. *Id.*
68. *Id.* at 176.

Conclusion

We have barely touched on the diverse perspectives of death and dying that exist in our society. There is a seemingly endless list. There are countless religious perspectives that we have not addressed including evangelical Christians, Catholics, Mormons, Christian Scientists. There are also the perspectives of groups identifiable without reference to religion such as gays and lesbians. With regard to the perspectives we have examined, we have barely touched the surface. *Diversity and End-of-Life Care,* a book on which I have heavily relied in preparing this section of this chapter begins with a proverb: "Every person is like all others, like some others, and like no others."[69] That book, the proverb, and this chapter of this book, are about "witnessing and appreciating individuality that is built on a foundation of common humanity."[70]

If we as legal professionals are to truly work with our clients to address the legal issues relating to their lives and the end of their lives, we must have an awareness of, an understanding of, and a respect for "the distinctiveness of culture, language, social circumstance, religion, personality, and gender [that] are key foundations by which individuals find meaning and purpose in their living an dying and come to terms with the loss and remembrance of family and loved ones."[71] We need not, and cannot, become experts in each of the perspectives held by our clients, but we can be aware of the diversity of perspectives and treat each of them with respect and understanding, and without judgment.

This is the last section of the last chapter dealing specifically with elder clients and their families. In Part Two we move on to consideration of some of the issues facing those clients—estate planning, end-of-life decisions, the Social Security Act and other laws, elder abuse, and ethical considerations.

---

69. Kenneth J. Doka and Amy S. Tucci, *Diversity and End-of-Life Care,* i. (Hospice Foundation of America 2009).

70. *Id.* at iii.

71. *Id.* at iii.

Part II

Estate Planning and Elder Law Issues

CHAPTER SIX

ESTATE PLANNING AND THE PERILS OF INTESTACY

At its best elder law starts with the young. While we tend to think of Elder Law in terms of old age and dying, we need not and should not wait until our clients are confronted with the immediacy of Alzheimer's or terminal disease to begin confronting the legal issues associated with the elderly anymore than we would wait until we are 65 to begin planning for retirement. Within the legal profession, financial and asset planning for old age and death is referred to as "estate planning," the subject of the next two chapters.

There are two common misconceptions among clients regarding estate planning. Both of these misconceptions are based on the belief that estate planning only deals with the distribution of their assets after they die. First, estate planning not only attempts to meet the client's goals for their assets after their deaths, it also attempts to maximize the benefits of those assets for our clients and their families during their lifetime. Second, in essence, estate planning is about assisting our clients in achieving peace of mind *now* about their future and the future of their families. In order to achieve that peace of mind we need to address more than simply financial assets. Advanced planning for other end-of-life decisions is covered in Chapter Eight.

Certainly assets are a major source of concern for our clients when they come to us for estate planning. They are concerned about protecting, preserving and maximizing those assets for their retirement and ensuring proper distribution of those assets after death. However, there is much more to life and death than money and tangibles. Estate planning is about choices, but not just choices in the distribution of assets. If we are to serve our clients we must give them the opportunity, information and advice they need to make choices regarding those other aspects of life, end-of-life, and death: Who will take care of their minor children if they cannot? Who will take care of the client if the client cannot do so himself? Who will make medical and end-of-life decisions for the client if she cannot? What will happen to her dead body?

These are all important issues for our clients and, therefore, they are important factors an effective and professional paralegal must understand. These issues will be dealt with comprehensively in Chapters Seven and Eight, but they should be kept in mind as we discuss the more concrete aspect of estate planning in this chapter.

A. Goals of Estate Planning

Goals of Estate Planning

Before we begin discussing the nuts and bolts of estate planning, it is useful to know why we do it and what we hope to gain by it. There are two ways to answer those questions. One way entails a positive statement of the benefits and goals of estate planning. The other involves explaining what happens if there is no estate plan. In this section we will discuss the goals. In the next section we will deal with the negative perspective and take a look at intestate succession—the state of affairs that occurs when there is no plan.

In essence, estate planning is about taking control of the future. We never, of course, have complete control, but we can provide for both our own future and the future of our families, even after we are dead. The first three goals for estate planning deal primarily with financial matters. As a result, it is not unusual for those of us who are not extremely well off financially to ask why we should be concerned with estate planning. That is where the last, and I believe, the most important goal comes in.

The first goal of estate planning is to provide for the client's desires for the distribution of his assets and for the care of those who have depended on him in life and will continue to do so after he dies. This goal has several aspects. First, we must make sure we have a firm understanding of what those desires are and then we must find a way to express those desires in a way that will clearly communicate them. The first is often the primary responsibility of the paralegal, requiring the paralegal to be quite skilled in understanding the law of estate planning and in understanding the client. The paralegal will also often prepare a first draft, expressing those desires in documents that will clearly communicate them.

The second goal is to give legal effect to those desires, i.e., to see that to the extent possible those desires are carried out for the client when the client is no longer able to do so himself. This is often a matter of using the right legal tools, tools that will create legally binding mechanisms ensuring that those desires are carried out. Here, too, the paralegal is often heavily involved. The paralegal must be able to gather the necessary information and understand each of the tools and how they work together well enough to assist the attorney in matching those tools with the client's desires.

The third goal is to maximize the amount of benefit that is passed on after the client dies. This, of course, involves minimizing the costs and taxes levied on those assets at the time of death. It may involve planning in order to meet Medicaid eligibility requirements as discussed in Chapter Nine. But, it also involves planning during the client's life to meet her life goals.

Proper estate planning will often involve members of the estate planning team other than the client, the attorney and the paralegal. Those members may include insurance agents, bankers, accountants, stock brokers, trust officers, and others.

The final goal is the most important—to minimize the stress, trauma, confusion, frustration of and *conflict between* members of the client's family. The better we do at accomplishing the first three goals, the more likely it is that we will have accomplished this one. Even when the family members do not like and do not agree with the wishes of the client, stress, confusion, frustration and especially conflict are reduced when the client's wishes are clear, clearly expressed, and legally binding.

Of course, while we can minimize these problems in some families, often they can never be eliminated. However, review each of the major disputes we discussed in Chapter Four for a moment. Careful consideration will reveal that each of them could have been minimized, if not avoided, with proper drafting of the relevant legal documents.

As discussed in Chapter Four, these conflicts are often based on motives other than money, so the purposes of and need for estate planning exist even when there is little or no money in the client's estate. For those so motivated, when there is no money to ignite the conflict, those conflicts shift to issues such as guardians for children, medical treatment, and burial.

These four are the primary goals of estate planning and they generally will apply to every client. In addition to these general goals, each client will have his own goals—the desires and wishes that give particularity to the general estate planning goals. In the next section, we will consider those goals.

Goals of the Estate Planning Client

Each client's desires, wishes, and goals will, of course, be as individual as the client herself. There is value, however, in considering the general nature of those goals. If we are to assist the client in reaching her goals we must be able to elicit from the client the information necessary for us to choose and use the correct tools for the job.

In this regard it is helpful to seek clarity from the client with respect to three sorts of goals—short-term, mid-term and long-term. These categories are fairly self-explanatory. A short-term goal may be to buy a new TV or car, or to go on a vacation in the next few months. Mid-term goals may be to graduate from college or buy a house. Long-term goals may be to fund a child's college education or our own retirement.

These goals change with each stage of a person's life. My goals now are far different than they were when I was in college and they changed when I graduated, first married, graduated from law school, had children, set up my first law office, and so on. Life can appear quite static from any one stage in one's life. It can be surprising how often those stages and a person's goals change. As a result, clients are advised to review their estate plans at least every five years.

Figure 5-1 shows the life stages of a hypothetical client named Melvin.[1] As we consider the processes and goals of planning and the consequences of not planning estates and end-of-life decisions in this chapter and Chapters Seven and Eight, it is helpful to reflect on this chart. What are Melvin's goals likely to be at each stage of his life? How are those goals likely to change as "persons of concern" come into and leave his life? If he does not make choices regarding to whom his estate goes and how those persons of concern are cared for, who will? If he does not make decisions regarding his own medical treatment, what his death will be like? What will happen to his body? Who will make decisions for him?

Before delving into estate planning, in the next section we will look at the answer to the question of what happens to his estate if a client does not make that decision himself—a process known as intestate succession. It will soon be clear why I refer to this answer as the "negative" explanation of why we do estate planning.

B. Intestate Succession

The short answer to the question "Who decides where our assets go, who oversees our estates, and who decides who will be guardians for our children if we do not have a plan?" is the state legislature. It is difficult for me to see

---

1. While the client is hypothetical, the life stages are based on the "real life" story of Melvin Dummar as depicted in the movie *Melvin and Howard* (MCA Universal, 1980). During the eleven year period depicted in the movie, Melvin moves from Stages 4 through 11 on the chart.

Figure 5-1

STAGES OF MELVIN'S LIFE

Persons of Concern

Stage 1	Minor	Mother Father Aunt
Stage 2	Single Adult	Mother Father Aunt
Stage 3	Married Adult	Wife Mother Father Aunt
Stage 4	Married with child	Wife Daughter Mother Father Aunt
Stage 5	Separated with child	Wife Daughter Mother Father Aunt
Stage 6	Divorced with child	Ex-wife Daughter Mother Father Aunt
Stage 7	Re-married to first wife	Wife Daughter Son?* Mother Father Aunt

* The question mark indicates there is some doubt as to whether Melvin is the biological father of the son.

Figure 5-1, *continued*

Stage 8	Divorced with children	Ex-wife Daughter Son? Mother Father Aunt
Stage 9	Married to 2nd wife	2nd Wife Daughter Son? Step–children Mother Father Aunt Ex-wife
Stage 10	Married to 2nd wife with adult children	2nd Wife Adult Daughter Adult son? Adult step-children Mother Father Aunt Ex-wife

Stage 11	Married to 2d wife
	with adult children and
	minor grandchildren,
	Parents deceased
		2nd Wife
		Adult Daughter with two
		  minor grandchildren
		Adult Son? with three minor
		  grandchildren
		Adult stepchildren
		Aunt
		Ex-wife

how the state government can possibly make a better decision in that regard that we can. Indeed, I am constantly surprised how many people, many of whom complain loudly and forcefully about government intervention in their lives, are willing to abdicate this aspect of their life, death, and the lives of their families after their death to the government. Yet so many do that we must understand the intestate process and be able to explain it to our clients and to the families of clients who chose to leave such choices to the state.

Intestacy

Intestacy is the distribution of an estate when there is no will. It is governed entirely by state statute. As is so often the case, this means that there is a great deal of variation from state to state. Attempts have been made to provide some uniformity to this process, most notably the Uniform Probate Code. However, the UPC in its original form was adopted by only sixteen states. Other states have adopted parts of the UPC, but often the state legislatures make significant changes during the process of enacting the code. In the end, concepts about what should happen to one's estate are so engrained at the state level that states only want uniformity if the other states will adopt what they already have.

Despite the variations in laws, there are some common terms and concepts in intestacy laws. One danger, however, is that people may be lulled into believing that because the terms are the same, the legal effect of using the terms is the same. It is often necessary to explain to clients that the same language in a statute that produced one result in Aunt Gladys' estate in Utah may produce a quite different result in dad's estate in Idaho.

Intestate succession is the scheme set forth by state statute that determines *who* gets *what proportion* of an estate when there is no will. The persons entitled to inherit if there is no will are referred to as the **intestate heirs,** or commonly just **heirs.** As it turns out it is important to be able to determine who a person's heirs are because they have certain rights even if there is a will. For example, heirs generally have the right to challenge the will. In order to exercise that right, they have the right to be notified of the person's death and the fact that an intestate estate administration is being established. They also have the right to petition to be appointed as decedent's **executor** or **executrix,** referred to as the **personal representative** under the UPC.

State intestacy laws are generally designed to keep the estate "in the family," meaning blood relatives except for the legal spouse. Thus persons related by blood or **consanguinity** inherit, and persons related by marriage or **affinity** do not. This has several consequences that may not fit well with our client's desires.

First, if there are no intestate heirs, the property **escheats** to state. This seldom actually occurs since it is almost always possible to find a blood relative, especially when there is money concerned. Recall, for example, how involved Louisa Mae's relatives became once she died. A more prominent example is that of Howard Hughes. Howard was a extremely wealthy, if eccentric, man. In 1976, Melvin Dummar, the man upon whose life the Stages of Melvin's Life shown in Figure 5-1 is based, claimed to have found a will executed by Howard that left a significant portion of his $2.5 billion estate to Melvin. That will was ruled to be a forgery. Since Howard had no surviving wife, children, or parents, his estate was evenly divided among 22 cousins.[2]

Second, there are a number of persons who may be of great concern to the client but who *can not* inherit if there is no will and will receive nothing without an estate plan. For example, **step-children** and a legal spouse's blood relatives are *not* heirs under intestacy laws.

Nor are **domestic partners** intestate heirs. The myth of **common law marriage** causes a great deal of confusion in this regard. Common law marriages can only be formed in eleven states and the District of Columbia. The requirements for a common law marriage vary within those twelve jurisdictions. As a result, people who believe they are "married" are not.

In one case in which I was involved, a couple had lived together for over thirty years telling everyone, including the man's children by a previous marriage that they were married. However, the jurisdiction did not allow for common law marriages. Being a bit "old fashioned," all the property he brought into the relationship and that was acquired during their lives together was in the man's name. When the man died, the woman had no rights to inherit. Her step-children, his children by a previous marriage who had had little to do with him and nothing to do with her since they began living together, were legally entitled to everything under the laws of intestacy and began eviction proceedings to remove her from the property. While I was able to make a claim that she had been his business partner, file an action for distribution of the "partnership assets," and achieve a settlement for her based on her services to the partnership, it was not nearly that to which she would have been entitled as a legal spouse or what he surely would have left her had he prepared a will.

This is also a problem for gay and lesbian couples in states that do not recognize their right to marry.

Growing a Family Tree

So who *are* a person's heirs? Who is entitled to inherit what proportion of the estate? In addition to a spouse, the decedent's **next of kin** will be the heirs. Next of kin are the closest blood relatives of the decedent. These are determined by their **degree of separation**, usually by reference to a chart such as shown in Figure 5-2. Charts showing degrees of kindred to several degrees are available on the internet and in several publications.

---

2. A woman named Terry Moore did claim to have married Hughes in 1949 and never divorced. Her claim was settled out of court.

Figure 5-2

DEGREES OF KINDRED CHART

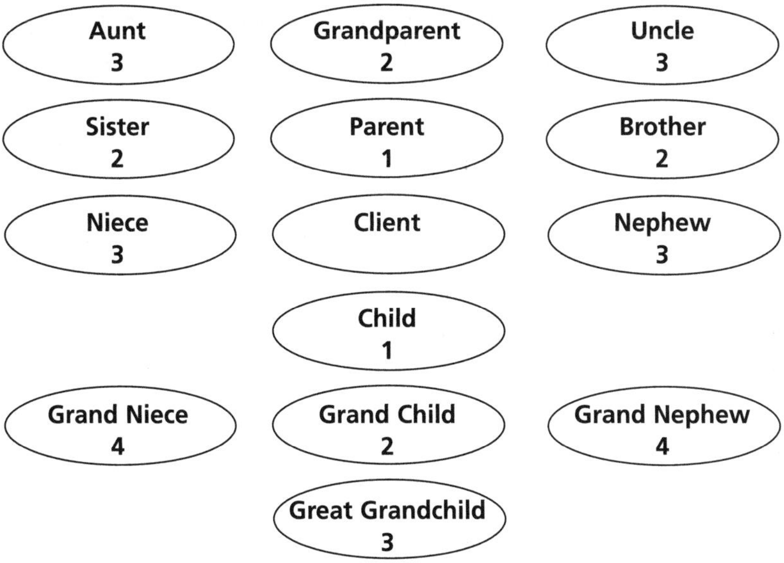

Aunt 3	Grandparent 2	Uncle 3
Sister 2	Parent 1	Brother 2
Niece 3	Client	Nephew 3
	Child 1	
Grand Niece 4	Grand Child 2	Grand Nephew 4
	Great Grandchild 3	

Because heirs have rights even when a client does create a will, it is always necessary that we gather information regarding the client's family, even if the client does not want to a member or any member of her family to receive any of her assets. In some instances we must know who is entitled to inherit so we can specifically note that the client intentionally left them out of the estate plan.

Because we do not know who will be alive when our client dies, it is necessary to have information regarding more than his immediate family. We need not carry this to extremes, but we should find out who his relatives are (or were) to at least the second degree. Depending on the circumstances, it may be necessary to go further.

As noted above, Howard Hughes' estate was inherited evenly by 22 cousins. First cousins are fourth degree on the degree of kindred charts.

While only blood relatives and spouses can inherit by law, we should also have information about non-blood relatives who are of concern to the client. For example, at Stage 9 of his life, Melvin may be concerned about his step-children either because he wants to provide for them or because he wants to make sure that anything that is his does not go to them through his new wife, but remains with his own children. Either way, we cannot devise a plan that effectuates the client's wishes about individuals unless we know what individuals are or may be involved.

When there is a substantial amount of information, simply gathering that information can cause more confusion than clarity unless the information is well-organized. For our purposes, this information is best organized through use of a family tree. We will want the family tree to allow us to determine quickly (1) the degree of kinship of the individual to our client, (2) whether the person is a lineal or collateral relative, (3) whether the individual is an ancestor or a descendent of the client, (3) and whether the individual is alive or dead at the time the family tree is made.

Before illustrating the process of growing a family tree, some content to some of the terms used in the last paragraph will be helpful. A **lineal** relative is one that is straight up or down from the client on the degrees of kindred chart. They include both the client's direct **ancestors,** those who came before the client and are above him on the chart, and his direct **descendents,** those who came after the client and are below him on the chart. The client's direct descendents—children, grandchildren, great-grandchildren, etc.—are his **issue.** Relatives that are not up or down from the client on the chart, but sideways from him are collateral relatives. These include his siblings, aunts, uncles, cousins, nieces, and nephews.

Now, let's start growing a typical family tree.

(1) We start with the client and the spouse if there is one. Although the spouse is not a blood relative, the spouse does inherit under intestacy laws.

Figure 5-3

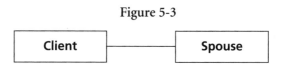

(2) Include an ex-spouse if the client had children with that spouse. The ex-spouse does not inherit from the client, but we need to have the relationship indicated. We may also want to include provisions in an estate plan to prevent the ex-spouse from inheriting through the children. For example, if Melvin dies leaving everything to his son and daughter, then his son died with no children of his own, Melvin's ex-wife would inherit from the son, including whatever the son still had left over from what he inherited from Melvin. It is sometimes helpful to indicate that the relationship has been severed through the line used to connect the two.

Figure 5-4

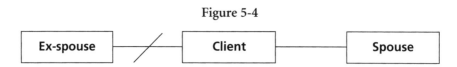

(3) Add the client's children, using lines to indicate with which spouse the client had the children. The numbers in brackets indicate the degree of separation from the client.

Figure 5-5

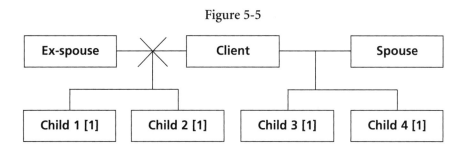

(4) Add lineal ascendants and descendents expanding with collateral kin, *keeping the branches level* at each generation. Note that in the next diagram the client's siblings are on the same level as she is.

Figure 5-6

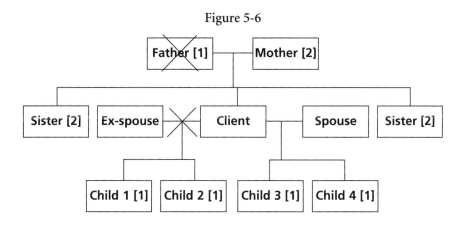

(5) Continue the process until the family has been diagramed sufficiently to tell the client's estate planning story at a glance indicating all persons of concern. Here's a example of a family tree for Melvin at Stage 11.

Figure 5-7 Melvin at Stage 11

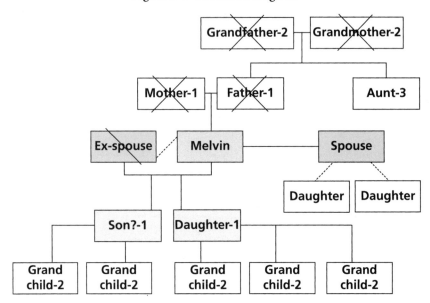

Once we have the family tree, we are prepared to assist the client in making an estate plan or to figure out who will inherit under the laws of intestacy. As we noted previously, the inheritance under an estate plan will be determined by the client, and inheritance under intestacy will be determined by state statute. That brings us to the next topic.

Words that Make Grown Lawyers Cry

State statutes will generally start with the spouse and children, each state having their own rules regarding how they split the estate. Some states will simply give each a share. For example, if there is a wife and four children, each will get one-fifth of the estate. Others will give the spouse the entire estate up to a certain amount, say $50,000, plus one-half of the rest with the other half being split equally between the children. In the end, you simply have to read the appropriate statute and break it down into its elements.

If there is no spouse and no children, the intestate heirs are grouped by degrees of separation into classes. Each degree of separation is its own class—those in the first degree of separation are one class, those in the second degree, another class, and so on. A person's class determines what share they get of the estate. There are different methods used to determine intestate distribution.

They are *per capita* and *per stirpes*, also called "**by representation.**" These words can lead attorneys to tears. It would be so much better if the statutes (and documents drafted for clients) simply state what was to happen with the estate. Instead, they use these terms that few people—lawyers included—really understand.

If *I* have it right, here is what happens in an estate depending on whether each class gets a share *per capita* or *per stirpes* using Mississippi law as an example. Under Mississippi law, (if we ignore certain provisions regarding exemptions and special allowances),

1. If a person dies intestate with no children, the entire estate goes to their spouse.
2. If there are children or descendents of those children who have not survived the decedent—whether the children are by the widow or a former marriage—the children and the widow/widower get equal shares.
3. If there is no widow or widower, the children each get an equal share.

That much seems fairly clear and simple. The next step is less clear. What happens if one of the decedent's children has died leaving two children? Do those two children split their parent's share or do they each rise up to that parent's level and take an equal share with the remaining parents?

Let's assume that our client, John, dies leaving an estate is worth $180,000. If he dies leaving a wife and two children, each will get $60,000. If he dies leaving a wife and two children, one of whom has three grandchildren, the wife and each child will still get $60,00 because we do not go beyond a living heir to that heir's descendants. But what happens if John dies leaving a wife, but one of the two children is dead leaving three grandchildren? This depends on which method the statute, will, or trust, says we must use.

Using *per stirpes* which means "by the root" each grandchild will one-third of the dead child's share. This is also referred to as "**by representation**" because each group of grandchildren represents, as a group, the share of their deceased parent. This applies not only to this child/grandchild example but to any group of heirs claiming through one person. In this example, but not the next, *per capita* gives us the same result. This method counts heads at the first class level, based on degrees of separation, which has one or more living persons and distributes the estate equally to each member of that class who are either alive or have surviving children. In this example, since one of the children is alive and there were two children in that class, the estate is divided into two parts. The living child gets one-half and the descendants of the other child get the other half in equal shares.

Let's try another example. In this example John had three children. One (Mark) is alive, one (Fred) died leaving two children, and another (Mary) died leaving three children. Using the *per stripes* method, Mark will receive one-third of the estate ($60,000), Fred's two children will each receive one-half of Fred's share or one-sixth of the estate ($30,000), and Mary's three children will each receive one-third of her share or one-ninth of the estate ($20,000).

Using the *per capita* method in this example, we again count heads at the first level having a surviving member. In this example this is again the child level, the first degree of separation. Since there were three children who either survived or died leaving children, the estate will be divided in thirds and Mark will receive one-third ($60,000). We then count all the heads at the next level with members surviving. In this case that level is the grandchildren, of which there are five and divide the remaining estate among them equally. So, each of Fred's children and Mary's children will receive one-fifth of the remaining two-thirds of the estate or two-fifteenths ($24,000). Fred's children get less than they would using the *per stirpes* method and Mary's children get more.

For our final example, assume John had a fourth child, Harry, who died leaving no children or descendants of his own. This will not change the result of either method. Since there is no one representing Harry, there is no change in the results using the *per stirpes* method. Since Harry did not have descendants, we do not count his head in the initial step, so there is no change in the *per capita* method.[3]

As you can see, it is unlikely the average person will understand the ramifications of the statutory intestacy scheme on the distribution of their estate. Thus it is unlikely they can affirmatively decide that it matches their desires.

---

3. Those of you enjoying this portion of the program may want to try a few more scenarios:

Assume John dies leaving

Two children, both dead, one with 2 children, one with 3 children

Two children, both dead, one with 2 children, one with 3 children, mother, father

No children, one brother who has two children, mother, father

No children, one brother who is dead leaving two children, mother, father

No children, one brother who is dead leaving two children, one sister who is dead leaving two children.

Also assume the law states:

IF NO CHILDREN OR DESCENDANTS: to the brothers and sisters and father and mother of the intestate and the descendants of such brothers and sisters in equal parts, the descendants of a sister or brother of the intestate to have in equal parts among them their deceased parent's share.

IF NONE OF THE ABOVE: in equal parts, to the grandparents and uncles and aunts, if any there be; otherwise, such estate shall descend in equal parts to the next of kin of the intestate in equal degree, computing by the rules of the civil law. There shall not be any representation among collaterals, except among the descendants of the brothers and sisters of the intestate.

Other Intestacy Issues

Each state's intestacy laws also deal with a plethora of other issues, including the intestate's debts together with exemptions and family allowances intended to protect some portion of the estate from creditors so that the family is not left destitute. Not surprisingly, in most cases this too would be better accomplished with estate planning. In addition, the statutes generally have special provisions dealing with half-blood relations, illegitimate children, adopted children, and **simultaneous death** (where distribution of the estate depends upon priority of death and there is insufficient evidence which person died first).

One of the more interesting issues, although it seldom applies, is the Oedipus problem. Oedipus is a character in Greek lore who an oracle predicted would kill his father and marry his mother. To prevent this from happening he was sent away as a baby and raised by another family, with no knowledge that the family was not his own. When he became an adult he argued with a stranger and killed him. It turned out the stranger was his real father. The issues for Greek playwrights were many. For us the only issue is whether Oedipus could inherit under the law.

The answer may depend on the particular language of the state statute. However, most states require that the killing be willful, intentional, or felonious. The Maine version of the UPC provides, "A surviving spouse, heir or devisee who feloniously and intentionally kills the decedent is not entitled to any benefits under the will or under this Article, and the estate of decedent passes as if the killer had predeceased the decedent."[4] Thus, arguments could be made that Oedipus did not intend to kill his father or was acting in self-defense. In any case, it appears clear that the statutes do not apply to situations where the heir caused the death through negligence, e.g., in a car accident.

Spousal Misconduct

We are far more likely to confront the issue of spousal misconduct than the Oedipus issue, and it is more likely that this issue will be of concern when developing an estate plan. In most jurisdictions mere spousal misconduct will not affect a spouse's right to inherit. A decree of divorce, annulment, or legal separation will terminate spousal rights to inherit, but simply filing for divorce or living separately will not, and incidents of adultery will not.

---

4. 18-A M.R.S.A. §2-803 (mainelegislature.org current through Dec. 31, 2009).

Some state statutes deal with this issue. Consider, for example, Missouri's statutory provision

> If any married person voluntarily leaves his or her spouse and goes away and continues with an adulterer or abandons his or her spouse without reasonable cause and continues to live separate and apart from his or her spouse for one whole year next preceding his or her death, or dwells with another in a state of adultery continuously, such spouse is forever barred from his or her inheritance rights, homestead allowance, exempt property or any statutory allowances from the estate of his or her spouse unless such spouse is voluntarily reconciled to him or her and resumes cohabitation with him or her.[5]

Other states will refer to bigamy and abandonment of marriage.

What is clear is that many of our clients will want to cut off a spouse's right to inherit well before the point where the statutory provisions go into effect. Estate planning can help deal with this issue, but there are some limits. A spouse generally has a right to "elect" against a will provision. This means the spouse can take whatever is left to him in the decedent's will *or* elect to take whatever share he would be entitled to under the laws of intestacy. So simply cutting the spouse out of the will does not prevent the spouse from inheriting.

Other estate planning tools can be more effective, including some that are put into place after the parties are already married. However, the best estate planning tool for dealing with this issue is through the use of a pre- or post-nuptial agreement, one of the estate planning tools discussed later in this chapter. We will discuss those tools after reviewing some of the basic estate planning concepts that must often be explained to clients.

C. Explaining Basic Concepts to Clients

In the day-to-day operation of the law office, the importance of the client interview is often forgotten. Certainly most offices make an effort to make an impression on the client in order to obtain and retain business. We make the client, to the extent possible, feel comfortable. We also do our best to be attentive, empathetic and not rushed, all while letting the client know just how important and busy the office is. In doing so, we can miss the real opportu-

---

5. Mo. Ann. Stat. 474.140 (www.moga.mo.gov current through August 28, 2009).

nity presented by the client interview—the opportunity to make the client part of the legal team.

Bringing the client on board not just as a source of work and a fee, but as a member of the team, can save the team a great deal of time, effort and frustration in all but the simplest of legal matters. It is during interviews that you can gain an understanding of the client, engage the client in the process, instruct the client, establish lines of communication, establish ground rules and set limits.

Many times the initial interview is limited to obtaining necessary information from the client and establishing the attorney/client relationship—setting the terms of employment and payment. We may go further and explain what the client can expect of us. However, the initial interview is an excellent opportunity to explain to the client what to expect of the process, what we expect of them over and above payment of our fee, and the basics they need to know to understand their role on their legal team.

For most clients this starts by clarifying basic terms and concepts. In order for the client to fulfill her role on the legal team she must have at least a basic understanding of the substantive and procedural law applicable to her legal matter. For example, in litigation most clients will start with some basic *misunderstandings* about (1) evidence, (2) their cause of action, (3) their role in the litigation and (4) court procedure. Clients have similar misunderstandings about deeds and the real estate closing process, will and the probate process, disability and the Social Security Disability claims process and so on. They obtain these misconceptions from friends, relatives, TV, movies and other sources of popular culture. Sometimes they will have understandings that are accurate for one state or one set of facts, but believe that the understanding has universal applicability. It will usually fall to the paralegal to correct these misconceptions. Often it will be necessary to explain each more than once in order to remove the misconceptions and instill the correct ones.

Written Informational Forms

It is helpful to have standard pre-prepared written explanations in the form of brochures, checklists, instructions or letters. Your office should have an ample and easily accessible collection of relevant instructional materials written in "plain language" in a system designed to ensure their delivery to the client at each step in the process. Keep in mind the need to make adjustments in such materials to take into account possible diminished vision as discussed in Chapter Two.

Remember also that not all clients have the same capacity or motivation to read or comprehend such aids. Clients are, after all, people and each person learns differently—some learn better through reading, but many learn best through hearing, through visual aids or through physical activity, i.e., walking through the process. Some clients do not read well (or at all) but will be reluctant to reveal this fact. Many clients will not realize the importance of reading and following written instructions. Many will read them with their own preconceptions or understandings of words which differ dramatically from the legal perspective from which they were written.

Communicating Understanding

Ultimately, the lawyer and you are responsible for knowing each client well enough to understand how best to not only communicate *with* the client but to communicate an understanding of the essentials *to* that client.

Start during your initial interview with the client:

- Establish the best physical method(s) of communicating with the client (phone, email, mail) as well as the best times to attempt that communication.
- In addition to oral explanations, use diagrams or walk them through some written instructions.
- Watch the client's body language, especially their eyes and face, for signs of understanding or confusion.
- Ask questions designed to ascertain whether the client understands what you or the attorney has said.
- Be aware that clients are often reluctant to discuss personal matters, even though they made the appointment for that purpose. They are especially reluctant when those personal matters concern death, illness and other matters they themselves would prefer to pretend did not happen to them or their family. Be patient. Assure them you understand. Explain why you need the information. Remind them that what they tell you will remain confidential.
- Be aware that clients do not know what you need to know. Some will be all too ready to talk, but will talk for quite some time without touching upon what you need. They do not know what is needed to produce an estate plan, you do. So it's up to you to ask. Explain to them what you need to know and why you need to know it.
- Be aware that the client does not understand terms that we take for granted and many, if not most, will not want to ask what those terms mean. It is not likely you will get a full and helpful response to the questions, "Did your wife have any intangible property?" unless you have clearly explained

the term "intangible property" (which means you need to have a clear understanding of it yourself). Better yet, ask simple, clear and direct questions designed to obtain the specific information you are seeking. Try, "Did you write any books, articles, songs or other similar works that were published?"

D. Clarifying Confusing Estate Planning Basics

It is not necessary to provide each client with a complete legal education. It is even possible to tell a client too much. The basics are all that is necessary. Also, I am not suggesting that you sit the client down and rattle off a bunch of definitions, even if those definitions are perfectly clear and cast in layperson's terms. A written form or brochure containing a clear simple explanation of basic terms will serve that function better. Rather, the effective paralegal will simply be aware *as they and the client are using terms* that many terms they are using carry specific legal connotations which need to be explained to the client.

For example when you first (and perhaps subsequently) use the term "intangible property" the client is unlikely to know what you are talking about so you need to explain the term to the client at that time. As discussed above, it is often best to avoid using terms with specific legal connotations altogether, but this is, unfortunately, not always possible.

Keep in mind that you cannot give a client legal advice, but explaining key basic concepts need not constitute the giving of advice.

Let's take a look at some of the legal jargon that can cause estate planning client confusion.

Estate

We can start with the word "estate," a word that has several connotations or meanings in everyday usage. If our clients looked the word up on Wikipedia (and far too many of us do) they might find:

> An estate comprises the houses and outbuildings and supporting farm-land and woods that surround the gardens and grounds of a very large property, such as a country house or mansion. It is an "estate" because the profits from its produce and rents are sufficient to support the household in the house at its center. Thus "the estate" may refer to all other cottages and villages in the same ownership as the mansion itself. An example of such an estate is Woburn Abbey in Bedfordshire, England.

I have had clients who have this very limited view of "estate" and believe they have no need for an estate plan because they rent rather than own their house. This is understandable since we tend to refer to houses and the buildings standing upon that ground as "real estate."

We know, however, and must sometimes explain, that when we are speaking of estate planning, the "estate" to which we are referring consists of *everything* our client *owns,* and for purposes of estate planning, everything the client *owes.*

Estate Planning

As stated above, we often need to make it clear than an estate plan is not simply a device for seeing that clients' assets are distributed as they would like after their death. It is also a plan for their estate during their life, intended to protect, preserve and maximize their assets to meet their goals during life. Planning should also include end-of-life decisions and decisions regarding disposition of one's body after death.

Estate Administration

Here attorneys and paralegals can begin to confuse even those clients who were otherwise thinking fairly clearly. Often while discussing estate planning with clients we will make reference to estate administration without making a clear distinction between the two. For many clients it simply makes no sense to say we are going to protect, preserve and maximize their estate with an estate plan that to the extent possible minimizes their estate. We understand that the estate to be administered (the probate estate) is not the same as the estate subject to the estate plan, but the client does not unless we explain it to him.

Domicile and Residence

When a person dies there can be questions regarding in which court her estate should be administered, i.e., which court has jurisdiction. This will usually be determined based on where the person was domiciled at the time of death. This can be difficult in situations where a person has two "homes." For example, when I lived in Maine, many of my clients were "snow birds"—they lived in Maine during the warm part of the year and lived in Florida or a similar location during the cold months. Sometimes the division of the year was almost equal. Other examples include college students who go "home" to a dorm or apartment for most of the year, but go "home" during breaks and on long weekends, military personnel who may live more than an entire year on tour, and merchant marines who spend months at sea.

Each of a person's "homes" may be a **residence**, a place where they live. There is no theoretical limit to the number of residences a person can have, but they can have only one domicile. Determining a person's domicile can be difficult, especially when a person is in the process of establishing a new one. Determining domicile for a particular purpose is often governed by a particular law, but in general **domicile** is the person's permanent home. Snow birds went south for the winter, but intended to return to Maine. Retirees often simply moved south permanently, but returned to Maine for extended vacations.

Which of a person's residences is that person's home—their domicile—will be determined by conduct and circumstances. One cannot maintain that she is domiciled in Maine, but spend eight months a year and have her driver's license, voter registration, passport, and the like all listing a residence in Florida.

The most difficult cases arise when a person is in the process of changing his domicile. He may have only been residing in the new location for a short time, perhaps a few weeks and not yet changed his driver's license, voter registration, etc., but if he has sold his home or given up his apartment in the old location, bought or rented a new residence in the new location, obtained a new job or begun a job search in the new location, and expressed an intent to stay in the new location, then his domicile is likely to be the new location.

Property Categories

"Property categories" is not a term frequently used when speaking to a client, but we do frequently speak in terms of categories of property in ways that confuse clients. It is especially confusing when they do not realize that the categories are not mutually exclusive, that is, they do not realize that property can be tangible, taxable, non-probate property.

Real and Personal

Real property is land and things permanently attached to land. **Personal property** is everything else. The distinction is clear when we think in terms of houses as real property and cars as personal property. But the distinction is not always as clear when the two are combined. For example, a house is real property and a mobile home on wheels is personal property. Simply taking off the wheels of the mobile home and leaving it sitting on cement blocks makes it immobile, but not real property—even if it hooks up to electricity and water lines. However, bolting the mobile home to a poured-cement foundation makes it real property even though it could theoretically be unbolted and moved. Similar difficulties occur within a building. A freestanding bookcase is personal property, but a bookcase built into or attached to a wall is real property.

Tangible and Intangible

Tangible property is anything capable of being touched, including both personal and real property. **Intangible property** are assets that cannot be touched such as bank accounts, an interest in a building, a right to collect royalties. This can be confusing to clients since they can touch their checkbook and savings account book. They can hold a stock certificate showing they are a shareholder in a business. The checkbook is tangible property, but it is worth little. The money in the account is not tangible, but is likely worth a whole lot more!

Probate and Non-probate

When a person dies leaving property through a will, the will must be proved to be valid, the property administered, i.e., someone has to see that the property is accounted for, debts are paid, and the property distributed to the person entitled to the property under the will. "Probate" technically refers only to the proving of the will which establishes an estate which must then be administered, but the term is usually used to refer to the entire process. The same is true if someone dies without a will or "intestate." The property owned by the person at the time of their death must still be administered.

This process can be time consuming, cumbersome and expensive, so a client will often want to avoid having her property go through the probate process. Soon we will discuss a variety of ways in which this can be accomplished. The basic goal is to set up a plan whereby the person's property goes directly to another person or entity rather than pass under a will through probate. Property that passes under the will through probate is **probate property**. Property that passes directly to another person or entity without going through probate is **non-probate property**.

Taxable and Non-taxable

When a person dies, the value of his estate may be subject to either an estate tax or an inheritance tax. As we will discuss in another section of this chapter, this is a fairly rare event. Some clients will want to make an estate plan that is designed to pass their property to another person or entity without the payment of tax. There are ways to do this, so it is possible for some of our client's property to be **taxable** and part of it to be **non-taxable**. The taxable property will be counted towards the value that can be taxed. The non-taxable property will not even be counted.

Combining Categories

These categories, with minor exception, are not mutually exclusive. A particular item of property can be personal, intangible, taxable probate property, or it could be real, tangible, non-probate, non-taxable property, and so on. Of course real property itself cannot be intangible, but the right to collect rent from real property would be.

E. Conclusion

Not everyone recognizes the need for estate planning. Often that non-recognition is the result of a lack of understanding of the goals and concepts of estate planning, and the perils of intestacy. Generally, estate planning is in the best interests of our clients. The effective, professional paralegal has a sound understanding of both estate planning and intestacy and possesses the ability to communicate that understanding to clients. Now that we have the basic under our belts, the next chapter will consider tools available for estate planning and matching those tools with our client's personal goals for effective estate planning.

CHAPTER SEVEN

UNDERSTANDING AND USING ESTATE PLANNING TOOLS

A. Property as a Bundle of Rights

In discussing property categories in the previous chapter, I used phrases such as "If a person dies leaving property" and "buys a new home." These phrases all imply that someone owns property. But, what does it mean to "own" property? The answer for purposes of estate planning can be somewhat surprising and quite confusing for clients.

One dictionary definition of "own" is "to have or hold as property: POSSESS." This definition is not satisfactory for our purposes. I can possess property without owning it. For example, you could loan me your car. I would possess it, but you would still own it.

Another dictionary suggests "to have control over," but this has the same defect and another besides, because I do not have complete control over property I am generally considered to own. For example, I own my house and the ground it sits on, but zoning ordinances and deed restrictions prevent me from opening a business in it. In addition, I cannot cancel my home insurance because the mortgage deed I signed to get the money to buy the house bargained away my right to do so. If I rent my house, I even lose the right to possess it! While I still "own" it, I have traded my right to possess the house for a certain period of time to another person in exchange for the right to be paid rent.

So it turns out that my house is not really a house at all. It is just a "bundle of rights." In addition to the "legal title," the bundle includes the right to possess the house, the right to decide whether to run a business in it, the right to have or not have it insured, the right to trade possession for rent, and many more. In our scenario, I have the right to possess the house, but traded it to a tenant for the right to be paid rent. The right to decide whether or not to use the house for a business belongs to the local government and home owners association, not to me. The right to decide whether or not to have the home insured was mine, but I traded it to the mortgage company.

Understanding this concept of property ownership can give us immense flexibility and power in estate planning. Let's say I want my children to have my house when I die. If I leave it to them in a will, it will have to go through probate which will take time and money. But if I give it to them now, I lose control over the property. If we have a falling out, they could kick me out of "my" house! If they let their drug and gambling problems get out of hand, their creditors could take the house away. There is no end to the unwanted consequences that could occur if I transfer the rights I have in my house to my children now rather than at the time of my death. Indeed, my estate planning problems revolve around the desire to transfer property without giving up control over it.

Now consider what can be done if we do not view the house as a single item of property, but as a collection of rights. One right is the right to live in the house and make all decisions regarding the house allowed by law and not contracted away. Another right is to have legal title to the house. I can give up the right to legal title (assuming I have not given up the right to give up that right in my mortgage deed), but keep all the other rights! I can transfer legal title to my sons now, but retain all other rights for the rest of my life. When I die, my interest in all those other rights will expire and go to the holders of the legal title, my sons.

This device is a "life estate." I convey legal title to my sons, but retain a life estate in the house. There are many such devices which can be used as estate planning tools. The trick is to select the best estate planning tool or tools to meet a particular client's goals. Before attempting this, we will take a look at some of the more commonly utilized estate planning tools.

B. Estate Planning Tools

This is not a Wills, Trusts and Estate Administration book. While we will look at several estate planning tools, we will not do a detailed analysis of any of them. Rather, we will attempt to gain an understanding of the basic requirements for each tool and an understanding of how viewing those tools through the "bundle of rights" lens enables us to meet the estate planning needs of our clients. Ultimately, the role of the paralegal in the estate planning process will likely include obtaining the necessary information from the clients, explaining the process to the clients, and assisting the attorney in developing the estate plan. None of these functions can be successfully and professionally accomplished without this understanding of the primary estate planning tools.

These tools are of two types. One type consists of actual documents used to convey, transfer, or distribute rights in assets—deeds, bills of sale, wills, trust agreements. The other consists of particular characterizations of the rights actually conveyed. For example, we took a brief look at a "life estate" in the last section. There is no document called a "life estate." A life estate is a method of transferring rights in assets that can be utilized in both deeds and wills. This will become clearer as we discuss the estate planning tools in more detail.

Each of the document devices will have its own requirements for validity — signatures, witnesses, notarization requirements, and the like. These requirements vary from state to state, but we can and will discuss some of the common requirements. You should be careful, of course, to check your state's specific requirements rather than rely on these generalizations. Keep in mind that one requirement will always be that the person executing the document must have the appropriate capacity to execute it. As discussed in Chapter Three, the standard for determining that capacity varies depending on the document and the jurisdiction.

Deeds and Bills of Sale

Deeds and Bills of Sale are documents by which interests in property are conveyed from one person or entity to another person or entity. Deeds are used to convey or transfer real property. Bills of Sale are used to convey or transfer personal property.

Deed Requirements and Characteristics

The requirements for a valid deed vary from state to state. Often there are statutory provisions relating to deed requirements,[1] but there are also requirements imposed through common law and common sense, e.g., a re-

---

1. See, e.g., Arizona Revised Statutes 33-401, "Formal requirements of conveyance; writing; subscription; delivery; acknowledgment; defects

   A. No estate of inheritance, freehold, or for a term of more than one year, in lands or tenements, shall be conveyed unless the conveyance is by an instrument in writing, subscribed and delivered by the party disposing of the estate, or by his agent thereunto authorized by writing.

   B. Every deed or conveyance of real property must be signed by the grantor and must be duly acknowledged before some officer authorized to take acknowledgments.

   C. For purposes of this section, a deed or conveyance containing any defect, omission or informality in the certificate of acknowledgment and which has been recorded for longer than ten years in the office of the county recorder of the county in which the property is located shall be deemed to have been duly acknowledged on and after the date of its recording."

quirement that the deed include a sufficiently clear description of the property being conveyed. To be valid a deed must generally:

1. Be in writing;
2. Contain a legal description sufficient to determine the property being conveyed;
3. Contain required "operative words of conveyance," e.g., "I, John J. Oldowner hereby grant, convey and sell to Jackie L. Newowner...."
4. Name and identify the parties as "Grantor" or "Grantee";
5. Be signed by all parties making the conveyance exactly as the names appear in the body of the deed;
6. Be delivered with the intent to pass title immediately;
7. Be accepted by the grantee(s);
8. Be acknowledged by the grantor(s) in front of a notary or other designated officer of the state.

Deeds are often designated by the extent to which a person is willing to warrant that they have the legal right to make the conveyance and defend against claims of third parties contesting that right. Thus a **Warranty Deed**[2] warrants the grantor has full right to convey the land and will defend against all-comers, while a **Quit-claim Deed** says nothing about what rights the grantor has, instead simply conveying whatever right she has. It may even turn out that the grantor has no right at all. This type of deed is sometimes referred to as a "**Release Deed,**" since the grantor is not claiming to actually have an interest in the property, but is just releasing whatever interest they might have; he does not convey the land, he simply releases or quits any claim he has to it. For example, if I am hesitant to buy land from Jones because I think Smith might claim an interest in it even though Jones tells me Smith has no claim, Jones might get a quit-claim deed from Smith to settle the issue to my satisfaction.

There are also "in-between" deeds called **Deeds without Warranty, Quit-claim with Covenant,** and the like. The effect of these deeds varies depending on the provisions of state law. Generally, they use words of conveyance rather than words of release, but limit the warranty. For example, a Quit-claim with

---

2. The exact language required for particular types of deeds or ownership interests can vary somewhat from state to state, and in some instances different language can be used to create the same interest in one state. Deeds using the complete language can be long, cumbersome, difficult to understand, and seem archaic. Some state have authorized forms that if used are deemed to satisfy the requirements. These deeds are referred to as "statutory short form deeds." See, e.g., Maine Revised Statutes Title 33, Chapter 12: SHORT FORM DEEDS ACT.

Covenant conveys the real property but covenants only that the grantor has not done anything to harm the title. There is no warranty that title was good to start with and no agreement to defend against the claims of others.

Bills of Sale

A bill of sale is a document that conveys an ownership interest in property other than real property. As usual, the requirements for a bill of sale vary from state to state. In its simplest form, a bill of sale will have a description of the article being conveyed, words of conveyance, the names of the parties, and the signature of the person making the conveyance, e.g., "On this 4th day of December, 2010, I, William Carowner, for consideration hereby acknowledged, sell, convey and deliver to Harry Carbuyer, one 1999 Toyota Corolla, VIN_____. Signed, William Carowner." Most of the discussion in this section regarding ownership and conveyance of "sticks" of interest in the bundle of rights regarding deeds also applies to bills of sale.

Deeds, Bills of Sale, and the Bundle of Rights

A deed or bill of sale can be used to convey any interest in property. I can convey all of my right, title, and interest, and warrant that I have all the right, title, and interest there is to have. Or I can convey only a portion of my rights. For example, I have an exclusive right to use my land, but I can convey a portion of that right to you allowing you to cross the land to, say, get from the road to the beach. This right-to-cross is normally referred to as an easement and the deed as an "easement deed."

A deed can also convey property to more than one person at a time. Undivided bundles of rights can be held by two or more people at a time, each having an undivided interest in the entire property. This combined ownership can take on several forms including joint tenancy and tenancy-in-common:

a. In a **joint tenancy,** the owners share equally in the ownership of the property. Two joint tenants do not each own half of the property; they each own a half interest in all of the property. With a joint tenancy each owner has a **right of survivorship** of the other(s). If one dies, their interest, at the moment of death, becomes the property of the remaining owners. To create a joint tenancy, specific language is required.

b. When the owners are **tenants-in-common** they also hold an undivided interest in the whole property, but there are a number of differences between tenants-in-common and joint tenants. The ownership interests do not have to be the same. One person could own a 50% share while the other 50% is divided 25% to a second person and 25% to a third. Regardless of the percentage, each has a full right to possess the property, i.e., one cannot exclude another just because they have a bigger share—even if the share is more than 50%. Perhaps more important for our purposes is the fact that when an owner dies, that person's share does not go automatically to the other owners. Instead, it goes to the deceased person's heirs (if they die without a will) or devisees (if they have a will devising the property).

There are other forms of ownership, most of which have to do with state laws regarding property owned by husbands and wives—tenancy by the entirety, community property, and marital property. These types of ownership are of some interest to estate planners, but more so to domestic relations attorneys. Tenancy by the entirety is essentially joint tenancy with rights of survivorship for husbands and wives, but even in states without tenancy by the entirety, husbands and wives can own property as joint tenants with essentially the same effect. We are going to focus here on joint tenancy and tenancy-in-common.

Joint Tenancy, Tenancy-in-common, and Estate Planning

You have likely already seen how just the ability to convey the bundle of rights in these two forms—joint tenancy and tenancy-in-common—can have significant implications for the use of deeds in an estate plan. If I want my life-partner to have my house when I die, I can convey title to myself and my partner as joint tenants. He will become the sole owner of the property when I die. No need for a will to accomplish this and no need for the time, delay, and expense of probate and estate administration! If, on the other hand, I and my second wife buy a house together, we may each want our share to go to our children by our first marriage. Voila!—a tenancy-in-common does the job.

There is a down side to this means of estate planning though. We start with my property and the assumption that I will want my life-partner to get my property when I die. But I may not die for many years. And my life-partner and I may not really stay partners for my entire life. If I convey a half interest in my property to her (as a joint tenant or tenancy-in-common) now, she will have that interest *now*. If I leave it to her in my will she gets it when I die, but if we are no longer partners I can change the will. If I convey it to her now, she gets whatever I convey to her now and I cannot change that no matter what happens in our relationship.

By using a deed, I avoid probate and estate administration, but I also lose control. This is the classic conflict confronted by the estate planner—the balancing of the client's desire to accomplish a transfer of her assets with a minimum of time, inconvenience, expenses, delay, and taxation against her desire to maintain control over the property during her lifetime. It is the same conflict discussed in the last section when we considered using a life estate to accomplish the transfer from parent to children rather than a current conveyance by deed of the entire bundle of rights or a conveyance at death by will of the entire bundle of rights.

Deeds and Life Estates

You already have a basic understanding of life estates based on the discussion thus far. A **life estate** is really just a characterization of a particular division of the bundle of rights that constitutes property ownership. In a life estate, the right for a particular person to enjoy the benefits (and perhaps the responsibility) of possession of property during the life of a person is separated from the right to the benefits of possession after that person's life has ended.

This description sounds a bit convoluted because of the reference to "a person." It is not clear exactly who has the property during whose life and who has it when who dies. That is because the one-sentence description actually covers several different possibilities.

One possibility we have mentioned already. I own property that I want to go to my sons when I die. I execute a deed conveying the property to them, but reserve a life estate to myself. I am the **life tenant.** My sons are the **remaindermen.** When I die, my interest expires and they have the entire property. They had the entire bundle of rights except for the one stick I held—the right to possess the property. When I die, that stick also belongs to them.

Another possibility is the reverse. Let's say I want to provide my mother with a place to live for her life, but I want to make sure I get the property when she dies and that the same property goes to my sons if I die. If I simply buy her a house by a deed in her name, the property is hers and she can leave it to anyone in her will, or it could be taken by creditors to pay medical bills and the like. If I buy the house as joint tenants with her, I will automatically get the property when she dies, but she gets it automatically when I die—it does not go to my sons. The solution may be to buy the property in my name and convey her *only* a life estate. She is the life tenant and I am the remainderman. The property **reverts** to me when she dies and I can leave to my sons in my will.

But we are not done yet. There is another possibility. It could be that I have two pieces of property, one in which I live. I would like to let my mother have the other for her life and then have it go to my son. I can convey the property to my son but subject to a life estate for my mother. She will be the life tenant and he will be the remainderman.

Just consider the possibilities! There is no end to the fun we can have devising devices to plan an estate. Look at what we have done with just Thing One and Thing Two. Let's move on to another thing.

Trusts

A trust is a particularly useful estate planning device as it allows us great flexibility in splitting up the bundle of rights that constitute property ownership. The basic split is between the legal title and the equitable or beneficial title. **Legal title** consists of having the property in one's name which gives the legal title owner the right to manage and control the property. **Equitable title** or **beneficial title** consists of the right to enjoy the benefits of ownership of property. In most cases, when we "own" property, we hold both the legal and equitable title.

When a trust is created, a person, the **trustor** or **settlor,** holding both the legal and equitable title to property (which can be real or personal, tangible or intangible) conveys legal title to one or more persons, the **trustee(s)**, but the right to manage and control the property must be exercised only for the benefit of another person(s), the **beneficiary**. So to create a trust, we need one or more settlors, property (called the "**corpus**") that is subject to the trust, one or more trustees, and one or more beneficiaries. There may also be a **remainderman,** a person or entity who gets the property once the trust ends. A trust ought to be, but need not be in writing. For estate planning purposes, it will be in writing. A trust is considered to be a separate legal entity for tax purposes and must file an annual return.

One person cannot be the settlor, the only trustee, and the only beneficiary. A trust requires separation of the legal title from the equitable title. If a person holds both the legal and equitable title alone, there is no separation and no trust. So, if Mary owns both the legal and equitable title and were to write a trust document saying "I hereby convey my house to me as trustee for the benefit of me," she has not actually created a trust since she will continue to hold both forms of title. Another person has to be included either as trustee or beneficiary. A trust is created if Mary's trust document says, "I hereby convey my house to me and my husband, Mark, as trustees for the benefit of me," or "I hereby convey my house to me as trustee for the benefit of me and my husband, Mark."

Note how useful a trust can be in resolving the conflict between the desire to be sure that a person's property be handled or distributed in a particular way in the future while maintaining control in the meantime. Rather than give my property to my sons now yielding control to them or keeping full control

Figure 6-1

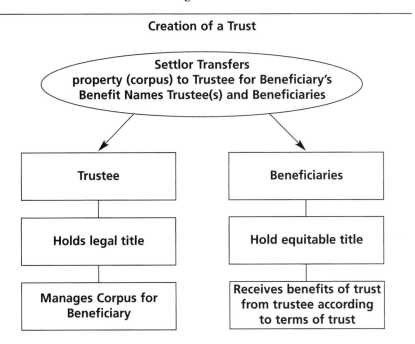

Creation of a Trust

Settlor Transfers property (corpus) to Trustee for Beneficiary's Benefit Names Trustee(s) and Beneficiaries

Trustee	Beneficiaries
Holds legal title	Hold equitable title
Manages Corpus for Beneficiary	Receives benefits of trust from trustee according to terms of trust

until my death and having the property pass to them through probate, I can create a trust giving the property to myself as trustee, for the benefit of myself and my sons, making it clear that I as trustee am to manage and control the property such that I receive all the benefits until I die. Then a successor trustee is to manage and control the property for my sons until they graduate from college, turn 25, or any other occasion I choose!

I can even direct that the property be used only for particular purposes such as covering the costs of education or to pay medical bills. If I am simply concerned that my beneficiaries are not mature or otherwise competent enough to manage funds, I can direct that the trustee make payments to third parties on behalf of the beneficiary rather than make payments to the beneficiary. The trustee could be directed to pay college tuition directly to the college, medical bills directly to the providers, rent directly to landlords, and so on.

The beneficiaries of a trust need not be named, but must be identifiable. I can set up a trust to provide scholarships for "students majoring in legal studies at the University of Mississippi beginning in 2020." While we do not presently know the names of the beneficiaries, we will be able to identify them when it is necessary to do so. The beneficiaries need not be human. Leona Helmsley

Figure 6-2

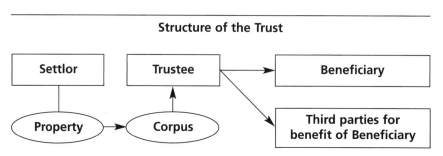

Structure of the Trust

famously left most of her fortune in trust for her dog and charities that benefit animals. In fact, beneficiaries need not even be living entities as trusts can be set up to, for example, provide perpetual care of a grave.

Trusts as Estate Planning Tools

This is not the place for an extensive exposition of trusts—the powers and duties of trustees, the termination of trusts, the many types and classifications of trusts, and the many rules and court doctrines that apply to them. Understanding of the usefulness of trusts as estate planning tools, however, does require some basics in this regard.

Trusts can be *inter vivos* or testamentary. An *inter vivos* trust (sometimes called a "living trust," thus often confused with a "living will" which is not a will or trust) becomes effective during the life of the settlor, while a **testamentary trust**, since it is created in a will only becomes effective when the person making the will dies. As noted above, the settlor can name herself as trustee of an *inter vivos* trust. Note again the flexibility this gives us for estate planning purposes. The main disadvantage of a testamentary trust is that the property that constitutes the corpus of the trust must go through probate and be transferred by the executor or other personal representative to the trustee, while the *inter vivos* trust avoids the probate process.

It is even possible to establish a trust with very little money. A **life insurance trust** can be set up as in *inter vivos* trust. The primary source of funds for the trust is a life insurance policy on the life of the settlor payable to the trust. During the settlor's life, he contributes enough each year to the trust to pay the premiums on the policy. If the life insurance were made payable to, say, the settlor's children, the settlor would have no control over those funds— they would be paid to and controlled by the children. It is seldom a good idea to pay substantial sums of money to an eighteen year old. Instead, the terms of the trust could require that the trustee use the funds to pay for education, housing, medical treatment, and the like until each child reaches a more mature age, say, 25 or 30. Or the trust could provide for the living expenses of a spouse during the spouse's life and then the remainder paid to the children. Or the trustee could be given the discretion to use the funds as she see fit for the benefit of several beneficiaries—often referred to as a "**sprinkling trust**" because the trustee can sprinkle the benefits as she believes is best. Or the trust could provide for those paralegal education scholarships. Or ... well, you get the idea.

The same can be accomplished through a will provision that distributes property to an already established trust. This is called a **pour-over trust** because the property pours-over into an already established trust rather than a trust set up in the will. There are several reasons for using this technique—the property remains unfettered by a trust during the testator's life time so the testator maintains control and avoids annual administration costs. The disadvantage is again that the property must go through probate before pouring over into the trust.

There are several other kinds of trusts designed for specific purposes—charitable trusts, marital trusts, Totten trusts, and so on. We will only discuss one more here—the **spendthrift trust**. Most trusts allow the trustee to control the rate at which the beneficiary receives the benefit of the trust income or corpus, or require that the trustee provide those benefits at a particular rate, e.g., $1,000 per month. Often the trust document will provide that the beneficiary will get the full corpus at some date in the future, e.g., when they turn 35. Often the primary purpose for setting up the trust is to provide control for someone who is a spendthrift—someone who is unable to control themselves or their finances.

Some beneficiaries are unwilling to wait. In some cases, the beneficiary will through gambling, drug use, unwise financial management or other problems, acquire creditors who are unwilling to wait. Impatient beneficiaries may try to sell their rights to the trust. For example, if I am going to receive $1,000 per month for the next 40 years, I will receive a total of $480,000. If I do not want to wait 40 years, I can sell now my right to receive the money in the future. No one would give me the $480,000 now and wait for the money to come in, but they may give me a lesser amount—$300,000 or other lump sum—thus enabling me to make an end-run around the wishes of the settlor who set up the trust. This can be avoided by making the trust a spendthrift trust. A typical spendthrift trust provision might read like this:

> The right of any beneficiary of a trust to receive the principal of the trust or any part of it, presently or in the future, shall not be alienable and shall not be subject to the claims of his creditors.

Since a creditor will not be able to collect against the trust, no creditor is likely to loan money with the trust as collateral or buy the beneficiaries interest in the trust. Keep in mind that whatever the beneficiary actually receives from the trust is subject to being taken by creditors, but the creditors cannot get at the trust itself.

Most states will enforce spendthrift trust provisions, but the statutes and case law of each state should be checked for exceptions and conditions. For example, Mississippi's Supreme Court has ruled that a spendthrift trust can be reached by involuntary creditors under certain conditions.[3]

Trust Administration

The nature and extent of effort required for trust administration varies with the nature and extent of the trust property and the trust itself. A trust that has only cash in a savings account with instructions that the money be held in the account accumulating interest until the beneficiary reaches a certain age is a far different animal in terms of administration than a trust that manages an apartment building. Many aspects of trust administration can be, and are, handled by paralegals.

Trusts are considered separate legal entities. That means they must obtain their own EIN (Employer Identification Number). This is true even if there is no chance that the trust will have any employees. Really it is a TIN or Taxpayer Identification Number similar to an individual's Social Security Number. The number is needed primarily because the trust is viewed as a separate taxpayer and must often file an annual tax return.

Aside from the tax aspects and obtaining an EIN, administrative duties include communicating with the beneficiaries, opening and maintaining bank accounts, investing and transferring funds in a way that preserves or increases the value of the corpus, paying creditors' claims, and making distributions to the beneficiaries. Each of these tasks is well within the perview of a paralegal.

Wills

The classic and basic estate planning tool is the Last Will and Testament. Wills are commonly used to provide for the distribution of assets after death, select the person or persons who will administer the estate, manage or avoid taxes, nominate guardians for children, set up trusts, and provide for funeral arrangements. While they are useful tools for these purposes, as we have seen they are not the only tools and they are not always the best tools for particular persons. While wills are the only tools by which we can select or nominate the persons who will administer our estates and be guardians for our children,

---

3. *Sligh v. First Nat. Bank of Holmes County*, 704 So. 2d 1020 (Miss. 1997).

trust and deeds can be set up and used during our lives to accomplish distributions, often with significant tax savings.

Many of the estate tools we have already discussed can be set up through a will—life estates, joint tenancies, and trusts, as examples. When we write a will for our clients we must ask not only to whom she wants the property to go on her death, but under what conditions and for how long. She may want her husband to retain the use of the marital home for his life, but want the home to go to her children by her first husband in the end rather than to his children. One way to accomplish this is to devise a life estate to the husband in her will with the remainder interest to her children.

The ability to have a will is regarded as a privilege rather than a right. This means that state legislatures can (and do) place conditions on who can make a will and how a valid will can be created. In fact, some statutes actually override provisions contained in a will.

The conditions on who can make a will and how to make a valid will are usually set forth by state statute. The person making the will is referred to as the "**testator**" if he is male and as the "**testatrix**" if she is female. The qualifications to make a will are deceptively simple. A typical statute will state, as does the Uniform Probate Code, "Any person 18 or more years of age who is of sound mind may make a will."[4] The age requirement is clear, definite, and firm. A will made on the day before the 18th birthday of the maker of the will is no will at all. The "sound mind" requirement is just as definite, but nowhere near as clear. The standard for determining **testamentary capacity** is discussed in Chapter Three.

The technical requirements for a valid will are also generally quite specific and the requirements are interpreted strictly. For example, statutes allowing **holographic wills**[5]—wills written entirely in the testator's handwriting—may require that the will be "subscribed" by the testator. Some courts interpret "subscribe" quite literally, i.e., "to write under." Thus, if a testator writes his name on the top of the will instead of the bottom, i.e., before the language devising his estate instead of after those provision, the will is not recognized as valid and the estate passes through intestacy.

Witnesses

State statutes govern the number of witnesses required, the qualifications for those witnesses, and the process of witnessing the will. Generally the witnesses

---

4. See, e.g., Me. Rev. Stat. Ann. tit.18-A, §2-501.

5. We will not discuss extensively here holographic wills or nuncupative wills (oral wills) both because they are rare and because they unlikely to be part of estate planning.

will be required to witness the signing of the will by the testator *and* by each of the other witnesses.

While the each statute should be examined carefully to determine the qualifications needed by witnesses, some general comments are in order. Witnesses:

- Should be acquainted with the testator/trix;
- Should have no interest as a beneficiary;
- Should actually see the Will being signed;
- Should be satisfied testator/trix knew document was Will;
- Should be satisfied testator/trix intended to make Will;
- Should be satisfied testator/trix was of sound and disposing mind and memory and capable of making a Will;
- Should also be competent to testify.

If a witness benefits under the will, most statutes provide that they will lose that benefit to the extent it exceeds what they would have gotten under intestacy, but some statutes have provisions that are more draconian.

Obviously, there is no way to guarantee that a witness will be competent to testify in the future when the will is presented for probate. **Probate**[6] of the will, i.e., the process of presenting the will to the court and proving it is indeed a valid will may require locating the witnesses and having them testify in person or by affidavit as to the circumstances surrounding the execution of the will by the testatrix.

However, many state statutes now provide for "**self-proving**" wills. Again, the provisions of the statute must be read carefully and followed strictly. Generally, these statutes require that the witnesses take an oath administered by a notary or other approved official, attesting that they witnessed the execution of the will and that the execution followed the required procedure. The statute will typically provide the exact language and procedure necessary to achieve a self-proving will.[7] There is seldom justification for missing the opportunity to make a will self-proving.

---

6. "Probate" is often used in a more generic sense referring to not only the proving of the will but to the actual administration of the estate left under the will.

7. See. e.g., Me. Rev. Stat. Ann. tit.18-A, §2-504: §2-504. Self-proved will

(a). Any will may be simultaneously executed, attested, and made self-proved, by acknowledgment thereof by the testator and affidavits of the witnesses, each made before an officer authorized to administer oaths under the laws of the state where execution occurs and evidenced by the officer's certificate in substantially the following form:

I, _____, the testator, on this _____ day of _____, 19____, being first duly sworn, do hereby declare to the undersigned authority that I sign and execute this instrument as my last will and that I sign it willingly (or will-

Will Issues—Spousal Election

There are many issues that can arise regarding the execution and administration of wills. Statutes will generally make specific provisions for what happens if a gift made under a will is no longer available when the testatrix dies, what happens if a person to whom a gift is made is no longer alive when the testator dies, and a host of other possible occurrences. From the point of view of the legal team, it is far better to consider all of these possibilities when drafting the will and making provisions best suited to meet the client's goals rather than leave them to the statutory scheme.

The actual structure of a will and the drafting of particular provisions are beyond the scope of this book. There are several excellent textbooks dealing with the structure and drafting of wills in general. It is likely that there are also articles or books designed to guide you through the provision of your own state's statutes. These books should be read and then kept handy for reference.

There is one issue we must consider here, however. That is the ability of state statutes to override the provisions of a will. This most commonly arises with regard provisions (or the lack thereof) relating to spouses and children.

---

ingly direct another to sign for me), as my free and voluntary act and that I am eighteen years of age or older, of sound mind, and under no constraint or undue influence.

Testator

We, _____ the witnesses, being first duly sworn, do hereby declare to the undersigned authority that the testator has signed and executed this instrument as his last will and that he signed it willingly (or willingly directed another to sign for him), and that each of us, in the presence and hearing of the testator, signs this will as witness to the testator's signing, and that to the best of our knowledge the testator is eighteen years of age or older, of sound mind and under no constraint or undue influence.

Witness

Witness

The State of _____

County of _____

Subscribed, sworn to and acknowledged before me by _____, the testator and subscribed and sworn to before me by _____, and _____, witnesses, this _____ day of _____.

(Seal)   (Signed)_____

(Official capacity of officer)

In most states, if a will made either before or after the marriage of a person omits mention of a spouse, that spouse will receive the same distribution they would have received if the person died without a will unless it is clear that the omission was intentional; for example, if the spouse was provided for in an *inter vivos* trust. The same is true of omitted children, referred to as **pretermitted children.** The statutes are often quite specific in governing when the omitted child receives a share of the estate and what share the child receives.[8]

Again, from the point of view of the legal team, it is far better to clearly state the client's intention in the will rather than allow these issues to be resolved by state statute. Even if the client would be happy with the statute as it is written in the state at the time the will is executed, assuming the client understood the ramifications of the statute, there is no guarantee the same statute will be in effect at the time the will is probated or that the client will still be domiciled in the same state when she dies.

Unfortunately, with regard to a spouse, even the clearly stated intention of the client may be overridden by state laws. The surviving spouse generally has the right to a **spousal election,** i.e., the right to take either what he or she is granted under the will or to take a share provided by statute. The Maine version of the Uniform Probate Code provides, "If a married person domiciled in this State dies, the surviving spouse has a right of election to take an elective share of ⅓ of the augmented estate under the limitations and conditions hereinafter stated."[9] These statutes are typically intended to prevent a testator from, for example, leaving his estate to his girlfriend instead of his wife.

The limitations and conditions contained in the statute are also beyond the scope of this book, but you should understand the concept of the **augmented**

---

8. See, e.g., Me. Rev. Stat. Ann. tit.18-A §2-302:
(a). If a testator fails to provide in his will for any of his children born or adopted after the execution of his will, the omitted child receives a share in the estate equal in value to that which he would have received if the testator had died intestate unless:
> (1). It appears from the will that the omission was intentional;
> (2). When the will was executed the testator had one or more children and devised substantially all his estate to the other parent of the omitted child; or
> (3). The testator provided for the child by transfer outside the will and the intent that the transfer be in lieu of a testamentary provision is shown by statements of the testator or from the amount of the transfer or other evidence.
(b). If at the time of execution of the will the testator fails to provide in his will for a living child solely because he believes the child to be dead, the child receives a share in the estate equal in value to that which he would have received if the testator had died intestate.
(c). In satisfying a share provided by this section, the devises made by the will abate as provided in section 3-902.
9. Me. Rev. Stat. Ann. tit.18-A §2-201

estate. Some people may attempt to get around the spousal election by giving their property to a boyfriend or a family member prior to death, or selling it to them for some nominal amount—a $1,000,000 building for $10. To prevent this from happening, the law includes the value of such transferred property in the estate for purposes of the spousal election.

The problem for the estate planner is obvious. We may draft a will that states precisely the intention and goal of our client only to have it overridden by the state statute. While the examples given above sound somewhat nefarious, it is our task to effectuate our client's wishes, not to judge them. In addition, there are many legitimate reasons to provide little or nothing for a spouse in a will. For example, the testatrix may have children by a prior marriage and want her estate to go to those children rather than to the spouse. Remember, anything that goes to a spouse when the client dies will go to the spouse's heirs or devisees at the spouse's death, so our client's property may end up going to her step-children rather than to her own children. Thus we must add at least one more tool to our estate planning toolkit—pre-and postnuptial agreements. These will be discussed in the next section.

Wills as Estate Planning Tools

Both the advantages and disadvantages of wills as estate planning tools are fairly obvious. They are extremely versatile since we can make specific distributions to specific persons or entities incorporating all of the tools already described. We can direct that property be conveyed in fee simple to individuals, to more than one person as joint tenants or tenants-in-common, as life estates, or in trust. There are, however, several downsides. First, they are effective only upon death and we do not know what the financial circumstances will be at the time of death, whether those we intend to receive property will survive the testator, and so on. Second, because they are effective only at death, they provide no assistance in addressing our clients' goals while they are living, i.e., they do not factor into asset management for purposes of retirement and the like. Finally, property that passes through a will is subject to estate administration, a process that can be long and expensive, and to estate taxes.

Despite the downsides, wills are an essential estate planning tool. For some clients it will be the only tool needed. More important, it is a needed tool for all clients. No matter how well we use other devices to transfer property during the life of a client, there is always the likelihood that there will be property not accounted for through those devices—some property that must pass to others at the time of death. If there is no will, that property will pass through intestacy.

There are many clauses that can be included in a will, but to address this issue we are most interested in the **residuary clause.** This is a clause that, after we have made all the specific gifts—the wedding dress to the eldest daughter or the large bequest to the favorite charity—disposes of all "the rest, remainder, and residue" of the client's estate. This is a catchall provision need to take care of anything that may not have been addressed by other means.

Even if we have set up an *inter vivos* trust for the client with specific beneficiaries provided when she dies, we need the will's residuary clause to "catch" anything not in the trust and direct it into the trust. Let's assume for example that we set up a trust to which the client conveys everything he owns (not a very practical thing to do). What if after the trust is established he inherits property from someone else, wins a lottery, or simply earns more money from a source not already in the trust? That additional trust must be re-directed to the trust through the will's residuary clause to prevent it from passing through intestacy.

Agreements

As discussed in the last section, state statutes can override provisions of wills. One major way in which statutes do this is to provide for the spousal election, the right of the spouse to choose to take what is given under their spouse's will. While there are sound public policy reasons for such laws, they can be an impediment to legitimate estate planning. This is especially true for older clients who are more likely to be on a second or third marriage, have children by a prior marriage, and have some sort of "nest egg" built up.

Let's take the example of Harry and Ruth. Harry, age 60, and Ruth, age 59, are considering marriage. Harry has two children by a previous marriage and Ruth has three. If either Harry or Ruth were to die unmarried, their entire estates would go to their children under the laws of intestacy or as directed by their wills. Let's say that Harry's estate is worth $1,000,000, so each child would get $500,000. If Harry marries Ruth, she will be entitled to an elective share of perhaps one-third of his estate, even if he leaves everything to his children in his will. So, if they are married on January 1st and Harry dies on January 10th, Ruth can elect to receive $333,333.33, leaving the same amount to each of Harry's children, even if Harry wrote a new will leaving everything to his children on January 9th.

Perhaps Harry would not object to his new wife receiving those funds to help get her through her final years financially, even though his intent was to leave his entire estate to his children and even though it is quite possible that Ruth already has her own nest egg sufficient to accomplish this purpose. But let's take it one step further. If Ruth now dies on January 11th, Harry's $333,333.33 will be divided among *Ruth's* children! It is highly unlikely that Harry would be happy with this result.

This is just one of a myriad of legal entanglements that can arise from marriage and affect estate planning. A short list of elder law areas affected by marriage includes a person's rights to pension payments, Medicaid and Medicare benefits, healthcare decisions, and estate taxes.

Fortunately, most of those entanglements can be avoided through the use of **prenuptial agreements.** These agreements, also called antenuptial agreements, are contracts between the parties in which the parties establish between them the rights each has to the property of the other and the obligations each has to the other. The agreements govern those rights and obligations during the marriage, in the event of separation or divorce, and on the death of a party.

Non-marital agreements, that is agreements made between non-married parties, can also be used to assist in effective estate planning. These agreements are often necessary because many couples engaged in life-long partnerships are not allowed to marry and are thus denied rights that would otherwise be automatically theirs under law as a result of the relationship of the parties. In many instances, each of the parties can grant these rights to the other party by virtue of written agreements.

Requirements

Since these agreements are contracts, all of the normal contract rules apply to their creation including the capacity requirements. Valid agreements will be enforced as contracts and are binding on a person's heirs. Often they are subject to special statutes in addition to the standard common law contract rules.

As is often the case, there has been a lack of uniformity among the laws of the various states. This lack of uniformity and resulting uncertainty is particularly troublesome with regard to these agreements due to the increasing number of marriages between persons previously married, the increased acceptance of prenuptial agreements, and the increased mobility of our population.[10]

---

10. Each of these factors is noted in the prefatory note to the Uniform Premarital Agreement Act:

> The number of marriages between persons previously married and the number of marriages between persons each of whom is intending to continue to pursue a career is steadily increasing. For these and other reasons, it is becoming more and more common for persons contemplating marriage to seek to resolve by agreement certain issues presented by the forthcoming marriage. However, despite a lengthy legal history for these premarital agreements, there is a substantial un-

The Uniform Premarital Agreement Act has been adopted in 27 states as of 2009. The basic requirements for a valid agreement are that it be in writing signed by both parties.[11] Interestingly, the Act provides that the agreement and written amendments to it made after marriage are enforceable without consideration, although it seems that by the nature of the agreement in most cases there will be at least mutual promises which constitute consideration under contract law.[12]

The UPAA does not itself require full disclosure of assets and other financial information prior to execution of the agreement, but to the extent that either party is waiving rights to which they would be entitled under law, there must be full disclosure for the agreement to be legally enforceable as a matter of common law.[13]

Some state statutes make the requirement explicit as does Missouri's which states,

> The rights of inheritance or any other statutory rights of a surviving spouse of a decedent who dies intestate shall be deemed to have been waived if prior to, or after, the marriage such intended spouse or spouse by a written contract did agree to waive such rights, after full disclosure of the nature and extent thereof, including the nature and extent of all property interests of the parties, and if the thing or promise given to the waiving party is a fair consideration under all the circumstances.[14]

While the UPAA specifically requires such agreements to be executed prior to marriage and effective only upon marriage, as indicated by the Missouri statute it is also possible in some states to accomplish the same ends in a **postnuptial** agreement. Here there is little to no uniformity at all. Some states may

---

certainty as to the enforceability of all, or a portion, of the provisions of these agreements and a significant lack of uniformity of treatment of these agreements among the states. The problems caused by this uncertainty and nonuniformity are greatly exacerbated by the mobility of our population. Nevertheless, this uncertainty and nonuniformity seem reflective not so much of basic policy differences between the states but rather a result of spasmodic, reflexive response to varying factual circumstances at different times. http://www.law.upenn.edu/bll/archives/ulc/fnact99/1980s/upaa83.htm (Last accessed May 2, 2010)

11. Uniform Premarital Agreement Act, Section 2.

12. *Id.*

13. For an interesting discussion of the differences between California and Arizona law in this regard in the context of a choice of law determination, see *In re Marriage of Bonds*, 83 Cal. Rptr. 2d 783 (Cal. 1999).

14. Mo. Rev. Stat. §474.120 (www.moga.mo.gov current through August 2009).

not enforce such an agreement on the public policy grounds. Ohio, for example, specifically prohibits such agreements by a statute which states,

> A husband and wife cannot, by any contract with each other, alter their legal relations, except that they may agree to an immediate separation and make provisions for the support of either of them and their children during the separation.[15]

Others states go well beyond the Missouri statute and have statutes that explicitly deal with postnuptial agreements on the same terms as prenuptial agreements. The Colorado Marital Agreement Act, for example, defines a martial agreement as "an agreement either between prospective spouses made in contemplation of marriage or between present spouses, but only if signed by both parties prior to the filing of an action for dissolution of marriage or for legal separation."[16]

Agreements as Estate Planning Tools

Marital and non-marital agreements are an invaluable, if underused, estate planning tool, allowing us to achieve our client's goals despite laws that might otherwise thwart those goals. Since they are intended to govern the rights and obligations of the parties during life as well as after death, they are particularly helpful in dealing with short, middle, and long term goals. There are a number of ways in which we must be particularly careful in using them, however.

First, both the laws governing marital agreements and the language of the agreements themselves are strictly construed. This means we must be particularly attentive in our legal research, analysis of the statutes and case law, drafting of the language used in the agreements, and the formalities required for a valid agreement.

Second, while all agreements are subject to claims of undue influence, fraud, and the like, marital agreements are particularly susceptible to such claims, especially with regard to the requirement of full disclosure. There are a number of steps we can take to reduce such claims and reduce the likelihood that any claims raised will be successful:

- Make a full record of the disclosures. Obtain confirmation from the party to whom the disclosure has been made. Have financial disclosure statements attached to the agreement and acknowledged by both parties. Many states have mandatory financial disclosure forms that must be filed by the parties in the event of a divorce. Use of those forms or forms which

---

15. Ohio Rev. Code § 3103.06 (codes.ohio.gov current through June 21, 2010).
16. Colo. Rev Stat. § 14-2-301 (1996)

disclose the same information may be useful in rebutting a claim that insufficient information was disclosed. They will not, of course, rebut a claim that false information was provided.

- Avoid any appearance of a conflict of interest on the part of the legal team. Each party must have their own *independent* advice. While we cannot force one of the parties to obtain their own legal counsel, we must make it *absolutely clear* that we represent only one party and are acting only in that party's interest. This is true even if the two parties come into our office stating that they have worked out an agreement and simply want us to formalize it.

- While we must encourage the party we do not represent to obtain their own legal counsel, we should not recommend or refer them to an attorney. Not only should the legal counsel be independent, but the process by which that counsel is selected should be independent.

- If the one party is not represented by their own attorney, include an acknowledgment in the agreement itself that the person has been advised to seek independent counsel and that we represent only the other party. The acknowledgment should include a statement that the party is specifically waiving the right to independent counsel. This acknowledgement should not be hidden among the many, many provisions that are commonly made part of such an agreement. Include it in large bold-face type immediately above the signature lines.

- Our clients should be encouraged to initiate discussion of prenuptial agreements sufficiently far in advance of the wedding to allow for full disclosure, careful consideration, and independent advice. While prenuptial agreements sprung upon the other party the night before the wedding have been enforced, they are particularly susceptible successful claims.

- Make as many provisions of the agreement as possible reciprocal. Even if as a practical matter one spouse is giving up nothing by releasing their rights to the other spouse's property (because the other party has no property), the provision in the agreement should state that each party is releasing their interest in the other party's property as a matter of basic fairness. Of course, there will be instances when there are good reasons to have a provision be unilateral. When that is the case, the agreement should include a statement of those reasons.

- Make sure the formalities for proper execution of the agreement are met before disinterested witnesses. We do not want the witnesses to Harry and Ruth's prenuptial agreement to be Harry's children or any of Harry's relatives. Have the agreement acknowledged as the parties' free act and deed before a notary even, if it is not required under state law.

Insurance

We will discuss one more estate planning tool before moving on—insurance. I am not in the business of selling insurance and I share the general distrust of insurance companies. However, there can be no denying the value of insurance as an estate planning tool. The idea behind estate planning is to protect our client's assets and provide for the financial needs of our client or our client's heirs. There is a form of insurance that can assist under the right circumstances in almost every aspect of estate planning.

Property insurance provides funding to replace assets lost due to fire or other casualty and liability insurance protects our client's assets from the financial consequences of the client's own negligence. However, given the needs and goals of the elder client, estate planning must consider short- and long-term disability insurance, health insurance (especially Medicare supplement insurance), nursing home or assisted living insurance, long term care insurance, and the like. Each of our clients faces the possibility, if not the probability, that they will need long term care of some sort. Few of our clients possess the resources to pay for that care. The issue for the estate planner will be the extent to which the client has the resources to pay for insurance that will cover that care.

Life insurance is, of course, a standard tool for estate planning. It is a tool that can be used creatively. Our clients generally look at life insurance simply as a way of providing for the financial security of their dependents after the client's death or to pay funeral costs or other expenses. However, it is a more versatile tool than that. Consider this dilemma:

Juan's only asset of substance is his house. It is worth about $100,000. The mortgage has been paid. What could be the problem? He has two children. Maria is strong and independent. She already has a job and is supporting herself. She is smart and wants a lot out of life. With the money for a college education, she could likely achieve much of what she wants. Miguel is disabled. He receives Social Security Disability (SSD) and Supplemental Security Income (SSI)—enough to pay for his basic needs and keep up the house if Juan dies, but he has no place else to live.

The dilemma is that if he leaves the house to both children and it is sold to provide each child with their share, Maria will receive the money she needs for college, but Miguel will lose his place to live and the SSI. The $50,000 will be quickly dissipated on his housing and care, and he will soon have nothing to show for it. On the other hand, if he allows Miguel to stay in the house, Maria will not receive any inheritance. How can he be fair to both of his children?

The answer may be insurance. For a fairly small premium, Juan can buy an insurance policy that will pay $100,000 to his beneficiary on his death. If he leaves the house to Miguel and names Maria as the beneficiary of the policy, each will receive $100,000 in value. While there is seldom a perfect solution to the fairness problem, life insurance can be an effective balancing tool in many instances.

Summary and a Caution

This brief overview of estate planning tools,[17] as well as the exercise in using them in the next section, presents a very simplified picture of each of the tools and

---

17. A more comprehensive, but still not complete listing of estate planning tools would include:

Ownership Forms
   Fee Simple
   Tenancy-in-Common
   Joint Tenancy
   Life Estates
Tools
   Gifts
      Inter vivos
      Testamentary
   Trusts
      Inter vivos
         Revocable
         Irrevocable
      Totten
      Marital Deduction
         QTIP
         A/B (Credit-Shelter)
      Charitable
      Life Insurance
      Spendthrift
      Sprinkling/spray
      Short-term
   Wills
      Pour Over Provision for existing trusts
      Specific Legacy
      Demonstrative Legacy
      General Legacy
      Residuary Legacy
      Testamentary Trusts
         Marital Deduction
            QTIP
            A/B (Credit-Shelter)
         Charitable
         Life Insurance
         Spendthrift

their use in estate planning. Each requires a great deal of thought in actual practice. Consider, for example, all that must be covered in a life estate. Let's say our client's mother who lives in Nebraska wants to leave him her cottage on a lake in Montana. In order to avoid a probate proceeding in Montana, she decides to convey the property to him now, but retain a life estate. Title will be in his name, subject to the life estate—her right to use the property while she is alive. Who will be responsible for insuring and maintaining the property? What rights will he have if she does not maintain the property? Can he enter the property against her wishes and do the maintenance himself? Who will pay the property taxes? Who will be able to deduct that payment on their income taxes? What happens if she goes into a nursing home with little hope of ever using the cottage again—must he leave the property untouched even if she lives in the nursing home for months or years?

These questions and more must be addressed for a simple life estate. Many more must be answered for trusts, wills, and marital agreements. Few are as simple as they appear. The effective, efficient, and professional paralegal will have checklists and interview sheets that facilitate his ability to obtain and use the necessary information.

Now that we have a basic understanding of some of the estate planning tools available to us, let's take an equally basic look at using those tools to meet our client's goals.

D. Matching Clients' Goals with Estate Planning Tools

In Chapter Six we discussed the different types of goals a client might have —short term, midterm and long term goals, and how they change as the client moves from one stage in his life to another. At that time we looked at the various hypothetical stages of Melvin Dummar's life. For purposes of this exercise, Melvin Dummar is at the beginning of Stage 9 of his life. Here is his current situation:

    Sprinkling/spray
    Short-term
  Life Insurance
    To estate
    To beneficiary
  Agreements
    Prenuptial
    Postnuptial
    Nonmarital

Melvin lives in Mississippi and has come to our office for estate planning. He and his second wife, Bonnie, are just starting out on their business which is a combination mini-mart/gas station. They lease the station but hope to purchase it over the next five years. They also lease a house on the adjoining lot which they also hope to purchase soon. The business (the lease of the property, contracts, goodwill, etc.) is now worth about $300,000 but should be worth over two million dollars by itself in a few years. He and Bonnie are joint tenants on the house lease and will take title the same way when they purchase it. It is worth about $250,000. They will purchase it with some money Bonnie has saved from her inheritance from her parents and a mortgage of about $200,000 to be paid off over 30 years. Other assets in his name alone include a car worth $15,000; a speed boat worth $10,000; stock investments worth $20,000; about $20,000 in two savings accounts, possibly some value still in his life story, and a life insurance policy with $250,000 face value (about $3,600 surrender value).

If Melvin died today he would be survived by Bonnie, his daughter who is newly married and is expecting a child, his son, two step-children, his ex-wife, Linda, who is remarried, and his aunt. He has some desires and some concerns:

1. If Bonnie survives him, he would like her to "have everything and be able to live as she has lived," but at the same time he wants to make sure that in the end his own children and/or grandchildren get his share of what he and Bonnie have acquired. He is especially concerned because this is a fairly new marriage. It looks as though it will work out well in the long run, but his prior history of two failed marriages concerns him.

2. His son has already inherited Melvin's propensity for recklessness with money. (Melvin's current financial condition is mostly the result of sound management by Bonnie). The son also gambles and may have a drinking problem. He wants to see that his son gets a share of his estate but does not want to simply leave him any money directly.

3. He still has fond thoughts of his ex-wife, Linda, but she is well taken care of by her current husband and, in any case, can take care of herself. If possible, he'd prefer that she not inherit anything of his from either his son or his daughter because he doesn't like her present husband.

4. He has come to regard his step-children as his children but has never adopted them. He does not want to ignore them in the estate distribution but he is aware that they will get a fair share of what he and Bonnie have built up through inheritance from Bonnie, who does not

feel the same way about her step-children as he does about his, primarily because they live with Linda and not with her.

5. He would like to make a "tithing" type gift to the Mormon Church, i.e., ten percent of his estate.

6. He has developed a distinct aversion to the court system as a result of his experience and would like to keep his estate out of court as much as possible.

7. He has no fondness for the government either and would like to minimize taxes.

8. He has a number of specific bequests to make, such as his hunting rifle to his best friend, but is concerned that as time goes on he may change his mind, people will die, etc., and he does not want to have to change his will every time something like that happens.

9. He wants to keep costs and hassles to a minimum.

The key to this exercise—the key to successful estate planning—is to match up the available estate planning tools with the client's goals, and arrive at a plan that effectively uses those tools to accomplish those goals to the extent they can be accomplished. Note that our role is not to judge those goals, but to fulfill them. When I use this exercise in class, many students will devise an estate plan that gives some item from the estate to Melvin's aunt. They do so because *they* would give something to *their* aunt. However, there is no indication in Melvin's list of desires and concerns that he wants to make any provision for the aunt! We must determine and effectuate our client's wishes, not ours.

For purposes of this exercise we will consider several, but not all of Melvin's desires. As we will see, there is no one tool and perhaps no combination of tools that will perfectly suit all of Melvin's desires. Our task is to achieve the plan that best implements his goals. It may be that some goals cannot be fully met and that Melvin will have to prioritize his goals.

Let's do a chart showing our client's wishes in one column. The second column is for the estate planning tools:

Goal	Tool

Melvin's first goal is to see that Bonnie is able to have full use of his estate during her life. There are a number of tools that could accomplish this goal as indicated in the next chart.

Goal	Tool

Bonnie to have full use of estate during her life	• Gifts in fee simple to Bonnie now
	• Gifts in joint tenancy with Melvin to Bonnie now
	• Gifts to Bonnie as a tenant-in-common with Melvin
	• Gift in fee simple to Bonnie in Melvin's will
	• Life estate in Melvin's will to Bonnie with the children as remaindermen
	• Conveyance to a trust
	    Inter vivos
	    Testamentary
	• Marital agreement

Children to have Melvin's estate on Bonnie's death	
Deal with son's recklessness	
Avoid probate	
Minimize costs and hassle	

As we examine the tools available to achieve the first goal we see that the use of some will eliminate the possibility of achieving other goals and thus must be eliminated. Others tools are not directly incompatible with other goals, but are not well suited to meet those goals. These tools should not be eliminated right away, however. If we do not find a tool or combination of tools that perfectly suits the client's needs, we will have to choose the best combination based on the client's priorities.

Looking at the available tools we see that we must eliminate "Gifts in fee simple to Bonnie now" as an option for several reasons. If we conveyed Melvin's estate to Bonnie now, (1) we would transfer ownership and control to Bonnie now putting Melvin in a very difficult position if the marriage is not successful, and (2) the transfer would be for more than just her life as the property would go to her heirs or devisees at her death rather than to his children. Unless there was a marital agreement requiring that she leave the property to his children in her will, we would be disinheriting Melvin's children. Even with a marital agreement requiring that Bonnie write a will, the practical problems that arise if she does not honor the agreement eliminate this tool. Similar considerations eliminate the present conveyance to Bonnie as joint tenants and tenants-in-common.

A life estate to Bonnie in Melvin's will is a viable tool. It meets the goal of allowing Bonnie full use of the estate during her life, but grants the property to his children on her death. However, it does not deal with the son's recklessness and would require probate since the property is passing through a will.

A trust is also a viable tool. If we transfer the property from Melvin to Melvin as Trustee for the benefit of himself and Bonnie during their lives, with his children as secondary beneficiaries, we have accomplished several goals. Melvin maintains control during his life and can pass that control on to Bonnie or someone else as successor trustee when his dies. The children become beneficiaries when both Melvin and Bonnie die. And, since this is an *inter vivos* trust, most of Melvin's estate will pass without the necessity of probate. The downside is the ninth goal—minimizing costs and hassle. Creating a trust this complex now will be costly, involving separate annual tax returns, and administrative costs. There is also the problem of conveying all assets, including assets not yet owned by Melvin to the trust.

A testamentary trust may eliminate some of these downsides, but does not comply with Melvin's goal to avoid probate. Thus at this point our chart might look like this:

Goal	Tool

Bonnie to have full use of estate during her life	• Life estate in Melvin's will to Bonnie with the children as remaindermen
	• Conveyance to a trust
	   Inter vivos
	   Testamentary
	• Marital agreement

Children to have Melvin's estate on Bonnie's death	• Life estate in Melvin's will to Bonnie with the children as remaindermen
	• Conveyance to a trust
	   Inter vivos
	   Testamentary

Deal with son's recklessness	• Life estate in Melvin's will to Bonnie with the children as remaindermen
	• Conveyance to a trust
	   Inter vivos
	   Testamentary

Avoid probate	• Conveyance to a trust *Inter vivos*
Minimize costs and hassle	• Life estate in Melvin's will to Bonnie with the children as remaindermen • Conveyance to a trust Testamentary

Now let's take a look at the goal of dealing with his son's recklessness. Simply leaving the estate to Bonnie for her life with the children as remaindermen will not help with this at all. At the very least we would have to create a spendthrift trust for the son and name the trust as the remainderman rather than the son. Similarly, any trust set up (either *inter vivos* or testamentary) should include spendthrift provisions. (Even the non-reckless daughter can benefit from the spendthrift provision.) So our chart would now look like this:

Goal	Tool

Bonnie to have full use of estate during her life	• Life estate in Melvin's will to Bonnie with a trust containing spendthrift provision and the children as beneficiaries named as remainderman
	• Conveyance to a trust containing spendthrift provision
	   Inter vivos
	   Testamentary
	• Marital agreement

Children to have Melvin's estate on Bonnie's death	• Life estate in Melvin's will to Bonnie with a trust containing spendthrift provision and the children as beneficiaries named as remainderman
	• Conveyance to a trust containing spendthrift provision
	   Inter vivos
	   Testamentary

Deal with son's recklessness	• Life estate in Melvin's will to Bonnie with the children as remainderman
	• Conveyance to a trust containing spendthrift provision
	   Inter vivos
	   Testamentary

Avoid probate	• Conveyance to a trust containing spendthrift provision *Inter vivos*
Minimize costs and hassle	• Life estate in Melvin's will to Bonnie with a trust containing spendthrift provision and the children as beneficiaries named as remainderman • Conveyance to a trust containing spendthrift provision with Bonnie as primary beneficiary and children as secondary beneficiary Testamentary

At this point we have developed the various options available to meet these client goals. They can be articulated to the client with their advantages and disadvantages, and the best option picked based on the client's priorities— minimizing probate, minimizing costs, or minimizing taxes. Other tools may be needed to accomplish the other goals, such as a charitable trust for the church. Other goals may be incorporated into the basic scheme chosen using the chart, such as specific bequests to his friend in a will. As discussed above, in any case the estate plan will include a will. Even if an *inter vivos* trust is chosen, a will should be used to gain the benefit of the residuary clause.

E. Taxes

Estate taxes, or rather avoiding estate taxes, will be a concern of many of our clients. For most of them, it need not be. The estate tax is a tax on the transfer of property at death. It is paid by the estate out of the property available to the estate, as opposed to an inheritance tax that is paid by the people inheriting the property. There is a federal estate tax and most states have a state estate tax.

According to the IRS, "Most relatively simple estates (cash, publicly traded securities, small amounts of other easily valued assets, and no special deductions or elections, or jointly held property) do not require the filing of an estate tax return. A filing is required for estates with combined gross assets and prior taxable gifts exceeding $1,500,000 in 2004–2005; $2,000,000 in 2006–2008; and $3,500,000 effective for decedents dying on or after January 1, 2009."[18] As a result, almost no estate pays a tax. For example, even in 2003 when the exemption amount was $1 million, only 121 of the 28,535 decedents in Mississippi had estate tax liability—99.8 percent of decedents paid no estate tax.

This is a difficult time to write about estate taxes as they are in a state of flux. As a result of legislation passed several years ago, the exemption amount has been increasing and the estate tax decreasing. In 2010 there is no estate tax at all. However, the legislation is set to expire in 2011, sending the law back to where it was in 2001. This has led to a great deal of wrangling in Congress. Some politicians refer to the estate tax as a "death tax" and argue it is wrong to tax someone just because they died. Others refer to the tax elimination as the "Paris Hilton Relief Act" since it would benefit only the very wealthy, who they argue are not in need of relief.

---

18. http://www.irs.gov/businesses/small/article/0,,id=164871,00.html (Last accessed May 3, 2010).

Given the current state of the law it is very difficult to plan for taxes in an estate plan—other than to advise clients to die in 2010 when there is no tax. However, a basic understanding of the tax is warranted. The estate plan should be structured to the extent possible while achieving our clients' other goals, so that the least amount of property is subject to the tax. We will start by looking at what is taxed.

The estate tax is based on the fair market value of the "**gross estate**" at the time of death. Our task, a task in which paralegals are quite involved, is to determine what goes into the augmented estate and what the value was at the time of death—not the value when it was bought by the decedent or even the value at the time of probate. For example, a share of stock bought for $100 in 2005 may have been worth only $50 dollars when the decedent died in July of 2009 during the recession, and $80 in May of 2010 as the stock market started its recovery. It is the July 2009 value that must be included in the estate.

According to the IRS, your gross estate includes the value of all property in which you had an interest at the time of death. Your gross estate also will include the following.

- Life insurance proceeds payable to your estate or, if you owned the policy, to your heirs.
- The value of certain annuities payable to your estate or your heirs.
- The value of certain property you transferred within 3 years before your death.
- Trusts or other interests established by you or others in which you have certain powers.

We will not go into this in great detail here, but even a cursory reading of this statement indicates some of the ways in which estate planning can reduce the gross estate. For example, life insurance policies can be properly structured to avoid ownership by the decedent, trusts can be written to avoid the decedent having the powers that will bring the trust value into the estate, and making transfers earlier rather than later to raise the chances of beating the three-year rule.[19]

Life estates are especially helpful in this regard as the title and primary value of the property can be transferred so that only the life estate remains with the decedent at the time of death. Since the life estate expires with the decedent it has no value to be included in the estate. However, there are other tax ramifications involved in the use of life estates and trusts to avoid estate taxes. Experts should

---

19. The proper timing of transfer is also an issue when attempting to establish eligibility for Medicaid payment for long-term nursing home care due to the 5-year "look back" rule. We will look more closely at this issue in Chapter Nine.

be consulted before using any estate planning tool simply to remove property from the gross estate. At this point, all you need to understand is that tax considerations can be a factor in choosing the correct estate planning tool.

Once the gross estate is established, certain deductions can be made to determine the **taxable estate.** The allowable deductions used in determining the taxable estate include:

1. Funeral expenses paid out of the estate
2. Debts you owed at the time of death
3. The marital deduction (generally, the value of the property that passes from the estate to the surviving spouse).

The taxable estate will be used in determining the tax, but it is not the amount that is taxed. This is because some of the estate value is exempt from taxes. This is the amount stated above as having moved from $1,000,000 in 2002 to $3,500,000 in 2009. So in 2009, *after* we have done whatever we can to prevent property from being included in the estate through estate planning, and *after* we tax all the deductions, we subtract $3,500,000 from the value before any tax is imposed. So if at this point the value is $3,499,999.99, there is no tax.

There is one catch or "complication." Won't it be easy to avoid all taxes just by giving away all our property to our kids? Well, Congress and the IRS thought of that and imposed a tax on some gifts—mainly the type of gift intended to avoid estate taxes. So the value of *inter vivos* gifts and the value of the estate are added together for purposes of taxes and there is one credit given for both of them. This credit is called the **unified credit.** It is this credit that determines the **Applicable Exclusion Amount,** that is, the amount we subtract from the taxable estate before calculating the taxes—the $3,500,000 in 2009.

Since the unification of the gift and estate taxes is meant only to prevent abuse of gifting to avoid estate taxes, the gift tax is not applied to what most of us think of as gifts—the new Wii for Christmas, the new laptop for graduation, and the like.[20] A separate **annual exclusion** applies to each person to whom

---

20. The general rule is that any gift is a taxable gift. However, there are many exceptions to this rule. Generally, the following are not taxable gifts:
- Gifts that are not more than the annual exclusion for the calendar year.
- Tuition or medical expenses you pay for someone (the educational and medical exclusions).
- Gifts to your spouse.
- Gifts to a political organization for its use.
- Gifts to qualified charities (a deduction is available for these amounts).

you make a gift. For example in 2006, the annual exclusion was $12,000. Therefore, you generally could give up to $12,000 each to any number of people in 2006 and none of the gifts would be taxable. If you are married, both you and your spouse can separately give up to $12,000 to the same person without making a taxable gift. If one of you gives more than $12,000 to a person in any one of these years, you may be able to take advantage of **gift splitting,** which allows one spouse to act as if they gave the gift even if the other spouse actually gave it.

As you can see, it is fairly easy to make large amounts of money "disappear" for estate tax purposes without exercising any of the more sophisticated estate planning tools. Let's assume our client has $10,000,000, a wife and four children. Using actuarial tables, we can determine he is likely to live another 20 years. Applying the 2009 tax rules:

- For twenty years he gives his wife $48,000 a year and they both give each child $12,000, a total of $96,000 a year with no tax. (Since gifts to spouses are not taxable and the $12,000 is the annual exclusion amount.) Over twenty years this is just under 2,000,000. So at death he has $8,000,000.
- In his will he gives his wife $4,500,000. There is no tax on this amount due to due to the marital deduction. This leaves $3,500,000 which ...
- In his will he gives to a trust for his children. There is no tax due to unified credit.
- Over the next ten years wife gives children $12,000 each ever year. This comes to $1,000,000 so at time of her death there's $3,500,000 left of the $4,500,000 he left to her in his will which ...
- In her will she leaves the $3,500,000 in equal shares to the four children. Again, there is no tax due because of the unified credit.

Again, while the federal estate tax can be an important factor for some clients, it is not likely to be a factor for most of our clients under current law. When it is, an expert should be consulted. You should also be mindful of the tax laws for the state in which you are practicing.

F. Estate Planning and the Elder Client

The purposes and goals of estate planning are no different for the elder client than any other. However, the goals of the elder client that must be met through the estate planning process will be quite different from those of younger clients. Of course, each client's goals will be unique to that client and that client's circumstances. However, there will be some common themes.

While a client in her thirties may be planning for retirement, this is a long-term goal, less immediate than the goals, say, of taking an annual vacation in the short term or buying a house in the mid-term. Even the long-term goal of planning for her children's college education is likely to take precedence over "old age issues."

This is, obviously, not the case for the elder client. For elder clients, managing their estate so that they can survive through and enjoy their retirement is their current, short-term goal. We are learning that for all too many of the baby boomers, this is a severe problem. Less immediate, but now of significant concern, is the likelihood of the need for "long-term" end-of-life care including the possibility of Alzheimer's or other disability. Long-term, the client hopes there is still something left over to pass on to their children.

Frequently, estate planning at this stage revolves around making arrangements to preserve whatever "nest egg" the client has through maximizing the use of Social Security, Medicaid, and Medicare. This may mean conveying that nest egg, or parts of it, to children according to a plan that complies with rules established by those programs. These programs will be discussed in Chapter Nine.

It also may mean planning for the transfer of control to children or others, so that financial decisions can be made when the client is no longer capable of making those decisions. Often this will require the use of **durable powers of attorney**, powers of attorney designed to be effective even when the person granting the power is no longer competent to make decisions. Some durable powers of attorney are designed to take effect *only* when the client lacks capacity. Durable powers of attorney are wonderful estate planning tools, but are susceptible to abuse.

Finally, estate planning for the elder client ought to include planning for medical and end-of-life decisions that must so often be made when the client is unable to make them himself. This is the topic of the next chapter.

CHAPTER EIGHT

PLANNING FOR THE END OF LIFE

A. Introduction—Death and Dying

As discussed in Chapter Five, in 1969 Elizabeth Kubler-Ross published *On Death and Dying* beginning the long process of changing the perception of the "right" way to care for the dying patients, a perception seemingly at the same time shared by the medical and legal professions, policy makers and general society but not shared by large numbers of individuals who comprised those same groups. While much progress has been made, society as well as the medical and legal professions has much work to do in dealing with the issues raised by death and dying.

Kubler-Ross pointed out that as a society our way of coping and dealing with death, dying, and dying patients had changed."[1] She went on to declare, "Dying nowadays is more gruesome in many ways, namely, more lonely, mechanical, and dehumanized; at times it is even difficult to determine technically when the time of death has occurred."[2] Dying had become lonely and impersonal because it occurred in impersonal hospitals connected to machines that were intended only to stave off death, rather than heal. She lamented that, "It would take so little to remember that the sick person too has feelings, has wishes and opinions, and has—most important of all—the right to be heard."[3] Unfortunately, it was not at all clear that patients did have a legal right to be heard. It was not until 1977 that California passed the Natural Death Act, the first such law.

Finally, the right was established by the U.S. Supreme Court in the matter of *Cruzan v. Director, Missouri Department of Mental Health.*[4] According to the opinion of the Court,

---

1. Elisabeth Kubler-Ross, *On Death and Dying* 6 (MacMillian Publishing Co., Inc. 1969).
2. *Id.* at 7.
3. *Id.* at 8.
4. 497 U.S. 261 (1990)

> On the night of January 11, 1983, Nancy Cruzan lost control of her
> car as she traveled down Elm Road in Jasper County, Missouri. The
> vehicle overturned, and Cruzan was discovered lying face down in a
> ditch without detectable respiratory or cardiac function. Paramedics
> were able to restore her breathing and heartbeat at the accident site,
> and she was transported to a hospital in an unconscious state. An at-
> tending neurosurgeon diagnosed her as having sustained probable
> cerebral contusions compounded by significant anoxia (lack of oxy-
> gen). The Missouri trial court in this case found that permanent brain
> damage generally results after 6 minutes in an anoxic state; it was es-
> timated that Cruzan was deprived of oxygen from 12 to 14 minutes.
> She remained in a coma for approximately three weeks and then pro-
> gressed to an unconscious state in which she was able to orally ingest
> some nutrition. In order to ease feeding and further the recovery, sur-
> geons implanted a gastrostomy feeding and hydration tube in Cruzan
> with the consent of her then husband. Subsequent rehabilitative efforts
> proved unavailing.[5]

Nancy's parents requested that the feeding and hydration tube be withdrawn,
and the State of Missouri refused.

In a lengthy opinion the court noted the history of litigation on the issue and
the interests to be balanced. The case did not involve just the right of a person
to refuse or direct his or her own medical treatment, but the right of others to
direct that treatment when the person was incapable of directing it. However,
the court did assume for purposes of the case that "the United States Constitution would grant a competent person a constitutionally protected right to
refuse lifesaving hydration and nutrition." The issue thus became to what extent a state could enact procedural safeguards to ensure that those making the
decisions for the incapacitated person were correct in their assessment of that
person's wishes. In *Cruzan*, the court determined that Missouri did not go beyond its bounds in requiring that such proof be by clear and convincing evidence.

The difficulty here is evident. It is only in the rare case that a patient will be
able to be informed of all the medical information necessary to make a decision to direct life-ending medical treatment *at the time the decision must be
made*. There are several issues, (1) how, then, could the right be exercised, (2)
how could a patient be made aware of this right, and (3) how could the right
be enforced if those who were providing the medical treatment refused to

---

5. *Id.*

honor the decisions. These issues were answered by the Patient Self Determination Act, passed by Congress in 1990.

B. Patient Self Determination Act

The American Bar Association explains the Patient Self Determination Act[6] this way:

> The PSDA simply requires that most health care institutions (but not individual doctors) do the following:
>
> 1. Give you at the time of admission a written summary of:
>   - your health care decision-making rights (Each state has developed such a summary for hospitals, nursing homes, and home health agencies to use.)
>   - the facility's policies with respect to recognizing advance directives.
> 2. Ask you if you have an advance directive, and document that fact in your medical record if you do. (It is up to you to make sure they get a copy of it).
> 3. Educate their staff and community about advance directives.
> 4. Never discriminate against patients based on whether or not they have an advance directive. Thus, it is against the law for them to require either that you have or not have an advance directive.[7]

I include this statement here because it is a concise, clear statement made in terms that can be conveyed to a client by a paralegal explaining the Act, keeping in mind that a paralegal cannot give legal advice, but can (and often does) explain law or legal concepts to clients. Of course, explaining rights as sensitive and complex as the PSDA is seldom as easy as reading from a text or providing that text to a client. It is important that you understand it well enough, though, to explain it fully to a client. However, also keep in mind that most states have developed explanations of that state's particular implementation of PSDA in terms that (at least theoretically) that state's citizens can understand.[8]

---

6. Federal Patient Self Determination Act, 42 U.S.C. 1395 *et. seq.*

7. "Law for Older Americans," Division of Public Education, *American Bar Association,* http://www.abanet.org/publiced/practical/patient_self_determination_act.html (Last accessed April 6, 2010).

8. A sample of the Mississippi booklet is available here: http://www.msdh.state.ms.us/msdhsite/_static/resources/75.pdf.

There are a number of questions likely to arise directly under the Act, and questions regarding the obligations of the medical provider. There are also questions regarding the various instruments by which a client can effectuate her rights to determine the course of her medical treatment. Questions regarding the obligations of the medical provider will be addressed in the remainder of this section. The various instruments used to effectuate client rights will be addressed in separate sections.

The PSDA contains requirements that some providers of health care—such as hospitals, nursing homes, hospices, home health agencies, and prepaid health care organizations—provide information to patients regarding advance directives and an individual's rights under state law to make decisions concerning medical care. The Act applies to health care institutions that receive federal funds rather than individual physicians. Since Medicaid and Medicare are federal programs providing federal funds, the Act applies to almost all health care institutions. The Act does not require states to make substantive changes to their laws, but such changes inevitably occur in order to preserve federal funding for entities providing health care in their jurisdictions.

The Act *does not* require a health care institution to honor the right of the client to terminate medical care. A health care provider, including physicians, can refuse to follow a client's direction, whether given directly or through a surrogate, for reasons of conscience. However, if they do so, they must transfer the client to another provider who will honor that direction. They must also inform the client from the outset of their policy regarding honoring such directives, so the client can choose another provider, if necessary.

The Act does require that a client's decision be honored by the client's family, agents, and surrogates. As we will discuss later, this is an important factor, as it serves the planning goal of minimizing conflict among the members of the client's family and stress on the person(s) who must effectuate the client's desires.

In a perfect world, we would each be able to make our own medical treatment decisions under all circumstances. (I am aware that for some people, in a perfect world there would be no need for such decisions to be made, but the legal profession seldom hypothesizes that much perfection.) In reality, our clients, and therefore we, must confront the fact that others will be making those decisions. As is often the case failure to make a decision is itself a decision. If we, or a client, fail to decide in advance how we want things done, or who we want to make decisions for us, we are in effect deciding that the state will make the decision for us through legislation. For example, as we discussed in Chapter Six, if we do not make a will, we have decided that our estate will be distributed according to the intestate distribution enacted by our state legislature.

In general, we have the right to make health care decisions, including decisions about nursing home care, for ourselves if we are 18 or older and are competent.

The nature, purpose, and reasonable risks and consequences of these treatments should be explained to us. The physician should explain to us:

- the pertinent facts about our illness and the nature of the treatment in plain language which is understandable to us
- explain to us why the proposed treatment is recommended
- inform us of all reasonable risks and material consequences or "side effects" associated with the proposed treatment
- tell us about any other types of treatment which we could undergo instead.

Alternatives to a person making the decision (in descending order) are:

- ▶ An advance directive, such as Individual Instructions, Advanced Health Care Directives, or Living Wills
- ▶ A designation, usually through an instrument such as a Power of Attorney for Health Care, of an adult of choice, called a surrogate, to make the decision
- ▶ A family member chosen by statute rather than the client may act as a surrogate to make the decision for the client
- ▶ An adult who shows care and concern and who is familiar with the client's values may make health care decisions
- ▶ A court might have to make the decision for you.

We will discuss each of these options in turn. It is my belief that these should be regarded as options in a descending order, i.e., that the first is better than the second, the second better than the third, and so on. However, throughout the discussion we must keep in mind that our role is to inform (and for the attorney to advise), not to convince or persuade, a client.

I view these options as belonging to one of three categories. In the first, the client makes as many health care decisions for himself in advance as he can and designates someone to make only those decisions which were not anticipated in advance. In the second, the client makes no decisions in advance except the designation of the person or persons who will make necessary decisions on her behalf. Finally, there is the option of taking no action. In this instance, the client should understand that taking no action is itself making a decision. The client decides to allow someone designated by state law to make the decisions on her behalf.

C. Making Medical and End-of-Life Decisions in Advance

There are many aspects of life and death which we cannot control. Leaving aside the fact that we may be able to lessen the chances of certain illnesses through adjustments in our lifestyle, especially our eating and exercise, we can seldom control or predict the onset of serious illness. We can, however, exercise some degree of control over how that illness will be handled within the medical care system.

It is, of course, not possible to anticipate every particular medical decision that may need to be made on your behalf when you are not capable of making those decisions yourself. We can be aware of the basic differences in approach to end-of-life and serious illness medical treatment, select from among those approaches the one that best conforms to our own, and take steps to notify medical care providers of our choice.

While there are many variations in approaches to serious illness and end-of-life medical treatment decisions, there are three major and somewhat opposing schools of thought. One is composed of those who believe, for religious or other reasons, that life must be prolonged at any cost, whether cost is measured in terms of finances, or physical or emotional pain to the patient. Many members of the medical profession hold this view. They are, after all, trained to provide medical treatment, rather than withhold it; to preserve life, rather than end it. As noted above, the PSDA does acknowledge that some medical providers may, for reasons of conscience, be unable or unwilling to honor any other choice. When this occurs, that provider must notify the patient and cooperate in transferring the patient to another provider who will honor the patient's decisions.

Another school of thought, also held for religious or other reasons, is that death is a process which at some point, despite medical intervention, is going to happen and that process should be made as smooth as possible for the dying person. The latter approach does not encourage or condone steps being taken to hasten the end of life, but does avoid extraordinary measures which serve no purpose other than to prolong life for someone in extreme pain or a vegetative state. This is often referred to as palliative care. It should not be viewed as an alternative to medical treatment but as a type of medical treatment—a medical specialty focused on relief of the pain, stress and other debilitating symptoms of serious illness. The goal is not just preservation of life, but the provision of a quality of life in the sense that suffering is minimized to the extent possible. The palliative care approach applies to all serious illnesses at any stage of life, not just those that occur at or cause the end of life.

In end-of-life situations palliative care is often provided through hospice care. The National Hospice and Palliative Care Organization (NHPCO) describes hospice care in this way:

> Considered the model for quality compassionate care for people facing a life-limiting illness, hospice provides expert medical care, pain management, and emotional and spiritual support expressly tailored to the patient's needs and wishes. Support is provided to the patient's loved ones as well.
>
> Hospice focuses on caring, not curing. In most cases, care is provided in the patient's home but may also be provided in freestanding hospice centers, hospitals, nursing homes, and other long-term care facilities. Hospice services are available to patients with any terminal illness or of any age, religion, or race.[9]

NHPCO estimates that over 38% of all deaths in the United States occur under the care of a hospice program.[10]

The third group believes that people, under certain conditions, should be able to hasten their own death, enabling them to have "Death with Dignity." Death with Dignity advocates encourage palliative care and advanced directives. However, they would go further. For example, the Death with Dignity National Center states,

> The greatest human freedom is to live, and die, according to one's own desires and beliefs. The most common desire among those with a terminal illness is to die with some measure of dignity. From advance directives to physician-assisted dying, death with dignity is a movement to provide options for the dying to control their own end-of-life care.[11]

At the time of this writing, only two states have enacted death with dignity laws—Oregon and Washington. While I approve of these laws because they enlarge the choices available to all, I will not discuss them extensively here because of their limited applicability.

From the point of view of the legal professional none of these approaches is correct, right, or better than the others. They are options that are approved

---

9. *NHPCO Facts and Figures: Hospice Care in America*, National Hospice and Palliative Care Organization at 3, http://www.nhpco.org/files/public/Statistics_Research/NHPCO_facts_and_figures.pdf (Last accessed April 10, 2010).

10. *Id.* at 4.

11. Death With Dignity National Center, http://www.deathwithdignity.org/ (Last accessed April 10, 2010).

by law. It is our role to understand each of the approaches and the laws that apply to them so that we can provide our clients with the best legal information and advice. This must be done in the most objective fashion possible.

The importance of the various methods of making advance decisions is that *the client* can make the decision that best suits their own beliefs. Having a living will or an advanced health care directive does not compel a client to choose an approach in opposition to their own beliefs. It simply allows them to make the decision rather than leave it to someone else, someone who may not share their beliefs.

We must be careful in discussing these options with clients that we do not judge their decisions or let them feel we do not approve of their decision. As noted previously, the elderly, especially those who are seriously ill, can be particularly vulnerable to outside influences. While many people become less concerned about what others think of them as they grow older, some others suffer from loss of a sense of self that can make them more susceptible to such influence. Our role is to assist the client in determining and effectuating their wishes, not to judge, shame, or persuade the client to our way of thinking.

There is a distinct ethical obligation in this regard. If your own beliefs make it unlikely that you can be objective in interviewing the client, explaining the options to the client, or otherwise assisting the attorney with the client, you should notify the attorney of that fact, so that other arrangements can be made to see that the client get the best objective assistance available.

While we often feel we know what another person would want, there is no way of being sure unless that person tells us. These instruments give our clients the ability to inform their families and their physicians what, at the time they executed the instrument, they believed they would want under a particular set of circumstances.

Certainly there are examples of people who feel strongly about these issues at one point in their life and then change their minds. Perhaps, they are certain they would never want to give up; they would want every effort made to preserve and extend their life until they are experiencing the pain and discomfort of a terminal illness. Shortly before this book was completed, *The New York Times* reported on a doctor who had spend her medical career providing and encouraging palliative care, but who chose to "fight to the end" when she was diagnosed with cancer, demanding treatments that were very painful and offered only a 2% chance of success.[12] The client can be reassured

---

12. "Helping Patients to Face Death, She Fought to Live," *The New York Times*," April 3, 2010, http://www.nytimes.com/2010/04/04/health/04doctor.html (Last accessed July 24, 2010).

that each of the documents can be changed or revoked to alter the choices made initially as long as the client remains competent to make the choice to change.

D. Options for Making Advance Medical and End-of-Life Decisions

Occasions when medical decisions may have to be made for us by others can arise at any stage of life. Accidents that can make emergency care necessary can also render us unable to make decisions regarding that care. For example, the doctor may decide that the best course of action is to remove a damaged kidney, but cannot do so without informed consent. I would rather have someone with my granted authority make that decision than have the doctor sew me back up, revive me, inform me, and then wheel me back into surgery. One of the instruments available to us is a medical power of attorney, which accomplishes this task.

Other instruments also provide our appointee with that kind of authority. Some of those documents are specially designed to deal with end-of-life decisions that occur when we have a terminal condition. Those documents deal with issues such as whether to initiate or continue medical interventions such as machines that keep us breathing, or the provision of nutrition through feeding tubes when we are in a vegetative state. We will begin our discussion with the most common documents used to deal with these end-of-life decisions.

Living Wills, Declarations to Physicians, and Other Advanced Directives

Every state now has legislation authorizing the use of some sort of advance health-care directive. Unfortunately, that legislation, much of which was passed in reaction to *Cruzon* and the Patient Self Determination Act, is not uniform in either substance or nomenclature. The documents authorized by the legislation are called "living wills," declarations to physicians, individual instructions, advanced health care directives, and other names depending on the jurisdiction.

Thus, while all states statutorily authorize powers of attorney for health care, and all but Massachusetts, Michigan and New York authorize living wills, there remains a great deal of confusion from state to state and client to client. The ABA notes,

> State legislation has been a mixed blessing. Although intended to facilitate the making of advance directives, many of the statutes may actually inhibit their use. The execution requirements are often detailed.

Restrictions on the types of treatment that may be withheld or withdrawn are common. There is little uniformity. The result is a system of fragmented, incomplete and often inconsistent legislation, both among states and within single states.[13]

In 1993 the National Conference of Commissioners on Uniform State Laws approved the Uniform Health-care Decisions Act, but at the time of this writing it had been enacted by only eight states: Alabama, Alaska, Delaware, Hawaii, Maine, Mississippi, New Mexico, and Wyoming.

Many of our clients are familiar with the term "living will," although some confuse it with a "living trust." The term is somewhat confusing. It expresses our "will" but it becomes effective during our lives, unlike an actual will that becomes effective upon our death. Further, it is designed to be a declaration of what medical care should be provided to us when we are dying! They may or may not have heard of the other terms by which these documents are called.

Due to the variety of these documents, we cannot discuss in detail the documents in each state. However, there are commonalities. Each of the states authorizing some form of living will, regardless of name, allows some document to be used to (1) designate an agent to make medical decisions for a person when that person is unable to make those decisions themselves, (2) give directions with regard to medical treatment intended to prolong life, (3) give directions regarding the provision of nutrition and hydration by artificial means, and (4) give directions regarding relief of pain.

For purposes of this section, I am providing a sample based on the Advanced Health Care Directive (AHCD) created by the Uniform Health-care Decisions Act. I do so for several reasons. First, it is comprehensive, meaning it combines in one document functions that are often covered in separate acts in some states. Thus, we will have some discussion of each of those separate documents under the umbrella of the AHCD. Second, as is the case with most uniform acts, the act incorporates those substantive provisions which are most common in the various existing state acts, while providing for simplified procedures. Third, having been enacted in eight states, it is the most common form available. Finally, I am hopeful that over time, more states will adopt the uniform act. It has been endorsed by the American Bar Association, the American Association of Retired Persons, and the ABA Commission on Legal Problems of the Elderly.

---

13. English, David M., "The Uniform Health-Care Decisions Act and its Progress in the States," *Probate and Property*, May/June 2001, American Bar Association, http://www.abanet.org/rppt/publications/magazine/2001/01mj/01mjenglish.html (Last accessed April 10, 2010).

Advance Health-Care Directive

Explanation

You have the right to give instructions about your own health care. You also have the right to name someone else to make health-care decisions for you. This form lets you do either or both of these things. It also lets you express your wishes regarding the designation of your primary physician. If you use this form, you may complete or modify all or any part of it. You are free to use a different form.

Part 1 of this form is a power of attorney for health care. Part 1 lets you name another individual as agent to make health-care decisions for you if you become incapable of making your own decisions or if you want someone else to make those decisions for you now even though you are still capable. You may name an alternate agent to act for you if your first choice is not willing, able or reasonably available to make decisions for you. Unless related to you, your agent may not be an owner, operator, or employee of a residential long-term health-care institution at which you are receiving care.

Unless the form you sign limits the authority of your agent, your agent may make all health-care decisions for you. This form has a place for you to limit the authority of your agent. You need not limit the authority of your agent if you wish to rely on your agent for all health-care decisions that may have to be made. If you choose not to limit the authority of your agent, your agent will have the right to:

(a) Consent or refuse consent to any care, treatment, service, or procedure to maintain, diagnose, or otherwise affect a physical or mental condition;

(b) Select or discharge health-care providers and institutions;

(c) Approve or disapprove diagnostic tests, surgical procedures, programs of medication, and orders not to resuscitate; and

(d) Direct the provision, withholding, or withdrawal of artificial nutrition and hydration and all other forms of health care.

Part 2 of this form lets you give specific instructions about any aspect of your health care. Choices are provided for you to express your wishes regarding the provision, withholding, or withdrawal of treatment to keep you alive, including the provision of and hydration, as well as the provision of pain relief. Space is provided for you to add to the choices you have made or for you to write out any additional wishes.

Part 3 of this form lets you designate a physician to have primary responsibility for your health care. After completing this form, sign and date the form at the end and have the form witnessed by one of the two alternative methods listed below. Give a copy of the signed and completed form to your physician, to any other health-care providers you may have, to any health-care institution at which you are receiving care, and to any health-care agents you have named. You should talk to the person you have named as agent to make sure that he or she understands your wishes and is willing to take the responsibility.

You have the right to revoke this advance health-care directive or replace this form at any time.

PART I
POWER OF ATTORNEY FOR HEALTH CARE

(1) **DESIGNATION OF AGENT:** I designate the following individual as my agent to make health-care decisions for me:

_____

(name of individual you choose as agent)

_____

(address) (city) (state) (zip code)

_____

(home phone) (work phone)

OPTIONAL: If I revoke my agent's authority or if my agent is not willing, able, or reasonably available to make a health-care decision for me, I designate as my first alternate agent:

_____

(name of individual you choose as first alternate agent)

_____

(address) (city) (state) (zip code)

_____

(home phone) (work phone)

OPTIONAL: If I revoke the authority of my agent and first alternate agent or if neither is willing, able, or reasonably available to make a health-care decision for me, I designate as my second alternate agent:

_____

(name of individual you choose as first alternate agent)

_____

(address) (city) (state) (zip code)

_____

(home phone) (work phone)

3

(2) AGENT'S AUTHORITY: My agent is authorized to make all health-care decisions for me, including decisions to provide, withhold, or withdraw artificial nutrition and hydration, and all other forms of health care to keep me alive, except as I state here:

_____

_____

_____

(Add additional sheets if needed.)

(3) WHEN AGENT'S AUTHORITY BECOMES EFFECTIVE: My agent's authority becomes effective when my primary physician determines that I am unable to make my own health-care decisions unless I mark the following box. If I mark this box [ ], my agent's authority to make health-care decisions for me takes effect immediately.

(4) AGENT'S OBLIGATION: My agent shall make health-care decisions for me in accordance with this power of attorney for health care, any instructions I give in Part 2 of this form, and my other wishes to the extent known to my agent. To the extent my wishes are unknown, my agent shall make health-care decisions for me in accordance with what my agent determines to be in my best interest. In determining my best interest, my agent shall consider my personal values to the extent known to my agent.

(5) NOMINATION OF GUARDIAN: If a guardian of my person needs to be appointed for me by a court, I nominate the agent designated in this form. If that agent is not willing, able, or reasonably available to act as guardian, I nominate the alternate agents whom I have named, in the order designated.

PART 2
INSTRUCTIONS FOR HEALTH CARE

If you are satisfied to allow your agent to determine what is best for you in making end-of-life decisions, you need not fill out this part of the form. If you do fill out this part of the form, you may strike any wording you do not want.

(6) END-OF-LIFE DECISIONS: I direct that my health-care providers and others involved in my care provide, withhold or withdraw treatment in accordance with the choice I have marked below:

[ ] (a) *Choice Not To Prolong Life*
I do not want my life to be prolonged if (i) I have an incurable and irreversible condition that will result in my death within a relatively short time, (ii) I become unconscious and, to a reasonable degree of medical certainty, I will not regain consciousness, or (iii) the likely risks and burdens of treatment would outweigh the expected benefits, or

[ ] (b) *Choice To Prolong Life*
I want my life to be prolonged as long as possible within the limits of generally accepted health-care standards.

(7) ARTIFICIAL NUTRITION AND HYDRATION: Artificial nutrition and hydration must be provided, withheld or withdrawn in accordance with the choice I have made in paragraph (6) unless I mark the following box. If I mark this box [ ], artificial nutrition and hydration must be provided regardless of my condition and regardless of the choice I have made in paragraph (6).

(8) RELIEF FROM PAIN: Except as I state in the following space, I direct that treatment for alleviation of pain or discomfort be provided at all times, even if it hastens my death:

_____

_____

(9) OTHER WISHES: (If you do not agree with any of the optional choices above and wish to write your own, or if you wish to add to the instructions you have given above, you may do so here.) I direct that:

_____

_____

_____

(Add additional sheets if needed.)

PART 3
PRIMARY PHYSICIAN

OPTIONAL

(10) I designate the following physician as my primary physician:

_____
(name of physician)

_____
(address) (city) (state) (zip code)

_____
(phone)

OPTIONAL: If the physician I have designated above is not willing, able, or reasonably available to act as my primary physician, I designate the following physician as my primary physician:

_____
(name of physician)

_____
(address) (city) (state) (zip code)

_____
(phone)

(11) EFFECT OF COPY: A copy of this form has the same effect as the original.
(12) SIGNATURES: Sign and date the form here:

_____   _____
(date)   (sign your name)

_____   _____
(address)   (print your name)

_____
(city) (state)

(13) WITNESSES: This power of attorney will not be valid for making health-care decisions unless it is either (a) signed by two (2) qualified adult witnesses who are personally known to you and who are present when you sign or acknowledge your signature; or (b) acknowledged before a notary public in the state.
ALTERNATIVE NO. 1

_____
Witness

I declare under penalty of perjury pursuant to Section 97-9-61, Mississippi Code of 1972, that the principal is personally known to me, that the principal signed or acknowledged this power of attorney in my presence, that the principal appears to be of sound mind and under no duress, fraud or undue influence, that I am not the person appointed as agent by this document, and that I am not a health-care provider, nor an employee of a health-care provider or facility. I am not related to the principal by blood, marriage or adoption, and to the best of my knowledge, I am not entitled to any part of the estate of the principal upon the death of the principal under a will now existing or by operation of law.

_____   _____
(date)   (signature of witness)

_____   _____
(address)   (printed name of witness)

_____
(city) (state)

_____
Witness

I declare under penalty of perjury pursuant to Section 97-9-61, Mississippi Code of 1972, that the principal is personally known to me, that the principal signed or acknowledged this power of attorney in my presence, that the principal appears to be of sound mind and under no duress, fraud or undue influence, that I am not the person appointed as agent by this document, and that I am not a health-care provider, nor an employee of a health-care provider or facility.

_____   _____
(date)   (signature of witness)

_____   _____
(address)   (printed name of witness)

_____
(city) (state)

ALTERNATIVE NO. 2

State of _____

County of _____

On this _____ day of _____, in the year ____, before me, _____ appeared _____ personally known to me (or proved to me on the basis of satisfactory evidence) to be the person whose name is subscribed to this instrument, and acknowledged that he or she executed it. I declare under the penalty of perjury that the person whose name is subscribed to this instrument appears to be of sound mind and under no duress, fraud or undue influence.

Notary Seal

_____
(Signature of Notary Public)

My commission expires: _____

_____

Part One of the AHCD appoints an agent for the client empowered to make healthcare decisions for the client. This power can be total as it normally is in the case of a medical or healthcare power of attorney discussed in the next section. Alternatively the power can be limited, directing that certain matters be decided in accordance with the specific instructions given in the Part Two of the AHCD. There are several good reasons why the client should use this alternative. First, it relieves the agent of the necessity of having to make those most serious decisions for you. Failing to state your own desires clearly on these issues imposes a tremendously heavy burden on the agent. In some instances the burden may be so great that the agent will be unable or unwilling to exercise the power granted to him. Thus, it is essential that alternates be named as provided for in Part One. Second, there are instances where the agent's personal beliefs may override his duty to effectuate what he believes you would want done. Third, disputes can arise among the family regarding what you would have wanted. Even though the agent will win those disputes legally, failure to make a clear statement creates unnecessary discord among the family members at a time of great sorrow and stress. Each of these reasons will be discussed more fully in following sections. Here, we will focus more on Part Two of the AHCD since it is the only document we will review that has the provisions dealing with end-of-life decisions.

Part Two of the AHCD deals with the four issues that arise when a person has a "terminal condition." The AHCD has the advantage of giving some definition to this concept—definition that can generally be understood by a lay person without a great deal of explanation. A terminal condition exists when the person has an incurable and irreversible condition that will result in death within a relatively short time, *or* the person becomes unconscious and, to a reasonable degree of medical certainty, will not regain consciousness, *or* the likely risks and burdens of treatment would outweigh the expected benefits. Other states have more specific, but often less understandable definitions. For example, the Wisconsin "Declaration to Physicians" form defines "persistent vegetative state" as a "condition that reasonable, medical judgment finds constitutes complete and irreversible loss of all the functions of the cerebral cortex and results in complete, chronic and irreversible cessation of all cognitive functioning and consciousness and a complete lack of behavioral responses that indicate cognitive functioning, although autonomic functions continue."

Note that in this respect the agent is not left without a role even though the client has made her wishes known. The physician will make an initial determination that the client has a terminal condition. However, she will not make the ultimate decision to *accept* the fact that the condition is terminal and effectuate the client's wishes.

The greatest difficulty with any of the documents available to enable a client to take control of his own end-of-life decisions is the reluctance, even in this era, of people to confront and discuss the inevitability of their own death. As discussed in Chapter Five, the present day American culture, more so than many others, tends to avoid discussion of death and dying, so our clients are frequently unprepared to make these decisions. Many have simply avoided even thinking about them until they come to our office. This reluctance to discuss death can make the legal team's task quite difficult. Both the attorney and the paralegal should themselves make every effort to become comfortable discussing the subject in order to make the client member of the legal team more comfortable with the subject. To the extent we can speak freely and dispassionately about death and the need to make legal preparation for death, we improve the chances the client will overcome their inherent reluctance.

Some clients, even once they are informed of the availability of advanced directives, will prefer to impose these most difficult decisions on others. Just as we should not judge our clients' ultimate decisions regarding, for example, the prolongation of life, we should not judge this decision. As we noted in Chapter Five, perspectives in this regard vary with cultural, ethnic, and religious background. Instead, we should dispassionately make sure they are fully informed regarding the consequences of leaving these decisions to other people. Once they are fully informed, the decision must be theirs.

Because the client has not or does not want to decide for themselves, they may ask you what you would do. Avoid engaging in discussing your personal preferences. In the first place, expressing your preference may be taken as advice. Assuming such advice is to be given in a law office, it must come from the attorney. At most, explain that such personal decisions are best made in consultation with their priest or rabbi and their family. (Even this is advice of a sort. While it is not really legal advice, it still would best come from the attorney.)

Regardless of what measures your state's legislature has enacted to deal with advanced medical and end-of-life decisions, you should become thoroughly familiar with both the substantive and procedural law governing their validity. Be able to explain their terms and effect in language a lay-person would understand. Practice by drafting and executing your own AHCD or other "living will" authorized by your state and encouraging members of your family to do the same. Be able to distinguish them from other means of dealing with health care and end-of-life decisions such as "Do Not Resuscitate" orders (DNRO) and medical powers of attorneys. DNROs are not usually prepared by attorneys or executed in law offices, as they are, unlike the other documents we have discussed, only executed by patients who already have a terminal condition. They direct that if a patient stops breathing, has heart failure or the like, no efforts be made to revive the patient. Like AHCDs the statutes governing them vary from state to state. Some allow non-hospital DNROs that must be honored by emergency response personnel. Such documents should follow the state rules precisely so that they can be immediately recognized and confirmed by the personnel. Since that personnel's authority is limited, any confusion will likely be resolved in favor of resuscitation.

Once completed, a copy of the AHCD should be provided to anyone designated to make healthcare decisions and to healthcare providers. It will remain valid until revoked in any manner that indicates intent to revoke. And it must be honored by the agent, family, surrogate or health care provider. There are, of course, some practical problems that arise if it is not honored, given the fact that the person making the AHCD is not able to bring a court action seeking its enforcement.

If the client anticipates traveling or maintains residences in different jurisdictions, they should execute AHCDs, living wills, or other directives that meet the requirements of each jurisdiction.

Medical Powers of Attorney

You may have gotten the impression from reading Section D that I am not a fan of medical or health-care powers of attorney. This is not the case. A durable power of attorney for health care ought to be a basic document in every estate plan prepared by an attorney. As noted in Section D, an AHCD prepared under the Uniform Health-Care Decisions Act starts with the appointment of an agent to make health care decisions for the person executing the AHCD. Also as noted in Section D, there is a role for such an agent even when the principal appointing the agent makes her own decisions in Part Two of the AHCD. I prefer the AHCD or a combination of a living will and medical power of attorney to a medical power of attorney standing alone because the principal does take control of his own life and the end of that life, rather than impose that burden on others.

So a paralegal must be prepared to explain both the substantive and procedural law regarding medical and health-care powers of attorney, and to draft one that will be valid under the applicable laws. Unfortunately, as with living wills and other AHCDs, there is a wide variance in both the substantive and procedural requirements. Some states provide forms designed for compliance with that state's law. The form devised by the Arizona Attorney General is quite specific, including language covering both what is and what is not authorized:

3. What I AUTHORIZE if I am unable to make medical care decisions for myself:
I authorize my health care representative to make health care decisions for me when I cannot make or communicate my own health care decisions due to mental or physical illness, injury, disability, or incapacity. I want my representative to make all such decisions for me except those decisions that I have expressly stated in Part 4 below that I do not authorize him/her to make. If I am able to communicate in any manner, my representative should discuss my health care options with me. My representative should explain to me any choices he or she made if I am able to understand. This appointment is effective unless and until it is revoked by me or by an order of a court.
The types of health care decisions I authorize to be made on my behalf include but are not limited to the following:
☐ To consent or to refuse medical care, including diagnostic, surgical, or therapeutic procedures;
☐ To authorize the physicians, nurses, therapists, and other health care providers of his/her choice to provide care for me, and to

obligate my resources or my estate to pay reasonable compensation for these services;

☐ To approve or deny my admittance to health care institutions, nursing homes, assisted living facilities, or other facilities or programs. By signing this form I understand that I allow my representative to make decisions about my mental health care except that generally speaking he or she cannot have me admitted to a structured treatment setting with 24-hour-a-day supervision and an intensive treatment program—called a "level one" behavioral health facility—using just this form;

☐ To have access to and control over my medical records and to have the authority to discuss those records with health care providers.

4. DECISIONS I EXPRESSLY DO NOT AUTHORIZE my Representative to make for me:

I do not want my representative to make the following health care decisions for me (describe or write in "not applicable"):

_____

_____

_____

These forms can be useful in the states for which they are authorized, but should—at most—be used in other states only as guides for the type of information that should be included in a medical power of attorney. It is the responsibility of the legal team to make sure the medical power of attorney signed by its client complies with the specific requirements of the jurisdiction in which it is executed. Special note should be taken of statutory requirements or limitations on who can be a witness and who can be appointed as an agent. If the client anticipates traveling or maintains residences in different jurisdictions, they should execute medical powers of attorney that meet the requirements of each jurisdiction.

It is essential that a medical power of attorney be durable. This will usually be accomplished by using language required by the statute enabling health care powers of attorney. These statutes are generally not the same statute that authorizes and controls durable powers of attorney covering other estate issues.

Most state statutes require that the power of attorney allow the maker of that power to express his or her wishes regarding health care in significant detail. The client should take full advantage of this ability.

First, it relieves the agent of the necessity of having to make those most serious decisions for the client. Failing to state the client's own desires clearly on these issues imposes a tremendously heavy burden on the agent. Principals frequently grant and agents frequently accept appointment without fully considering this burden. It is not at all unusual for the person who must make the decisions to express surprise and confusion when actually confronted with the necessity of making the decisions. Keep in mind that the agent is most likely someone close to the client—a spouse or child who is already under a great deal of stress dealing with the illness or infirmity of the loved one. They may be quite emotionally distraught and physically exhausted when called upon to make the decision. A well-crafted statement of the client's desires allows other members of the family and the medical providers to assure the decision maker that they are "doing the right thing." In some instances, the agent may be unable to exercise the power granted to him. It is essential that alternates be appointed.

In addition, it is not unusual for disputes to arise among the family regarding what the client wanted. Each of the children may be convinced that they know best what a parent would want. Each wants to believe they are the aged parent's closest confidant. Again, we must recognize that the family members themselves are likely to be emotionally distraught and could be under great physical strain as they maintain their vigil at the bedside of their parent. At times like these, sibling rivalries and animosities that may have lain dormant tend to rise to the surface. Even though the agent will win those disputes legally, failure to clearly express the client's wishes creates unnecessary discord among the family members at a time of great sorrow and stress.

Finally there is the possibility that the agent's personal beliefs as to what *should be done* will make them less than objective, especially at this time of stress and confusion, when it comes to determining the wishes of the principal. The agent does have a duty to comply with the principal's wishes and courts can terminate the agent's authority if the agent does not comply in good faith with that duty. However, there is little basis for making a determination of bad faith if there is no clear record of the client's wishes. Each of the other interested parties will have their own understanding and likely be able to testify as to conversations they had with the client wherein the client expressed a preference to them. Given the susceptibility of elder clients to undue influence and manipulation, the natural tendency of people to tell their listeners what they want to hear in order to avoid unpleasant discussions, the natural tendency of listeners to hear what they want to hear, and the vast variety of motivations in play under these circumstances, a court is unlikely to resolve such disputes against the person bearing the client's medical power of attorney.

Perhaps the best illustration of the problems that can arise when a person has not provided a clear, written expression of their desires regarding medical treatment is the well-known case of Terri Schiavo. This case is best known for the legal and political maneuvering that surrounded it. Terri, at the age of 26, collapsed and entered into a persistive vegetative state. She was fed by a feeding tube for eight years. Terri did not have a living will or a durable medical power of attorney, but her husband and legal guardian testified that she had told him she did not want to be kept alive by extraordinary means. Her husband eventually petitioned the appropriate court under Florida law for permission to withdraw the feeding tube. The trial court applied the "clear and convincing evidence" standard and granted the petition. However, her parents, who thought they knew Terri's wishes better than her husband, questioned his motives, and filed multiple appeals which prolonged the litigation —and Terri's vegetative state—for five years. In each of the more than twenty hearings on the matter, the court ruled in the husband's favor as required by state law.

Even after losing the appeals, Terri's parents continued their efforts to override the decision of the person granted the power to make the decision for Terri under state law. They convinced the Florida legislature to pass "Terri's Law," a law specifically designed to deal with this one case, giving Florida's governor 15 days to have the feeding tube reinserted. Once the tube was reinserted, Terri's husband challenged the constitutionality of "Terri's Law" and it was struck down by the Florida Supreme Court.

Terri's case became a "cause celebre" for politicians. Congress became involved and passed a special law transferring jurisdiction of the case to federal courts. The law had not changed, however, and the federal courts came to the same conclusion as the state. After federal court appeals ended with the Supreme Court denying certiorari, the feeding tube was removed and Terri died.

The lessons to be learned from Terri's case are many. Most are aimed at politicians, courts, and legislatures. For our purposes, the most important lesson is the basic one: the recognition that inter-family disputes can and will arise over medical treatment of those who cannot make medical decisions for themselves and the ability to avoid those disputes by execution of clear, written advanced statements whether in living wills, AHCDs, or as explicit statements of desire in durable health-care powers of attorney.

Surrogates

Medical treatment decisions must still be made in the absence of an advanced directive. In many situations this means the attending physician will, by default, make those decisions. We must keep in mind that a decision to do nothing is still a decision. Unfortunately, most people still do not have advanced directives. Consider, for example the situation in New York State:

> Most adults in New York do not prepare advance directives. Despite vigorous efforts to educate people regarding the wisdom of executing advance planning mechanisms, only a small proportion of patients have a health care proxy or a living will. A 2001 study of New York seniors found that two out of three seniors responding had not completed advance directives despite the fact that all of the research sites had previously conducted programs to educate them about the importance of having a health care proxy. When asked whom they trust the most to make medical decisions for them, the vast majority (79%) mentioned a spouse or other family member. Only 17% mentioned their physician. *More than half of those studied indicated they believed family decision making was legal in New York State without a designated health care proxy even after reading a statement that the law states otherwise.*[14] (Emphasis added)

It appears then, that our clients may not be executing advanced directives not because they want their primary physicians making these decisions for them, but because they do not understand the need for the directives. It is the responsibility of the legal team to make the law in this regard clear to our clients.

The above quote from the New York City Bar comes from a report urging passage of a statute allowing health care decisions to be made by surrogates. At least 28 states have enacted statutes authorizing decisions by surrogates. Those statutes will establish a hierarchy for designation of that surrogate. A typical hierarchy will establish a member of the following classes of the patient's family who is reasonably available, in descending order of priority, may act as surrogate:

a. The spouse, unless legally separated;
b. An adult child;
c. A parent; or
d. An adult brother or sister.[15]

---

14. "Report on Legislation by the Committee on Health Law and the Committee on Bioethical Issues," New York City Bar, http://www.nycbar.org/pdf/report/FHCDA_Pos_Paper_032006.pdf (Last accessed April 11, 2010) citing Results of Literacy Study Reinforce Need for the Family Health Care Decisions Act, Sarah Lawrence College, Health Advocacy Program.

15. This is the hierarchy established under the Uniform Health-Care Decisions Act.

If none of these individuals is reasonably available, an adult who has exhibited special care and concern for the patient, who is familiar with the patient's personal values, and who is reasonably available may act as surrogate.

There are obvious problems with this hierarchy. A person's marriage could be so irretrievably broken down that he is on the way to file for divorce when, like Terri Schiavo, he collapses and enters a persistent vegetative state. Yet, it will be that person's estranged spouse who makes the decision on whether to "pull the plug." It was my practice whenever consulted about a divorce to have the consulting client execute an AHCD before they left the office.

More important, perhaps, is the difficult position in which it leaves those persons whose closest relationship is with someone other than a member of their family when that person is not a spouse. This is an increasingly important issue as non-standard families become more prevalent. Under this hierarchy, a life-long partner has less standing than a brother or sister, even though that brother or sister may have spent decades shunning their sibling because he or she chose a person of the same sex as their partner. This occurs despite the fact that the partner is most likely to have "exhibited special care and concern for the patient, who is familiar with the patient's personal values." In these situations it is especially important that the client have designated a surrogate with an advanced directive. It is the responsibility of the legal team to inform the client of these options and explain them clearly and objectively, and of the attorney to advise the client of the benefits given their personal circumstances, regardless of the personal beliefs of the members of that legal team regarding the appropriateness of their choice of a life-partner.

The Uniform Health-Care Decisions Act does not establish a particular burden of proof for the surrogate to meet in the event of a dispute, relying instead on the hierarchy to provide a person whose judgment will suffice in lieu of a court decision based on conflicting evidence. The surrogate does have a duty to carry out the wishes of the incapacitated person to the extent they are known to the surrogate, to act in the best interest of the incapacitated person when the wishes are not known. In determining the patient's best interest, the surrogate generally must consider the patient's personal values to the extent known to the surrogate.

In a minority of states without the UHCDA, the burden of proof may be "clear and convincing evidence" of the incapacitated person's wishes. If the person's wishes cannot be proven, some courts will make the decision based on the "best interest" of the person. The "clear and convincing" standard is the most demanding standard used in non-criminal proceedings. The New York City Bar report quoted above argues against the standard, stating considerations such as the reluctance of people in our culture to discuss death:

The "clear and convincing" evidence standard does not work. Rather than facilitate a health care provider's ability to follow patient choice about treatment, this standard poses a formidable barrier to both families and providers. A majority of courts in other states has found the "clear and convincing" evidence standard to be unworkable and overly burdensome in these cases.

The "clear and convincing" standard is predicated on the notion that a person, while *competent*, would have clearly expressed his or her wishes regarding end-of-life decisions in some manner. However, for many people discussion of end-of-life matters is a personally uncomfortable subject, such that they refrain from expressing their wishes in this area. In addition, the cultural backgrounds of some New Yorkers make it extremely difficult, if not impossible, to even mention their own death and dying, let alone to articulate "clear and convincing" plans for it.[16]

As previously mentioned, this reluctance to discuss death can make the legal team's task quite difficult. Both the attorney and the paralegal should themselves make every effort to become comfortable discussing the subject in order to make the client member of the legal team more comfortable with the subject. To the extent we can speak freely and dispassionately about death and the need to make legal preparation for death, we improve the chances the client will overcome his inherent reluctance.

There is another problem with statutory-imposed hierarchies that we must discuss before leaving this topic. If more than one member of a class assumes authority to act as surrogate, and they do not agree on a health-care decision and the supervising health-care provider is so informed, the supervising health-care provider shall comply with the decision of a majority of the members of that class who have communicated their views to the provider. *If the class is evenly divided concerning the health-care decision and the supervising health-care provider is so informed, that class and all individuals having lower priority are disqualified from making the decision.* Thus if there are two parents who disagree or four siblings evenly divided, we go back to the default position. When the two parents are divorced, it is quite likely that the default position will result in litigation. Thus, while this book focuses on the elderly, I take this opportunity to note that I advise all adults to prepare AHCDs, especially unmarried children of divorced parents.

---

16. *Id.*

Finally, be aware that, as is the case with laws of intestacy, step-parents, step-children, and step-siblings have no place as family on this hierarchy. The step-parent may have raised the child from infancy to adulthood and the step-child may have taken care of the step-parent in the decade preceding the need for the decision, but with regard to each other, they have no legal part in the decision making process unless we get to the point that "an adult who has exhibited special care and concern for the patient, who is familiar with the patient's personal values, and who is reasonably available may act as surrogate."

The surrogacy statutes can be altered on an individual basis by a person while that person has the capacity to alter them. A person at any time may disqualify another, including a member of the individual's family, from acting as the person's surrogate by a signed writing *or by personally informing the supervising health-care provider of the disqualification.* In other words, the person need not take the affirmative step of selecting a surrogate. She can take the negative action of eliminating one or more individuals from the hierarchy, leaving the hierarchy to designate the surrogate from among the remaining qualifying person. For example, she could inform the supervising health-care provider that she does not want her estranged husband to be considered in the hierarchy.

Some statutes disqualify certain persons from acting as a surrogate. This is generally to prevent conflicts of interest and undue influence. For example, the UHCDA prohibits an owner, operator, or employee of a residential long-term health-care institution at which the patient is receiving care from being a surrogate for a patient unless that person is related to the patient by blood, marriage, or adoption, except in the case of a patient of a state-operated facility who has no person listed in the hierarchy reasonably available to act as a surrogate.

A surrogate is required to communicate his or her assumption of authority as promptly as practicable to the members of the patient's family specified in the hierarchy who can be readily contacted. A supervising health-care provider may require an individual claiming the right to act as surrogate for a patient to provide a written declaration under penalty of perjury stating facts and circumstances reasonably sufficient to establish the claimed authority.

E. Other Issues

The decisions that can, and should, be handled through advanced directives do not end with medical treatment or even with death. They include the donation of organs, autopsies, and arrangements for dead bodies.

Anatomical Gifts

The prefatory note for the Revised Anatomical Gift Act states the need for donations of organs for transplant and the need for a mechanism to facilitate donation:

> As of January, 2006 there were over 92,000 individuals on the waiting list for organ transplantation, and the list keeps growing. It is estimated that approximately 5,000 individuals join the waiting list each year. See "Organ Donation: Opportunities for Action," Institute of Medicine of the National Academies (2006) www.nap.edu. Every hour another person in the United States dies because of the lack of an organ to provide a life saving organ transplant.
>
> The lack of organs results from the lack of organ donors. For example, according to the Scientific Registry of Transplant Recipients in 2005 when there were about 90,000 people on the organ transplant waiting list, there were 13,091 individuals who died under the age of 70 using cardiac and brain death criteria and who were eligible to be organ donors. Of these, only 58% or 7,593 were actual donors who provided just over 23,000 organs. Living donors, primarily of kidneys, contributed about 6,800 more organs. Between them about 28,000 organs were transplanted into patients on the waiting list in 2005.[17]

The first Anatomical Gift Act was approved for adoption by states in 1968, and it was quickly adopted by all the states. A revised version was approved in 1987. The revised version has only been adopted by 28 states leaving some variance from state to state on the rules regarding anatomical gifts. While the method by which a person declares his intent to donate organs is controlled by the states, the U.S. Department of Health and Human Services oversees the process by which organs are procured ("harvested") and distributed.

The 1987 Act was intended to simplify gifting procedures and to encourage donations by (1) allowing public agencies to participate in the arrangement of donation, (2) requiring hospitals to ask patients near death if they are willing to be come donors and to discuss the issue with patients' families and (3) encouraging the use of devices such as driver's license application forms to raise the issue and allow donation election.

Although the original Act has been in existence since 1968, there is still a fair amount of confusion and misunderstanding among the public (and some legal professionals) regarding anatomical gifts. The legal professional should be well

---

17. www.anatomicalgiftact.org (Last accessed July 24, 2010).

versed in the topic and prepared to explain the process to the client. Again, the specifics of state law vary, but there are some generalities we can discuss here.

Any individual who is eighteen (18) years of age or over and who is competent to execute a will may give all or any part of his body for any one or more of the purposes specified in the Act (research, transplant, therapy), the gift to take effect upon death. Minors can make a gift only with their parents' signatures added. A gift can be made by will. This portion of the will becomes effective immediately without the necessity of probate. In general though gifts are and should be made through an Organ-tissue Donor's Card that, unlike a will, is kept with the person. The donation can be a general one or designated for a specific use or specific donee.

While the U.S. Department of Health and Human Services oversees the donation harvesting and distribution process, there are private organizations that seek to assist in that process by registering potential donors so that the information is available to agencies facilitating transplants. The oldest and largest of these is *The Living Bank International* located in Houston, Texas.[18] The United Network for Organ Sharing (UNOS) maintains a national waiting list.[19] When an organ becomes available, the list is reviewed to determine who will receive the organ based on factors such as distance from the donor, blood and tissue type, current physical condition and length of time on the waiting list. Since time is very important, local recipients are considered first, then regional and national recipients.

Donations can be made by persons other than the donor. Unless the physician has knowledge that contrary directions have been given by the decedent, the following persons, in the order of priority stated, may give all or any part of a decedent's body for any one or more of the purposes specified:

1. The spouse, if one survives
2. An adult son or daughter
3. Either parent
4. An adult brother or sister
5. The guardian of the person of the decedent at the time of his death
6. Any other person or agency authorized or under obligation to dispose of the body.

Note that in this hierarchy the spouse can make the decision even if there is a legal separation and there is no provision for "exhibited special care and concern for the patient, who is familiar with the patient's personal values." If there

---

18. www.livingbank.org
19. www.unos.org

is known to be a controversy within the class of persons first entitled to make the gift, the gift will not be accepted. Telephonic consent to gift is acceptable.

Contrary directions are best given by the decedent in writing. A simple statement that the decedent refuses or declines to make any anatomical gifts and that any such gifts authorized by other persons after her death are against the person's wishes will suffice.

A donation can be revoked by the donor orally or in writing provided the statutory requirements are made. It cannot be revoked by anyone beside the donor, so once the person dies, there is no need to obtain the consent of anyone, including the person's spouse or family.

Dead Bodies

A person's wishes for disposal of his dead body should also be made clear in advance. This avoids disputes over whether the body should be buried or cremated, and over the particular ceremonies and rites to be followed. State laws vary on enforcement of will provisions regarding burial. There are practical problems that arise from the fact that the dead body must be dealt with well before probate of the will. Some states require that the burial provisions be honored only if the decedent has made prior financial arrangements for those provisions.

When the decedent has left no specific instructions, she has in effect made a decision that someone else will make that decision. Each state sets forth a hierarchy for designation of the person who will take possession of the body and responsibility for it. A typical statute provides that if a decedent has left no written authorization for the cremation and/or disposition of the decedent's body as permitted by law, the following competent persons, in the order of priority listed below, may authorize the type, method, place, cremation and/or other disposition of the decedent's body:

a. The surviving spouse;
b. The surviving children who are at least eighteen (18) years of age and can be located after reasonable efforts;
c. The surviving parents;
d. The surviving siblings who are at least eighteen (18) years of age and can be located after reasonable efforts;
e. A person in the class of the next degree of kinship, in descending order, who, under state law, would inherit the decedent's estate if the decedent died intestate who are at least eighteen (18) years of age and can be located with reasonable effort;

f. A person who has exhibited special care and concern for the decedent and is willing and able to make decisions about the cremation and disposition;

g. In the case of indigents or any other individuals whose final disposition is the responsibility of the state or any of its instrumentalities, a public administrator, medical examiner, coroner, state-appointed guardian, or any other public official charged with arranging the final disposition of the decedent may serve as the authorizing agent;

h. In the case of individuals who have donated their bodies to science or whose[20] death occurred in a nursing home or private institution and in which the institution is charged with making arrangements for the final disposition of the decedent, a representative of the institution may serve as the authorizing agent in the absence of any of the above;

i. In the absence of any of the above, any person willing to assume responsibility for the cremation and disposition of the decedent.

Note again that in this hierarchy the spouse can make the decision even if there is a legal separation and the provision for a person who "exhibited special care and concern for the patient, who is familiar with the patient's personal values" is far down the line.

I represented a wife in a rather acrimonious divorce that ended with a judgment after trial. The husband, who had left the state to live with another woman, died before the appeal period. Since the appeal period had not yet expired, we took the position that my client was still the spouse. She was thus entitled to take control of the estate as a widow rather than be governed by the divorce judgment. She also was able to take possession of the body and make the decision regarding its burial. To my surprise, she did so claiming that it was in the best interest of their children that he have a full ceremonial burial attended by a united family. However, it does seem unlikely that he would have chosen to have her make decisions regarding the manner and place of his burial.

Autopsies

State statutes generally provide that autopsies may be performed without the consent of the decedent or her family for purposes of public health and in criminal cases. Each state also provides for autopsies for other purposes with the consent of the decedent or others as provided by statutes.[21] Some living

---

20. See, e.g., Georgia Living Will O.C.G.A. §31-32-3, http://www.halt.org/living_wills/georgia.pdf (Last accessed April 11, 2010).

21. For example, Mississippi's Code, §41-37-25 provides:
An autopsy may be performed without court order by a qualified physician when authorized

will forms include a statement giving the agent the ability to authorize an autopsy. An advanced directive regarding an autopsy can be especially important for members of some religions. For example, there is a general prohibition under Jewish law, subject to some exceptions, against autopsy. Living will forms that deal with the requirements of Jewish law are available.[22]

---

by (a) the decedent, during his lifetime, or (b) any of the following persons who shall have assumed custody of the body for the purpose of burial: a surviving spouse, either parent or any person in loco parentis, a descendant over the age of eighteen years, a guardian, or the next of kin. In the absence of any of the foregoing persons any friend of the deceased who has assumed responsibility for burial, or any other person charged by law with responsibility for burial, may give such consent. If two or more persons have assumed custody of the body of an adult for purposes of burial, the consent of one such person shall be deemed sufficient.

In the case of a minor, however, the consent of either parent shall be deemed sufficient, unless the other parent gives written notice to the physician who is to perform the autopsy of such parent's objection thereto prior to the commencement of the autopsy. In the event that neither parent has legal custody of the minor, the guardian shall have the right to authorize an autopsy. The fees provided in this chapter for autopsies in criminal investigations shall not be applicable to this section.

No autopsy shall be held under this section over the objection of the surviving spouse, or if there be no surviving spouse, of any surviving parent, or if there be neither a surviving spouse nor parent, then of any surviving child.

22. See, e.g., the United Synagogue for Conservative Judaism's website, http://www.uscj.org/ Jewish_Medical_Direc5334.html (Last accessed May 20, 2010) and The Rabbinical Council of America Halachic Health Care Proxy, http://www.rabbis.org/pdfs/hcp.pdf (Last accessed May 21, 2010).

CHAPTER NINE

PUBLIC BENEFIT PROGRAMS

A. Introduction

The focus of this book is the elder client rather than elder law. Nonetheless, our quest for greater understanding of the elder client has included review and examination of over a dozen laws particularly applicable to the elderly, including the Uniform Probate Act, the Uniform Guardianship and Protective Proceedings Act, and the Patient Self Determination Act. In the next chapter we will consider laws designed to deal with abuse and neglect of the elderly. In this chapter we will review laws that cover topics essential to the understanding of most elder clients' daily lives.

Regardless of the legal issue that brings an elder client into the law office, most clients elder clients will have an overriding concern: "How am I going to pay for this?" This concern relates not just to the legal services they are about to receive but to every aspect of their lives—housing, food, medical care and so on. For many clients, being elderly means finding ways to finance life. While this is in a way true of all of us, the elder client generally no longer has the ability to produce income that the younger client has, so "making ends meet" has a much different meaning for the elder client.

Even for most of those clients who planned for this period of their lives using all of the estate planning tools discussed in Chapters Six and Seven, the question remains whether they will outlive their resources. In 2004, the Congressional Budget Office forecast a relatively rosy outlook for about three-quarters of baby boomers, the generation now arriving at retirement age, stating, "Compared with their parents at the same age, baby boomers typically have higher income, are preparing for retirement at largely the same pace, and have accumulated more private wealth. On the whole, boomers are on track to have higher income in retirement than their parents and appear much less likely to live in poverty after they retire."[1] For the remaining quarter, "Within that over-

---

1. "The Retirement Prospects of the Baby Boomers," *Congressional Budget Office,* March 18, 2004, http://www.cbo.gov/doc.cfm?index=5195&type=0 (Last accessed May 22, 2010).

all picture, however, about a quarter of baby boomer households have so far failed to accumulate significant savings. They appear likely to depend entirely on government benefits in retirement."[2]

More recent assessments are not as optimistic given the recession that began in 2007. In May of 2010, ABC News reported, "According to the Center for Economic and Policy Research, baby boomers age 46 to 54 have watched their net worth drop an average 45% over the past five years. Even more troubling, boomers between the ages of 55 to 64—those nearing and already in retirement— have seen their net worth cut nearly in half (49%)."[3]

This is particularly troubling as many in this retirement group are facing the prospect of being financially responsible for their parents and/or their children even during retirement. *SeniorJournal.com* reported on a survey indicating:

> [M]ore than one in three Baby Boomers (37 percent) will be financially responsible for parents or children during retirement. And 7 percent of boomers will be financially responsible for both parents and children in retirement. That is on top of the extensive debt that three out of five Baby Boomers (58 percent) surveyed expect to pay off during retirement:
> - 25 percent paying credit card debt
> - 37 percent paying car notes
> - 27 percent paying a mortgage on their house
>
> The survey also revealed that Baby Boomers have saved an average of only 12 percent of the total they will need to meet even basic living expenses in retirement.[4]

The bottom line here is that while a quarter of baby boomer households appear likely to depend entirely on government benefits in retirement, a far larger number are likely to rely heavily on those benefits. In this chapter we will review the major laws affecting those benefits and the agencies that oversee them. We will not attempt to master those laws,[5] but to gain sufficient grasp

---

2. *Id.*

3. Tony Christensen, "How To Retire Even If The Market Crashes," *ABC News.com,* May 19, 2010, http://abcnews.go.com/Business/Retirement/saving-retirement/story?id=10639193 (Last accessed May 22, 2010).

4. "Baby Boomers Are The 'Sandwich-ed Generation,' As Financial Obligations Prevent Real Retirement," *SeniorJournal.com,* December 4, 2001, http://seniorjournal.com/NEWS/Retirement/12-05-1Sandwished.htm (Last accessed May 22, 2010).

5. For those seeking greater mastery of those laws I recommend, Ralph C. Brashier, *Mastering Elder Law,* Carolina Academic Press (2010) upon which I have drawn heavily for this chapter.

of the laws to aid in understanding the legal and financial environment in which many of our clients exist when seeking our services.

The benefits at which we will look most closely are Social Security, Supplemental Security Income, Medicare, and Medicaid. Before examining those programs, we will review the Federal Age Discrimination in Employment Act, since for many baby boomers one option will be to work longer and retire later than originally planned.

B. Age Discrimination in Employment Act (ADEA)

The Age Discrimination in Employment Act[6] was enacted in 1967 "to promote employment of older persons based on their ability rather than age; to prohibit arbitrary age discrimination in employment; to help employers and workers find ways of meeting problems arising form the impact of age on employment."[7] It applies to persons who are at least 40 years old.

The Act governs employers, employment agencies, and labor unions. It is administered by the Equal Employment Opportunity Commission (EEOC)[8] which has issued regulations pursuant to the ADEA.[9] The Act and regulations cover a wide range of actions, but the primary focus is preventing:

1. hiring, firing, or other discriminating against persons with respect to compensation, terms, conditions, or privileges of employment because of a person's age; or
2. limiting, segregating, or classifying employees in any age-related way that adversely affects a person's status as an employee.

The ADEA also governs, in substantial detail, employee pension benefit plans.

---

6. 29 U.S.C. §§ 621–634.

7. 29 U.S.C. § 621.

8. "The U.S. Equal Employment Opportunity Commission (EEOC) is responsible for enforcing federal laws that make it illegal to discriminate against a job applicant or an employee because of the person's race, color, religion, sex (including pregnancy), national origin, age (40 or older), disability or genetic information. It is also illegal to discriminate against a person because the person complained about discrimination, filed a charge of discrimination, or participated in an employment discrimination investigation or lawsuit." "About the EEOC: Overview," *EEOC*, http://www.eeoc.gov/eeoc (Last accessed May 22, 2010).

9. 29 C.F.R. 1625.1 *et seq.*

The ADEA does not cover small private employers. This can be a concern because we so often hear that small business is the cornerstone of employment in the United States. While it is true that "small business" as defined by the Small Business Administration employs over half of all private business employees, the SBA's definition of a small business is one with fewer than 500 employees.[10] Fortunately, the ADEA defines an "employer" as a business with twenty or more employees on a regular basis.[11] An employer must be an industry affecting commerce. This includes non-profit and charitable enterprises when the other requisites are met.

While the ADEA defines employer as including a state, the United States Supreme Court ruled that the provision ran afoul of states' sovereign immunity provided under the Eleventh Amendment to the Constitution.[12] This prevents private citizens from bringing an ADEA action against a state, but not the EEOC, which can bring an action against a state on behalf of an individual. Individuals may also bring actions under state ADEAs which exist in most states.

There are exceptions to the provisions of ADEA that can be used as defenses. The primary defenses[13] are:

1. The Bona Fide Occupational Qualification.[14] This allows an employer to show (the employer has the burden of proof) that its action is reasonably necessary to the essence of the business and meets other criteria. A typical example is a mandatory retirement age for airline pilots;
2. Reasonable Factor Other Than Age. In my experience employers often rely on the claim that an employee was terminated due to a reduction in force or a corporate reorganization when faced with a discrimination or "whistleblower" claim. The employer has the burden of proof when making this defense;
3. Bona Fide Seniority Systems. This defense is, I believe, used more frequently with regard to discrimination claims other than those based on age. It allows the employer to recognize factors such as length of service on the job and may thus be used to justify, say, promoting a white male with 20 years service or a Latino female with 2 years service. The requires that the

---

10. "SBA Office of Advocacy Frequently Asked Questions," *SBA Office of Advocacy*, at 1, http://www.sba.gov/advo/stats/sbfaq.pdf (Last accessed May 22, 2010).

11. 29 U.S.C. §630(b).

12. *Kimmel v Board of Regents*, 528 U.S. 62 (2000).

13. This list is from, Ralph C. Brashier, *Mastering Elder Law*, Carolina Academic Press (2010) at 191–193, but the characterizations of the exceptions are mine. For a fuller explanation of ADEA, these exceptions, and other exceptions see Brashier's work.

14. This and other exceptions are also defenses under the Civil Rights Act of 1964.

system be bona fide, i.e., that it not just be a cover for intention to discriminate;

4. Bona Fide Employee Benefit Plans also provide a defense, allowing employers to abide by the terms of such a plan when they are legitimate plans rather than an excuse to discriminate; and,

5. Good Cause. Of course, ADEA like other laws is not intended to allow workers not to work or to otherwise violate the terms of their employment. Employers frequently defend against ADEA claims by asserting they had a good cause other than age for their action.

ADEA actions are started by filing a charge with the EEOC. EEOC is required to attempt to resolve the charge and any conduct violating ADEA through conciliation, conference, and persuasion. The employee must allow 60 days for this process before commencing a lawsuit unless the EEOC notifies the employee that the informal process has failed prior to that time.

The ADEA provides for a variety of remedies depending on the facts of the case. The court can issue injunctions against the employer and award damages to the employee. Damages may include back pay and benefits such as pension and insurance payments. Wages and benefits earn in new employment are set-off against the damage award. The employee has a duty to seek new employment and otherwise mitigate damages.

The court can also order reinstatement for an employee. However, if this is not possible given the relationship between the employer and employee, the court can award the employee damages based on future losses or "front pay."

C. Social Security

Overview

Social Security began in 1935 as part of the New Deal. It was originally designed solely as a safety net for old age, but now covers disabled workers and their families, survivors of deceased eligible individuals, and includes the Supplemental Security Income (SSI) and Medicare programs. SSI provides assistance for elderly, blind, and disabled people who met income and asset criteria.

Social Security itself is not a "**means test**" program, i.e., a program in which eligibility is determined in part based on the resources (assets and/or income) available to an applicant. A person is entitled to its benefits because she, or someone on whom she was dependent, contributed to the program, regardless of what other income may be available to her. Most employees are all likely familiar with the Social Security deduction that is made in paychecks, although some individuals employed by the federal government prior to January 1, 1984, railroad workers, and employees of some state entities such as school districts, are exempt because they are covered by another plan.

In addition to the employee's payroll deduction, the employer pays a matching amount. Presently each contributes 6.40% of the employee's income up to wages and salary totaling $106,800 as of 2010 to the Social Security. Self-employed persons pay both shares of the tax. This contribution is often indicated as a FICA contribution on payroll stubs since it is made mandatory by the Federal Insurance Contributions Act. Each party also contributes 1.45% of all wages and salaries as Medicare taxes, the Hospital Insurance Trust Fund used for Medicare Part A hospital coverage.

There is a great deal of controversy over the funding and viability of the Social Security System. The system is designed to collect contributions from people currently in the workforce and make benefit payments to people currently retired from the workforce. The system is an insurance system, rather than a savings system. As I have made contributions to the system over the last 43 years, I have not contributed to my retirement fund, but to funding the retirement of people who were already retired. The money I paid has been immediately paid out to retirees, for example, my grandmothers, mother, and stepfather. My retirement will be funded by workers working when I retire.

A number of problems and issues have developed in this system. The primary problem is that people are living longer. They are thus retired longer and collect benefits longer. As the baby boomer generation retires, there will be fewer and fewer workers *per retiree* even if there are more workers. At some point, Social Security will be spending more than it receives. That point is a moving point. It has gotten closer during the recession that started in 2007 because fewer people have been employed while the number of retirees has not gone down significantly.

This problem has not gone unnoticed. In 1983 Congress passed legislation intending to resolve the problem. The payroll tax was increased, the level of earnings subject to the tax was increased, and the full-retirement age was increased to the present 66 with another scheduled increase to 67 in 2022.

Another problem arises from the fact that money not used to pay benefits and administrative expenses is held in the Social Security Trust Fund and invested in U.S. Government Bonds. The government thus borrows the trust fund money to pay for operating costs and covering the budget deficit. This means that the government is going to have to pay the money back in order for benefits to be paid once current employee/employer contributions are not enough to pay current retiree and other benefits.

It appears that reforms will be necessary or the system will collapse, although some experts point out that there is only a problem if the U.S. Government votes not to raise the money necessary to honor the bonds. However, legislative action on Social Security quickly becomes a "hot button" issue for a politician. Regardless of the solution proposed, outrage is expressed by some interest group or groups. Al Gore famously promised to put Social Security in a "lockbox" during the 2000 presidential election. Politicians and commentators refer to Social Security as the "third rail" of politics, likening it to the electrified rail on subway—to be avoided at all costs.

The Social Security controversy is also likely to be a "hot button" issue with clients. It is a political issue rather than a legal issue. While you should understand the basics of the controversy, the topic should be avoided when communicating with clients. If the client brings it up, politely redirect the conversation. As legal professionals, our concerns with Social Security are purely legal: who is entitled to what benefits and how we can ensure our clients receive the benefits to which they are entitled.

Eligibility and Benefits

Eligibility for Social Security must be established by working and making payments into the system for the required number of quarters (unless the benefits are being claimed as a spouse or dependent of an eligible person). **Quarters** are the credits that must be accumulated in order to receive benefits. For persons born after 1929, 40 quarters must be accumulated—the equivalent of ten years. However, the quarters do not have to be earned consecutively. The 40 quarters could theoretically be earned one quarter each year for 40 years.

Once a person has racked up 40 quarters, they are eligible for retirement for life. Working more quarters does not in itself increase benefits. However, it pays to keep on working. This is because the benefit to which a person is entitled is determined by averaging what is earned over the person's career. Social Security refers to this as **Average Indexed Monthly Earnings** (AIME). Generally the higher the lifetime earnings are, i.e., the more you worked, the higher the AIME will be, and the higher the benefits will be.

The Social Security Administration provides a Benefits Calculator that can be used to estimate benefits for person who has accumulated enough credits and is not already receiving benefits or entitled to benefits from another public pension plan. You may want to try it yourself so that you are familiar with it when mentioning it to clients. Here's the link: http://www.ssa.gov/estimator.

A client's earning records and estimated benefits can also be obtained from the Social Security Administration (SSA) using Form SSA 700, "Request for

Earnings and Benefit Estimate Statement" form. The form can be obtained from the local Social Security Office or by calling 800-772-1213. (This is a 24/7 number.)[15] Again, it is a good idea to request a form for yourself so you can describe the process to clients from personal experience.

The SSA also sends out Benefit Estimate Statements automatically, but few clients seem to save them. Having these statements is useful for retirement planning purposes. The statements list the total wages for each year, the number of quarters earned, the estimated monthly retirement and disability benefits, an estimate of contributions to the system made by the individual, and an estimate of the person's family benefits if the person dies.

SSA calls the benefit amount the **Primary Insurance Amount (PIA)**. The actual amount of the benefit depends not only on the earnings record but on when the person elects to retire. This amount is subject to an automatic **cost of living adjustment (COLA)** each year. You are likely to hear clients express concern over the likely amount of the COLA each year and to express disappointment when the COLA is announced.

The entire benefit can only be collected when the eligible person reaches **Full Retirement Age (FRA)**.[16] The Full Retirement Age is increasing and depends on the year of birth. It ranges from 65 for those born in or before 1937 to 67 for those born in 1960 or later. SSA provides a chart for determining an individual's Full Retirement Age at this link: http://www.socialsecurity.gov/pubs/retirechart.htm.

A person does not have to wait until FRA to collect retirement benefits. Once he reaches the age of 62, an eligible individual can elect to take early retirement. Doing so reduces the amount of the monthly benefit since payments are based on the average length of time a person lives after retirement. Retiring early means the total money to be paid out must be stretched, on average, over a longer period of time, thus requiring that each payment be for less. On average, the retiree will collect the same amount of money over the course of their retirement. According to SSA, if your full retirement age is 67, the reduction for starting your benefits at

- age 62 is about 30 percent;
- age 63 is about 25 percent;

---

15. There is also a number for the deaf and hard of hearing: 800-325-0778. This number is only available on non-holiday Mondays through Fridays from 7 a.m. to 7 p.m. More contact information is available on the SSA website: http://www.ssa.gov/pgm/services.htm.

16. The SSA now tends to refer to this as "Normal Retirement Age (NRA). See, e.g., http://www.socialsecurity.gov/OACT/COLA/rtea.html (Last accessed May 23, 2010).

- age 64 is about 20 percent;
- age 65 is about 13 and 1/3 percent; and
- age 66 is about 6 and 2/3 percent.[17]

Conversely, if retirement is delayed, the monthly benefit goes up. The percentage increase also goes up until the retiree reaches the age of 70, after which there is no benefit to delaying receipt of benefits.

Benefits can be directly deposited into the retiree's bank account. This eliminates the possibility of the check being lost or stolen, so all clients should be advised to enroll in direct deposit. The funds are fully available when credited to the account, so there is also no delay in using the funds after deposit as there can be with a check. The client can enroll at their bank or through SSA online using this link: https://secure.ssa.gov/acu/ACU_PPA/ main.jsp?URL=/apps6z/DD/ main.jsp&LVL=5.

Retirement Earnings Test

Once a person reaches FRA, they can continue to work and still receive full benefits. However, if an individual elects to receive benefits early, there are limitations on how much they can earn from employment, including self-employment until they reach FRA. Other income such as interest, dividends, and pensions does not affect benefits.

Under the **Retirement Earning Test**, Social Security withholds benefits if earnings exceed a certain level, called a retirement earnings test **exempt amount**. One of two different exempt amounts applies, depending on the year in which FRA is reached. These exempt amounts generally increase annually with increases in the national average wage index.

SSA determines the exempt amounts using procedures defined in the Social Security Act. SSA's example for 2010 states that, for people attaining FRA after 2010, the annual exempt amount in 2010 is $14,160. For people attaining FRA in 2010, the annual exempt amount is $37,680. This higher exempt amount applies only to earnings made in months prior to the month of FRA attainment.

SSA withholds $1 in benefits for every $2 of earnings in excess of the lower exempt amount. It withholds $1 in benefits for every $3 of earnings in excess of the higher exempt amount. Earnings in or after the month in which FRA is reached do not count toward the retirement test.

---

17. "Age To Receive Full Social Security Retirement Benefits," *SSA*, http://www.social security.gov/pubs/retirechart.htm (Last accessed May 22, 2010).

Representative Payees

When Social Security beneficiaries are unable to manage their own funds, the payments can be made to another person on their behalf. This person is referred to as the **representative payee**. For children, the payee will normally be the child's guardian. For adults, convincing evidence of the beneficiary's incapacity is required. While a court determination such as the appointment of a guardian or conservator will normally satisfy this requirement, it is not required. However, SSA will require evidence from a qualified medical practitioner and may require other evidence such as an interview with the beneficiary or statements from relatives. Since the representative payee will have complete control over the funds, a situation ripe for abuse, SSA will also require information regarding the payee and his suitability to act as payee. A beneficiary may object to the appointment of a representative payee and can as for a reevaluation if circumstances change.

The representative payee is required by law to use the funds in the beneficiary's best interest. She must keep records of how the money is used, including receipts. The beneficiary's funds must not be commingled with the payee's own funds. Accumulations of more than $500 should be invested or placed in interest bearing accounts. SSA can invoke civil fines for misuse of funds by a payee and assessments of up to twice the amount of the funds misused. It can also refer the matter for criminal prosecution. A conviction can result in fines and/or imprisonment for up to five years.

Benefits for Family Members

Even if he or she has never worked, a spouse and child of an eligible individual may collect Social Security benefits. When the spouse or child is able to receive benefits and the amount of benefits that can be collected depend on several factors, including

- whether the eligible person is alive or dead
- the age of the spouse applying for benefits
- whether there are dependent children and the age of those children
- whether the eligible person and the spouse are at Full Retirement Age
- whether the spouse has also accumulated enough credits to be eligible for benefits
- whether the spouse is still working.

An unmarried ex-spouse can also qualify for benefits based on marriage to a person who is eligible for benefits provided they were married for at least ten years immediately before the divorce.

Benefits to family members do not decrease the benefit to the eligible individual. There are limits to how much will be paid to family members. The total depends on the benefit amount and the number of family members who also qualify on the eligible person's record. The total varies, but generally the total amount a family can receive is about 50 to 80 percent of the full retirement benefit. However, if an ex-spouse receives benefits, it does not affect the amount that can be paid to the current family. In theory, a person could be married three or four times for ten years each and each of the ex-spouses could collect a spouse's benefit without diminishing the amount paid to the person's current family.

Under some conditions, even the parents of a deceased eligible person can receive benefits based on that person's eligibility. In addition to age and similar requirements, the eligible person must have been providing more than one-half of the parent's support at the time of the eligible person's death or disability. This provision can even apply to stepparents if the stepparent relationship began before the eligible person reached sixteen years of age.

SSA also pays a lump sum death payment to the survivors of an eligible person. Who receives the payment depends on who the survivors are, starting with the spouse. The payment is $255.

Benefit Election Strategy: The Paralegal's Role

Obviously, when and whether our client and his family qualify for benefits and when each qualifying person elects to receive benefits can be an important part of retirement planning. Thought must be given not only to what benefits are available but to the strategy for implementing those benefits. For example, the SSA points out:

> If you are full retirement age, you can apply for retirement benefits and then request to have payments suspended. That way, your spouse can receive a spouse's benefit and you can continue to earn delayed retirement credits until age 70. If your spouse has reached full retirement age and is eligible for a spouse's benefit and his or her own retirement benefit, he or she has a choice. Your spouse can choose to receive only the spouse's benefit now and delay receiving retirement benefits until a later date. If retirement benefits are delayed, a higher benefit may be received at a later date based on the effect of delayed retirement credits.[18]

---

18. "Benefits for your spouse," *Social Security Online Retirement Planner*, http://www.social security.gov/retire2/yourspouse.htm (Last accessed May 23, 2010).

Strategic election of benefits requires that the paralegal obtain detailed information from the client regarding the client's family as well as the Earnings and Benefit Estimate Statement.

If your office does not already have a comprehensive interview form and checklist to obtain the necessary information, it is well worth developing one. Take the time to review all of the requirements for benefits for the client, for spouses, ex-spouses, and children and design an interview form and checklist that elicits all the necessary information including names, addresses, Social Security Numbers, work history, dates of marriages and divorces, and the like. Using this information the legal team can make a retirement plan that maximizes benefits.

Taxation of Benefits

Whether Social Security benefits are taxed depends on the income of the person receiving the benefits. To determine whether benefits will be taxed, compare the base amount for the client's filing status with the total of:

1. One-half of the benefits, plus
2. All other income, including tax-exempt interest.

The **base amount** is:

- $25,000 for single taxpayers, heads of household, or qualifying widow(er)s,
- $25,000 for married taxpayers filing separately and lived apart from their spouse for all of the tax year,
- $32,000 for married taxpayers filing jointly,
- $-0- for married taxpayers filing separately and lived with your spouse at any time during 2009.

Generally, up to 50% of benefits will be taxable. However, up to 85% of benefits can be taxable if either

- The total of one-half of the benefits and all other income is more than $34,000 ($44,000 if married filing jointly).
- The taxpayer is married filing separately and lived with his or her spouse at any time during the tax year.[19]

---

19. "IRS Publication Number 915, Social Security and Equivalent Railroad Retirement Benefits," *Internal Revenue Service*, http://www.irs.gov/publications/p915/ar02.html#en_US_publink100097869 (Last accessed May 23, 2010).

Taxes raised from the taxation of benefits goes to the Social Security Trust Fund and Medicare's Hospital Insurance Trust Fund.

D. Social Security Disability (SSD) and Supplemental Security Income (SSI)

Social Security Disability

Social Security Disability (SSD) benefits are not age based, so they are not strictly speaking a topic for elder law. In fact, a person receiving disability benefits will have his or her benefits converted to retirement benefits when they reach retirement age. However, disability benefits are an important part of the Social Security program and can be used to provide income to clients who become disabled before reaching retirement age.

SSD benefits are not a "means test" based benefit. The criteria for receiving benefits is not tied to a person's income or assets. Instead they are tied to the amount of credit a person has accumulated in the Social Security system prior to becoming disabled. Because a person can become disabled at any time, even prior to having the opportunity to work 40 quarters, the amount of credit required is age related.

To qualify for benefits, the client must have contributed to Social Security both long enough and recently enough. If the disability occurs before age 24, one and a half years of work during the three-year period before the disability begins is generally needed. Between 24 and 30, the client must generally have worked for half of the period between age 21 and the time of the disability. After age 30, the amount of work needed depends on the age when the disability occurred, and the client must have worked for five years out of the 10 years immediately before becoming disabled.

Disability

In order to meet the SSA definition of disabled, a person must be unable to engage in **substantial gainful activity**. This means that the person's physical or mental disability prevents her from doing do any kind of work given her age, education, and experience, not just be unable to do the work they were doing. Thus a young college educated construction worker may have an accident that prevents him from doing construction work, but not prevent him after training to do office work. However, if the construction worker had only a third grade education, he may be found unable to work because he is not qualified for any kind of work that does not require heavy physical labor.

In order to qualify, a disability must be one that will last at least 12 months or lead to death. Grounds for disability include AIDS if that is the basis for the client to be unable to work. They also include drug addiction and alcoholism, but the person must enter rehabilitation treatment and benefit payments last only 36 months. Blindness is also grounds provided the person's vision cannot be corrected.

The disability determination is based on the information available to SSA so it is important that they be provided with all relevant information. Often this is done by giving SSA authority to obtain medical records from the client's physicians. The application for disability can be filed in person, online, or over the phone. Attorneys who specialize in SSD work tell me initial applications are almost always denied. The applicant must ask that the decision be reconsidered. When they do so, the decision is reviewed by another SSA employee. Most applications continue being denied after reconsideration. At this point the applicant can appeal the decision to an Administrative Law Judge. At this level more applications are approved, but there additional appeals available if the application continues to be denied.

The criteria for determining disability and the proper procedure for obtaining a disability determination can be fairly complex. Unless thoroughly familiar with both the impairments that qualify for a disability determination and the procedure to be followed, a legal professional ought not to venture an opinion or attempt an explanation on whether a client meets the criteria. Clients frequently state that a relative or friend knows a relative or friend who receives SSD for a condition "just like mine" or "not nearly as bad as mine." We should not reinforce such preconceptions, but wait until the client's medical records have been thoroughly reviewed. This is especially true since the determinations are based on factors other than the actual medical condition, such as age and experience.

Benefits

There is a five month waiting period before disability benefits are paid, but once payment occurs, it will relate back to the date of disability or 12 months whichever is shorter. Thus, the application should be made as soon as the possibility of a qualifying disability is discovered. The process can take quite some time, with the initial claims being processed in about 90 days.

The benefit payment is usually the same as the Primary Insurance Amount (PIA) but may be adjusted to account for Workers Compensation and other payments received by the applicant.

Benefits end when the disabled person returns to work and begins making "substantial earning," generally average earnings of $500 or more per month.

However, there are special provisions for trial work periods during which benefits will not be reduced or eliminated. Benefits also end if the disability ends even if the claimant does not actually return to work.

Spouses, ex-spouses, and children can all qualify for benefits. For example, a disabled surviving spouse or ex-spouse aged 50–59 can receive disabled surviving spouse's benefits provided he meets other requirements. Special provisions also exist for disabled children depending on a child's age and the age at which they became disabled.

A person receiving SSD for two years is automatically eligible for Medicare. This is a substantial benefit since medical costs associated with many disabilities are often a tremendous burden.

Supplemental Security Income (SSI)

In 1973 Congress added Supplemental Security Income provisions to the Social Security Act. This program is based on a means test, rather than on accumulated credits in the Social Security system, so no prior work record is needed.

SSI makes payments to people who are disabled, blind, or age 65 or older and who have little income or resources. SSI is not financed by Social Security taxes. Disability is determined in the same way as it is for SSD, but eligibility is determined by income and assets rather than by accumulated quarters. Clients who qualify for SSI generally also qualify for other governmental aid such as food stamps and Medicaid.

Not all assets are counted in determining eligibility. For example, a client's home and certain personal property usually including a car are not counted. Resources such as cash, bank accounts, stocks, bonds, real estate other than the home and the like are counted. These cannot total more than $2,000 for one person and $3,000 for a couple.

Income considered for SSI purposes is quite comprehensive. It includes, wages, self-employment earnings, Social Security, pensions, Workers' Compensation payments, interest, dividends, royalties, winnings, unemployment compensation, and gifts. Income can also include non-cash items supplied to the client by others such as food, clothing and shelter unless the provider is a nonprofit corporation. In addition to income and assets requirements, there are also residency and citizenship requirements.

The client can have some income and still get SSI. The allowable income is determined by the state of residence. The SSA provides a Benefits Screening Tool on its website. Here is the link: http://connections.govbenefits.gov/ssa_en.portal.

E. Medicare and Medicaid

Healthcare is a major concern for elder clients and paying for healthcare is an even larger concern. Many elder clients must choose between paying for healthcare and paying for other basic needs, such as food and shelter. Often healthcare loses. There are two basic programs designed to assist the elderly in meeting medical and long-term care expenses, Medicare and Medicaid. They are administered by the Centers for Medicare and Medicaid Services, a division of the Department of Health and Human Services. The CMMS website URL is http://www.cms.gov.

The laws and rules governing these programs are too complex to be covered thoroughly here. As with the other programs in this chapter, the goal is to gain a basic understanding in order to better understand issues confronting our elder clients, rather than a mastery of the topic. This discussion does not take into account changes that may occur as a result of the recently enacted health care reform.

Medicare

Medicare is a health insurance program. Coverage was originally provided in two parts and those two parts continue to be the primary coverage. Part A provides coverage for care in a hospital, skilled nursing facility, home health care, and hospice care. There is no premium for Part A for most people because it is paid for with the 1.45% Medicare taxes on all wages and salaries contributed by employers and employees to the Hospital Insurance Trust Fund. Part B provides coverage for doctor's bills, outpatient hospital care, and other medical services. Most people pay a monthly premium for Part B. Part C is an optional type of coverage referred to as a "Medicare Advantage Plan" offered by private companies under contract with Medicare.

In 2006 Prescription Drug Coverage (Part D Coverage) was made available to everyone with Medicare. Medicare Prescription Drug Coverage is insurance. Private companies provide the coverage. Beneficiaries choose the drug plan and pay a monthly premium. Like other insurance, if a beneficiary decides not to enroll in a drug plan when they are first eligible, they may pay a penalty if they choose to join later.

In order to qualify, a person must be age 65 or older, disabled (as described in the section of this chapter on SSD), or have End-Stage Renal Disease (permanent kidney failure requiring dialysis or a kidney transplant). Eligibility based on disability occurs only after the person has been receiving SSD benefits for two years. People receiving Railroad Retirement benefits or Railroad Retirement disability are also eligible.

Medicare Part A Coverage

Medicare Part A coverage is not unlimited. As with private insurance programs, there are enrollment periods and there is an annual deductible that increases each year. In a benefit period, after the deductible, Medicare pays all hospital expenses for 60 days and all expenses except for a co-insurance deductible for the next thirty days. Each participant also has "reserve days" that can be used for hospitalizations of more than 90 days. These days are subject to a larger co-insurance deductible. Private insurance policies call medi-gap insurance are available to cover the co-insurance deductibles.

Most medically related services are covered, including a semi-private room (private rooms may be covered if medically necessary.) However, "extras" such as telephones, televisions, and private-duty nursing are not covered.

Under some circumstances, *limited* home care and *limited* hospice care are covered.

Medicare Part B Coverage

Medicare Part B requires premium payments by the enrolled individual. Premiums are based on a sliding-scale with premiums in 2009 as low as $96.40 a month for persons with a Modified Adjusted Gross Income of $85,000 or less for an individual and $170,000 or less for a couple to $308.30 a month for individuals with greater than $213,000 and couples with greater than $426,000 in income.

Part B also has a deductible which increases each year. It was $135 in 2009. There is also a co-insurance requirement of 20%, meaning Part B will pay 80% of the approved amount for a service. Physicians who take Medicare patients agree to limit their charges to the approved amount. Because that approved amount is less than what other insurers pay, some doctors will not take Medicare patients or limit the number of Medicare patients they take.

Most physician services are covered by Part B. While it does not cover most routine medical examination, it does cover a broad range of preventive services. Examples of services not covered are hearing aides, acupuncture, cosmetic surgery, and routine dental and foot care.

Medicare Part C Coverage

Part C coverage, often called a "Medicare Advantage Plan," is available for those who elect to enroll. Those eligible for Part A and enrolled in Part B are eligible to enroll in one of these plans offered by private companies under contract to Medicare. Medicare pays the private plan to provide the overage. In essence a Medicare Advantage Plan company is an HMO, a Health Management Organization. While the enrollment in these plans is increasing, the enrollment varies from state to state and plan to plan.

These plans cover all the benefits offered by Medicare Parts A and B, and may offer additional benefits. Out-of-pocket costs such as deductibles and co-insurance payments vary from plan to plan. The additional benefits are provided by limiting the coverage to "in-network" providers, i.e., doctors who have agreed to abide by the plan rules in exchange for payment for services to patients covered by the plan, by requiring a referral to see a specialist, requiring prior authorization for certain procedures, and other standard HMO provisions.

Medicare Part D Coverage

Medicare Part D is the Prescription Drug Coverage Program which began in 2006. In most cases coverage is provided as a separate drug plan, but may also be included in a Part C Medicare Advantage Plan. These plans are offered by private companies under contract with Medicare. An eligible person must elect to enroll in the plan. The plans vary in costs and coverage, including deductibles and co-payments.

While the plans vary, there are a number of rules governing Part D plans. For example, they are required to cover almost all of the drugs in six classes: anti-psychotics, anti-depressants, anti-convulsants, immunosuppressants, cancer, and HIV/AIDS, but may cover as few as two drugs in other categories. Coverage for other classes such as drugs for erectile dysfunction are not required by the rules, but may be provided by the plans anyway. As long as they are consistent with the program's rules, a plan may have its own rules. They often do have rules relating to obtaining prior authorization for certain drugs and limitations on the quantity of medication or the number of refills allowable in specified time periods.

As in other private prescription drug coverage plans, the amount of co-payments is often determined by whether the drug is generic, preferred or non preferred. These are premium based plans so eligible persons should examine the company rules, the amount of co-payments and other cost factors before enrolling.

Low Income Programs

In addition to the standard Medicare program, there are special programs available for low income individuals. In addition to normal Medicare eligibility the individual must meet other economic criteria. These programs are for people who are at or near the federal poverty level. Each program is designed for a particular level of poverty and has its own economic resources requirements. For those who qualify, the Qualified Medicare Beneficiary program pays the Medicare premiums, deductibles, and co-insurance costs; the Specified Low-Income Medicare Beneficiary program, and the Qualified Individual Program-1 pay the Medicare Part B premium.

Medicaid

Medicaid[20] is a program to assist the poor in obtaining medical care. It is not specifically age related, but since so many elderly are poor and need expensive care such as nursing home care, the elderly are the recipients of a great deal of the aid provided by the program. The program is administered by the federal government which sets the ground rules but run by the states.

The Medicaid program is intended to cover catastrophic illness for the poor. The eligibility requirements are based on financial need. Those requirements are set by each state. However, being poor is not enough. Medicaid is available only to certain low-income individuals and families who fit into an eligibility group that is recognized by federal and state law.

According to the Centers for Medicare and Medicaid Services, many groups of people are covered by Medicaid. The rules for counting your income and resources vary from state to state and from group to group. There are special rules for those who live in nursing homes and for disabled children living at home.[21]

Because the eligibility requirements are set by each state, it is not possible to review them here. An updated copy of the requirements for your state should be kept in your office for easy reference. Although these requirements are set state by state, there are establish national rules of concern in every state.

Medicaid Look-back Rule

Because long-term healthcare costs are so high, it is not unusual for them to wipe out a person's entire estate, making impoverished people out of persons who would not otherwise be poor. A long stay in a nursing home facility could quite easily run through tens of thousands of dollars that would otherwise have been available to pass on to a client's spouse and children. Once all that money is gone, a client could then apply for Medicaid and have that program cover the costs.

Not surprisingly, it is also not unusual for an estate planner to try to avoid the loss of a client's assets by simply transferring them to the client's children

---

20. 42 U.S.C. § 1396 et. seq.

21. "Medicaid Overview," *Centers for Medicare and Medicaid Services*, https://www.cms.gov/MedicaidGenInfo (Last accessed May 23, 2010).

just before the client enters a nursing home and immediately applying for Medicaid to pay the bill. In order to prevent this, a provision was included in the Medicaid program to "look back" at transfers made prior to the Medicaid application and count property that had been transferred out of the estate. Originally 12 months, the look-back period is now five years.

If certain transfers were made within the look-back period, then the person making the transfer is penalized by not being eligible for coverage for a period of time. The period of the penalty depends on the amount of the value of the transfer. It is determined by dividing the amount of the transfer by the average monthly costs of nursing home care in the state or local community. For example, if a transfer of $120,000 occurs and the average monthly cost of care is $20,000, then the person making the transfer will be denied benefits for six months.

Rules Regarding Trusts

You can see how this relates to estate planning as we discussed it in Chapters 6 and 7. When establishing our client's goals, it is quite likely that one goal would be to avoid being declared ineligible for Medicaid assistance if it becomes necessary. Our client is likely to want to convey out her assets early to avoid the look-back rule, but at the same time not give up control of the assets until she needs to. One tool for accomplishing this would be a trust.

Recognizing the usefulness of trusts as tools to create Medicaid eligibility, Congress has included provisions in the Medicaid statutes to limit their use for this purpose. A revocable trust, that is, a trust that can be cancelled by the trustor at any time or under specific conditions is treated for practical purposes as if it did not exist. Irrevocable trusts fare better, but if any portion of the trust *could be* used for the benefit of the individual applying for Medicaid, then that entire portion is considered to be a resource available to the applicant.

There are some exceptions or exemptions from the rules for certain trusts. One is a trust that contains the assets of a disabled person established for his benefit by a parent, grandparent, legal guardian, or court; provided that the trust provides that when the person dies the remainder of the trust is paid to the state to the extent of payments made by Medicaid on his behalf. A second is a trust whose corpus consisted only of pension, Social Security, or similar income. A third is a "pooled" trust set up for people who are disabled. These trusts are established and managed by nonprofit associations. The assets are pooled for management, but a separate account is maintained for each beneficiary of the trust.

This type of trust is commonly used in personal injury work. Say a woman was severely injured in a car accident and was permanently disabled. The person who caused the accident may have little insurance and no assets. We may be able to get her a $100,000,000 judgment, but all she will collect is $50,000 or $100,000 depending on the insurance. This amount would quickly be used up by Medicaid expenses, so we would set up a "special needs trust" for her using the insurance proceeds. The money would be available to address needs not covered by Medicaid and she would still be eligible for Medicaid, but if there was any money left when she died, it would go to repay Medicaid.

These trusts are quite complex and must conform in every respect to the Medicaid rules and regulations. In many regions there are attorneys who specialize in public benefits law and are very familiar with these trusts. I recommend that anyone not intimately familiar with them consult with such an attorney before discussing them with a client.

Spend-downs

When assets are counted for Medicaid purposes, there are some assets that are not counted. At times our client's will have too many counted assets to qualify for Medicaid. When that happens we look to see if we can "spend down" those assets or convert them into not-counted assets in order for the client to be eligible. For example, if the client has too much cash, they could invest it in their home which is exempt, prepay funeral expenses, or pay off debts.

Medicaid Liens

Some assets, even though they are considered exempt for purposes of Medicaid eligibility, are subject to being used to reimburse the state for benefits paid on the owner's behalf. Medicaid statutes provide for liens on that property under certain conditions. The rules are different depending on whether the state is trying to collect during the life of the owner or after his death.

During the life of the owner, liens can be placed on the property if it is done pursuant to a judgment that the benefits were incorrectly paid. Also a lien can be placed on an institutionalized person's real property under certain conditions and subject to restrictions in favor of the person's spouse, children, and other family members. The state can also make recovery against a person's estate for amounts incorrectly paid and under some other conditions. Again, this is a subject that should be reviewed based on our client's specific circumstances with an attorney who specializes in public benefits law before it is discussed with a client.

F. VA Benefits

Veterans benefits can be a significant resource for elderly clients and their families. Benefits include a veteran pension, disability compensation, and healthcare. Given the costs of healthcare, that benefit is paramount. In addition, there are benefits relating to education, vocational rehabilitation, and burial. Finally, there are benefits relating to dependents and survivors.

Almost any person who has actively served (full-time service) in any branch of the military and who received a discharge other than "under dishonorable conditions" is likely eligible.

The VA pension program provides for payments to low-income disabled veterans and veterans over the age of 65. Widows and widowers may also benefit from this program. This program requires that the veterans have a certain amount of time in service and that part of that service be during a period of war.

However, the benefit of most use to most of our elder clients is likely to be health care. The United States Department of Veteran Affairs makes this statement regarding VA Healthcare:

> VA provides a Medical Benefits Package to all enrolled Veterans. This comprehensive plan provides a full range of preventive outpatient and inpatient services within VA health care system. Also, once you enroll in the VA's health care system, you can be seen at any VA facility across the country.
>
> VA operates an annual enrollment system that helps to manage the provision of health care by providing an overall population of beneficiaries. Additionally, the enrollment system ensures that Veterans who are eligible can get care and ensures that care is given to Veterans who are eligible. VA applies a variety of factors in determining Veterans' eligibility for enrollment, but once a Veteran is enrolled, that Veteran remains enrolled in the VA health care system.
>
> Do You Qualify? There are many ways that a Veteran may qualify to receive top-notch VA health care at over 1,400 medical centers and clinics across the nation. The VA has highly trained physicians and clinicians that allow the VA to address many specialties. You may also be able to receive assistance with prescription medication. VA health care is portable. Once enrolled, you may receive care at your home facility as well as the nearest VA facility while traveling.[22]

---

22. "VA Health Care Overview," *United States Department of Veteran Affairs*, http://www4.va.gov/healtheligibility (Last accessed May 23, 2010).

Not everyone speaks as highly of VA healthcare as the VA does, and there are frequent stories in the news regarding the VA's failings. However, as legal professionals we would be remiss in our duty to our clients if we do not encourage them to take advantage of this option when it is available to them.

CHAPTER TEN

ELDER ABUSE

A. Elder Abuse—Statistics, Definitions, and Classifications

Elder abuse has been mentioned frequently in previous chapters. We saw some examples that focused primarily on financial issues when discussing the family as caregivers, including the daughter who used her deathbed vigil to isolate and gain an advantage over other family members. We also looked at abuse by guardians, including the case of Brooke Astor, whose son was accused of misusing $14 million of her money and forcing her to sleep in a cold bedroom in a "torn nightgown" that "smells probably from dog urine." She was denied medicines and forced to eat "pureed peas, carrots and oatmeal."[1] The case was settled out of court, but the son was ultimately convicted of defrauding his mother and sentenced to one to three years in prison.[2]

We noted that even public guardians are not free from taint in this regard. The National Association of Attorney Generals' *NAAGazette* noted the 2009 sentencing of a former Buchanan County, Mo., public administrator to three years' imprisonment for embezzling over $119,000 from Social Security payments intended for clients served by her office.[3]

---

1. "Obituary: Brooke Aster," *Guardian*, August 16, 2007, http://www.guardian.co.uk/news/2007/aug/16/guardianobituaries.usa (Last accessed April 3, 2010).

2. *The New York Times,* December 21, 2009, http://topics.nytimes.com/top/reference/timestopics/people/m/anthony_d_marshall/index.html (Last accessed April 3, 2010).

3. "Protecting the Protected: Overseeing Adult Guardianship," *NAAGazette*, National Association of Attorney Generals, http://www.naag.org/protecting-the-protected-overseeing-adult-guardianship.php (Last accessed April 3, 2010).

Statistics and Definitions

Unfortunately, these examples do not give the whole picture of elder abuse and neglect. It is generally acknowledged that "currently a clear picture of the incidence and prevalence of elder abuse in the United States is sadly lacking— and that such a picture 'is essential if social policy is to be created to impact prevention and treatment' "[4] Incidence rates are estimated, depending on the methodologies used, from 1.2% based on reports of abuse to Adult Protective Services in the year 2000 to 5%, as estimated by the U.S. Senate Special Committee on Aging in 2003.

One problem with such estimates is the limits on the sources of data. The ABA Commission on Law and Aging suggests that surveys based on reports of abuse to Adult Protective Services be supplemented by sources such as healthcare data from Medicare claims, Medicaid Fraud units and nursing home enforcement; criminal justice data; and informal sources such as AARP member surveys. Survey data may be helpful in giving a full picture of the extent of abuse.[5] Each of the other sources requires that abuse be actually reported or discovered. In reality, many cases of abuse are not reported. In many instances, the abuser and abused are the only ones who know of the abuse. The abusers will not report it and the abused cannot, either because they are not physically or mentally able to or because they fear the consequences. After all, they are at the mercy of their abusers if the report is not found valid and may perceive themselves as having no other source of care if it is found valid.

Another difficulty with drawing conclusions from existing data arises from differences in definitions of "elder abuse" and "elder mistreatment." The ABA White Paper noted that the NCEA used this definition:

> [E]lder abuse is a term referring to any knowing, intentional, or negligent act by a caregiver or any other person that causes harm or a serious risk of harm to a vulnerable adult. The specificity of laws varies from state to state, but broadly defined, abuse may be: physical abuse, emotional abuse, sexual abuse, exploitation, neglect, abandonment.

While the National Research Council report uses the term "elder mistreatment," defined as:

---

4. Erica F. Wood, "The Availability and Utility of Interdisciplinary Data on Elder Abuse: A White Paper for the National Center on Elder Abuse," *American Bar Association Commission on Law and Aging for the National Center on Elder Abuse* 7 (May 2006).

    5. *Id.*

(a) intentional actions that cause harm or create a serious risk of harm (whether or not harm is intended) to a vulnerable elder by a caregiver or other person who stands in a trust relationship to the elder, or (b) failure by a caregiver to satisfy the elder's basic needs or to protect the elder from harm The report explains that the term "mistreatment" is meant to exclude cases of self neglect, as well as cases of victimization by strangers.[6]

The U.S. Administration on Aging's National Center on Elder Abuse now provides this information on definitions at its website:

> Federal definitions of elder abuse, neglect, and exploitation appeared for the first time in the 1987 Amendments to the Older Americans Act. These definitions were provided in the law only as guidelines for identifying the problems and not for enforcement purposes.
>
> Definitions in state law vary considerably from state to state in terms of what constitutes abuse, neglect, or exploitation of the elderly. Researchers also have used varying definitions to describe and study the problem.
>
> Broadly defined, however, there are three basic categories of elder abuse:
> • Domestic elder abuse
> • Institutional elder abuse
> • Self-neglect or self-abuse
> While state definitions may vary, in most states, definitions of elder abuse generally fall within these three categories.
>
> **Domestic elder abuse** generally refers to any of several forms of maltreatment of an older person by someone who has a special relationship with the elder (a spouse, a sibling, a child, a friend, or a caregiver), that occur in the elder's home, or in the home of a caregiver.
>
> **Institutional abuse**, on the other hand, generally refers to any of the above-mentioned forms of abuse that occur in residential facilities for older persons (e.g., nursing homes, foster homes, group homes, board and care facilities). Perpetrators of institutional abuse usually are persons who have a legal or contractual obligation to provide elder victims with care and protection (e.g., paid caregivers, staff, professionals).

---

6. *Id.* at 8.

Definitions and legal terms vary from state to state in regards to the types of domestic elder abuse that NCEA recognizes, as well as their signs and symptoms.[7]

It is important that the legal professional know the legal definitions of elder abuse, mistreatment, and neglect set forth in statutes covering the jurisdictions in which they practice. It is equally important that the legal professional understand her legal obligations under those statutes and how those obligation relate to their ethical obligations. Finally, it is essential that the legal professional recognize the signs of abuse and neglect. *Keep in mind that your elder client may be unable or unwilling to speak frankly about abuse they are experiencing, especially in the presence of a family member or other person who has assisted them in getting to your office.*

Regardless of the limitations on data sources, we can glean some information and that information confirms that elder abuse is a significant problem. Based on the information presently available here is what we do know, based on an NCEA survey of Adult Protective Services reports done in 2004:

National Trends—Abuse of Vulnerable Adults of All Ages
- APS received a total of 565,747 reports of elder and vulnerable adult abuse for persons of all ages (50 states, plus Guam and the District of Columbia). This represents a 19.7% increase from the 2000 Survey (472,813 reports).
- APS investigated 461,135 total reports of elder and vulnerable adult abuse for persons of all ages (49 states). This represents a 16.3% increase from the 2000 Survey (396,398 investigations).
- APS substantiated 191,908 reports of elder and vulnerable adult abuse for victims of all ages (42 states). This represents a 15.6% increase from the 2000 Survey (166,019 substantiated reports).
- The average APS budget per state was $8,550,369, compared to an average of $7,084,358 reported in the 2000 Survey (42 states).

Statewide Reporting Numbers
- APS received a total of 253,426 reports on persons aged 60+ (32 states).
- APS investigated a total of 192,243 reports on persons aged 60+ (29 states).
- APS substantiated 88,455 reports on persons aged 60+ (24 states).
- APS received a total of 84,767 reports of self-neglect on persons aged 60+ (21 states).

---

7. " Elder Abuse/Mistreatment Defined," *National Center on Elder Abuse*, http://www.ncea. aoa.gov/NCEAroot/Main_Site/FAQ/Basics/Definition.aspx (Last accessed May 25, 2010).

- APS investigated a total of 82,007 reports of self-neglect on persons aged 60+ (20 states).
- APS substantiated 46,794 reports of self-neglect on persons aged 60+ (20 states).
- The most common sources of reports of abuse of adults 60+ were family members (17.0%), social services workers (10.6%), and friends and neighbors (8.0%).[8]

We also know that up to 90% of mistreatment cases are perpetrated by family members, abusers are primarily men, and about 60% are adult children or spouses/partners of the abused.[9]

Types of Elder Mistreatment

Undue Influence

Undue influence is the most subtle type of mistreatment, and therefore the most difficult to detect. Since the elder person is unduly influenced through fear, dependence, diminished capacity and other factors, the victim is unlikely to be both willing and capable of reporting the abuse. Many will not even be consciously aware of the undue influence. This topic has been discussed in detail in previous chapters,[10] so here I will only list some of the signs that *may* indicate undue influence is being exercised over a client. These signs include:

- The helper speaks for the client;
- The client repeatedly asks the helper to answer a question for him or her;
- The client consistently looks to the helper before answering a question;
- The client stops or changes an answer after the helper looks at, touches, or makes a movement towards the client;
- The helper frequently corrects the client's answers;
- The helper refuses or is reluctant to allow the client to speak privately with the attorney or paralegal;
- The client appears confused or influenced by medication or alcohol.

---

8. "The 2004 Survey of State Adult Protective Services: Abuse of Adults 60 Years of Age and Older" *The National Committee for the Prevention of Elder Abuse and The National Adult Protective Services Association,* Prepared for the National Center on Elder Abuse, at 5, http://www.ncea.aoa.gov/NCEAroot/Main_Site/pdf/2-14-06%20FINAL%2060+REPORT.pdf (Last accessed May 25, 2010).

9. Nancy R. Hooyman and H. Asuman Kiyak, *Social Gerontology: A Multidisciplinary Perspective,* 362 (7th ed., Pearson 2005).

10. Chapter Two, pages __–__ and Chapter Four, pages __–__.

Neglect

While we have ethical or moral obligations to help others, not everyone has a responsibility to provide care for others. At least thirty states have made the moral obligation to provide care for parents a legal obligation through enactment of "filial responsibility laws."[11] These statutes vary widely in definition of the duty, exceptions, defenses, and penalties.[12] The National Center for Policy Analysis reports:

> States with filial responsibility statutes take a variety of approaches to enforcement: 21 allow some sort of civil court action to obtain financial support (or cost recovery) and 12 specify a criminal penalty for filial nonsupport; three states allow both civil and criminal actions. Of course, in many cases state filial responsibility laws limit children's liability under a variety of conditions, such as whether the adult child has enough income to actually contribute, or if the adult child's financial circumstances change, or if they were abandoned or deserted by the parent.[13]

The reasoning behind these statutes is set forth in a South Dakota Supreme Court opinion:

> It is certainly reasonable to place a duty to support an indigent parent on that parent's adult child because they are direct lineal descendants who have received the support, care, comfort and guidance of

---

11. Alaska, Arkansas, California, Connecticut, Delaware, Georgia, Idaho, Indiana, Iowa, Kentucky, Louisiana, Maryland, Massachusetts, Mississippi, Montana, Nevada, New Hampshire, New Jersey, North Carolina, North Dakota, Ohio, Oregon, Pennsylvania, Rhode Island, South Dakota, Tennessee, Utah, Vermont, Virginia, and West Virginia., according to Jane Gross, "The New Old Age: States With Filial Responsibility Laws," ttp://graphics8.ny times.com/packages/pdf/health/NOA/30states.pdf (Last accessed May 25, 2010). Gross provides complete statutory citations for each of the listed states.

12. The Montana statute is, however, fairly typical:

Montana Code Ann., 40-6-301. Duty of child to support indigent parents.

(1) It is the duty of every adult child, having the financial ability, to furnish and provide necessary food, clothing, shelter, medical attendance, and burial, entombment, or cremation costs for an indigent parent, unless, in the judgment of the court or jury, the child is excused by reason of intemperance, indolence, immorality, or profligacy of the parent.

(2) If a county pays for burial, entombment, or cremation costs under 53-3-116, the county may seek reimbursement under this part, if applicable.

13. Matthew Pakula, "The Legal Responsibility of Adult Children to Care for Indigent Parents," *National Center for Policy Analysis*, July 12, 2005, http://www.ncpa.org/pub/ba521/ (Last accessed May 25, 2010).

that parent during their minority. If a parent does not qualify for public assistance, who is best suited to meet that parent's needs? It can reasonably be concluded that no other person has received a greater benefit from a parent than that parent's child and it logically follows that the adult child should bear the burden of reciprocating on that benefit in the event a parent needs support in their later years.[14]

While duties may arise as a result of these statues, most duties to provide care for the elder client normally arise out of either an express contract for formal care in an institution or in the home, or through a voluntary undertaking. The latter is the normal basis for obligations assumed by family members, friends, and neighbors. Once the volunteer has assumed the obligation, they cannot neglect or abandon that duty without ensuring that someone else has taken their place.

Signs of neglect include a lack of good personal hygiene, inadequate or inappropriate clothing, inadequate health care, malnutrition, and bedsores. However, depression, fear, or anxiety can also be indicators of neglect, as can be external indicators such as non-working or inadequate toilets, heat, air-conditioning, or utilities.

Physical Abuse

Some elders are subject to physical violence from their caregivers. Many social and psychological factors may be behind this treatment, ranging from a sense of frustration, exhaustion, and being overwhelmed on the part of the caregiver, to just plain meanness. Regardless of the motivation behind it, the elderly are susceptible to being hit, pushed, shaken, slapped, unnecessary restraints, forced feeding, and the like, just as young children are. Certainly the elderly are susceptible to falls and other accidental injury, however, any bruises, welts, or other injuries should raise some suspicion, extra vigilance, and discreet inquiry.

Financial Abuse

Much financial abuse is the result of greed on the part of a member of the elder client's family. Jane A. Black notes as examples, "a daughter uses her power of attorney over Mom's bank accounts to withdraw her life savings; a niece coerces her elderly aunt to designate her as the beneficiary of her life insur-

---

14. *Americana Healthcare Center v Randall*, 513 N.W. 2d 566, 573 (S.D., 1994)

ance policy; a nephew dupes an elderly uncle into signing a power of attorney and the nephew makes thousands of dollars worth of "gifts" to himself each month from the uncle; a son caring for Dad pays for substandard care to preserve assets he stands to inherit."[15] Black correctly points out that each of these acts is a type of theft or fraud similar to that for which Brooke Astor's son was convicted.

Black goes on to document through examination of case law, a "glaring" abuse of powers of attorney and to analyze statutes intended to curb this practice. Those statutes may enhance penalties for certain crimes committed specifically against elderly persons, create a presumption that a transfer of real estate, personal property, or money for less than full consideration by an elderly person with whom the victim has a fiduciary relationship is the result of undue influence, freezing assets that were exploited from an elderly victim, considering the elderly age of a victim as an aggravating factor that should be taken into account for sentencing purposes. Black notes that about ten states address financial exploitation of the elderly through statutes that specifically address misuse of power of attorney.[16]

In addition to abuse by family members and guardians, the elderly are particularly likely to be victims of identity theft, telemarketing fraud, and scam artists. Some of these cases can be horrific. In January of 2010, *The Los Angeles Times* reported on the case of Walter Sartory, brilliant and wealthy but a paranoid schizophrenic who was abducted, drugged, and his body set on fire. A housekeeper and her son have been charged with murder.[17]

Many states have laws designed to deter this type of abuse including laws that give all persons the right to cancel home-solicited contracts within a specified number of days. In addition, some protection can be gained by the client registering for the "Do Not Call List."

Legal professionals may be in an unique position to spot financial abuse of their elder clients by watching for unusual changes in their finances from one meeting to another, and discussing the use of powers of attorney and other delegations of authority with the client and the agent created under those instruments. Be especially attentive to explanations or descriptions of transac-

---

15. Jane A. Black, "The Not-So-Golden Years: Power of Attorney, Elder Abuse, and Why Our Laws Are failing a Vulnerable Population," at 3, http://www.stjohns.edu/media/3/8975 642417e64df288d548955d2dcc73.pdf (Last accessed May 25, 2010).

16. *Id.* at 16.

17. "A mad scheme to kill a scientist," *The Los Angeles Times,* January 07, 2010, (Last accessed January 10, 2010.

tions given by the client and the agent. Be concerned if they differ in any significant way.

Self-Neglect

For most older persons, independence is a key element of maintaining their self-esteem and sense of self. Being able to "do" is part of who they "are." This need for independence must be respected, even when the person behaves in a way that we find eccentric or even distasteful. However, when the person's behavior threatens their own safety or the safety of others—once person can no longer or will not provide for his or her own basic food, shelter, medical care, and general safety needs, it is a matter of self-neglect. Self-neglect should be viewed as a possible lack of competency. The NCEA, lists these signs of possible self-neglect:

- Hoarding
- Failure to take essential medications or refusal to seek medical treatment for serious illness
- Leaving a burning stove unattended
- Poor hygiene
- Not wearing suitable clothing for the weather
- Confusion
- Inability to attend to housekeeping
- Dehydration[18]

According to NCEA, self-neglect accounts for the majority of cases reported to adult protective services. Not surprisingly self-neglect is often paired with declining health, isolation, Alzheimer's disease or dementia, or drug and alcohol dependency.

A finding of self-neglect does not automatically mean the client will be placed in an institution. Supports in the community may allow them to continue living on their own. Conditions like depression and malnutrition may be successfully treated through medical intervention. However, if the problems are severe enough, a guardian may be appointed and in the most severe cases, institutionalization may be required. Generally, state intervention should be limited to the amount necessary given the extent of the individual's diminished capacity.

---

18. "Frequently Asked Questions," *National Center on Elder Abuse,* http://www.ncea.aoa.gov/NCEAroot/Main_Site/FAQ/Questions.aspx (Last access on May 25, 2010).

B. Governmental Action — Adult Protective Services

Federal Government

The Federal Government does not participate directly in providing services to prevent or react to elder abuse, instead taking the role of educating, coordinating, and funding state agencies in the fight. In 1987 the Older Americans Act was amended to provide guidelines for identifying abuse. Since then, NCEA reports:

> In 1992, Congress created and funded a new Title VII, Chapter 3 for prevention of abuse, neglect, and exploitation. Title VII Vulnerable Elder Rights Protection also includes provisions for long-term care ombudsman programs and state legal assistance development.
>
> In 2000, provisions were added to Title VII to encourage states to foster greater coordination with law enforcement and the courts.
>
> In the 2006 amendments to the Older Americans Act, new language was added to Title II and Title VII emphasizing multi-disciplinary and collaborative approaches to addressing elder mistreatment when developing programs and long-term strategic plans for elder justice activities. New language in Title VII also expands the options for States and tribal organizations to use some portion of the Title VII allotments for detection, assessment, intervention in, investigation of, and response to elder abuse, neglect, and exploitation, in addition to prevention and treatment. And, for the first time, "elder justice" and "self-neglect" are defined in the OAA.
>
> As the years have gone by, Title VII Vulnerable Elder Rights Protection has proven instrumental in promoting public education and interagency coordination to address elder abuse. The Long-Term Care Ombudsman program is also established in Title VII.[19]

The health care reform bill enacted in 2010 includes additional legislation affecting the elderly: the Elder Justice Act, the Nursing Home Transparency and Improvement Act, and the Patient Safety and Abuse Prevention Act all directed at additional funding for the prevention of elder abuse, coordinating existing agencies and preventing nursing home abuses.

---

19. "Older Americans Act," *National Center on Elder Abuse*, http://www.ncea.aoa.gov/NCEAroot/Main_Site/Library/Laws/Older_Americans_Act.aspx (Last accessed May 25, 2010).

State Government

Adult Protective Services

All states have laws providing adult protective services for vulnerable adults. Exactly who is protected, what protection they are provided, and how those protections are afforded varies from state to state. NCEA provides a fairly comprehensive "Analysis of State Adult Protective Services Laws" on its website.[20]

NCEA provides this information regarding APS services in general:

> Adult Protective Services (APS) are those services provided to insure the safety and well-being of elders and adults with disabilities who are in danger of being mistreated or neglected, are unable to take care of themselves or protect themselves from harm, and have no one to assist them.
>
> Interventions provided by Adult Protective Services include, but are not limited to, receiving reports of adult abuse, exploitation or neglect, investigating these reports, case planning, monitoring and evaluation. In addition to casework services, Adult Protection may provide or arrange for the provision of medical, social, economic, legal, housing, law enforcement or other protective, emergency or supportive services.
>
> In most states, APS caseworkers are the first responders to reports of abuse, neglect, and exploitation of vulnerable adults. A **vulnerable adult** is defined as a person who is being mistreated or is in danger of mistreatment and who, due to age and/or disability, is unable to protect himself or herself.
>
> Most APS programs serve both older and younger vulnerable adults. In some states, APS is responsible only for cases involving older adults (eligibility may be based on age, incapacity or vulnerability of the adult). A few APS programs serve only younger adults ages 18–59.
>
> APS Interventions
>
> • Receiving reports of elder/vulnerable adult abuse, neglect, and/or exploitation
> • Investigating these reports
> • Assessing victim's risk
> • Assessing victim's capacity to understand his/her risk and ability to give informed consent

---

20. http://www.ncea.aoa.gov/NCEAroot/Main_Site/Find_Help/APS/Analysis_State_Laws.aspx (Last accessed May 25, 2010).

- Developing case plan
- Arranging for emergency shelter, medical care, legal assistance, and supportive services
- Service monitoring
- Evaluation[21]

Other State Legislation

As discussed in the section of this chapter on financial abuse, states have become quite creative in enacting legislation intended to combat elder abuse. These statutes include provisions to limit abuse of powers of attorney, criminalize elder abuse, enhance sentencing for crimes against the elderly, and mandate reporting of suspected abuse.

C. Mandated Reporting

Seldom do APS investigators simply happen upon elder abuse. APS depends on citizen reporting of abuse. By the very nature of the victim, i.e., "vulnerable" adults, it is highly unlikely the victim will report the abuse. Many abusers count on this fact in the exploitation of the victim.

However, much abuse goes unreported for reasons including a natural reluctance to become involved in "messy" situations, especially situations often viewed as being private family affairs, reluctance to take action on suspicion, and fear of retaliation. Some people simply take a "not my job" attitude towards the problem.

Most states have enacted legislation that either mandates or encourages reporting. These statutes, like most others dealing with elder law topics, vary widely from state to state. Some states mandate reporting by specific classes of people, usually healthcare professionals, social workers, and law enforcement personnel. Others cast a much broader net to include *anyone* who has reason to suspect elder abuse.

The Mississippi Vulnerable Adult Act, for example, contains a long list of identified classes of persons who must report, including health professionals (including those that rely solely on spiritual healing), accountants, and bank employees. However, the law clearly states that regardless of the list, "*any per-*

---

21. "About Adult Protective Services," *National Center on Elder Abuse,* http://www.ncea.aoa.gov/ncearoot/Main_Site/Find_Help/APS/About_APS.aspx (Last accessed May 25, 2010).

son ... who knows or suspects that a vulnerable adult has been or is being abused, neglected or exploited shall immediately report such knowledge or suspicion to the Department of Human Services or to the county department of human services where the vulnerable adult is located."[22] (Emphasis added.)

Of particular import for us is the fact that such statutes may apply to attorneys—indeed the Mississippi statute's first identified profession for mandatory reporting is the attorney profession. This appears to create an ethical dilemma for attorneys and their paralegals. The statutes require reporting even if the knowledge or suspicion comes to the attorney as part of attorney-client communications that would otherwise be considered confidential and subject to the attorney-client privilege.

The solution to this dilemma is likely to lie within the specific rules of professional conduct governing the jurisdiction in which the attorney practices. The ABA Model Rules of Professional Conduct, Rule 1.6.b.6 provides that an attorney may reveal privileged communications "to comply with other law or court order."[23] Thus, the rule allows attorneys to report in jurisdictions with mandatory reporting statutes. With regard to other professions, some commentators have suggested that failure to make a mandated report constitutes malpractice.[24] This may also be the case for attorneys.

A secondary concern is whether the attorney has an obligation to advise a client that the attorney/client privilege does not protect communications that may reveal elder abuse. In previous discussions, I noted that a power of attorney gives the agent authority to act on the principal's behalf, not to exploit the principal. If the principal is our client, there is no problem with reporting an agent who is exploiting the client. However, the issue is more complex if our client is the person doing the exploitation. They may confide in us on the assumption that what they say is confidential when, in some jurisdictions, we may be mandated to report. In these circumstances I believe the attorney has an obligation to advise the client of this exception to the attorney/client privilege before engaging in communications with the client.

The more dangerous territory is voluntary reporting. Reporting statutes often provide immunity from liability for reports made in good faith, and establish a presumption of good faith. Some statutes that provide for voluntary reporting provide that the reporter's identity may only be revealed as ordered

---

22. Miss. Code Ann. 43-47-7 (LexisNexis current through 2009 3rd Extraordinary Session).

23. Rule 1.6.b.6, ABA Model Rules of Professional Conduct (2004), http://www.law.cornell.edu/ethics/aba/current/ABA_CODE.HTM#Rule_1.6 (Last accessed May 25, 2010).

24. Ralph C. Brashier, *Mastering Elder Law*, 18 (Carolina Academic Press 2010).

by a court for good cause.[25] The content of the report is also usually confidential. All of this does not necessarily protect the legal professional if the report is a violation of the attorney/client privilege.

When we suspect a non-client is abusing our client, the obligation to report even if reporting is not mandated appears clear. This may not be the case, however, when the client directs us not to report. However, in circumstances of obvious abuse and exploitation, a direction not to report may be a form of self neglect or the result of undue influence. In such a case, I would err on the side of reporting unless there was some clear indication that reporting would violate an ethical obligation. In my view the overriding obligation is to act in the best interest of the client.

When we learn through privileged communications, however, that our client is the abuser, voluntary reporting must be carefully considered under the particular rules of professional conduct governing our jurisdiction. Under the ABA Model Rules, there appears to be enough leeway to make the voluntary report. Rule 1.6.b provisions for revelation of otherwise confidential information include:

Rule 1.6: Confidentiality of Information

b. A lawyer may reveal information relating to the representation of a client to the extent the lawyer reasonably believes necessary:
1. to prevent reasonably certain death or substantial bodily harm;
2. to prevent the client from committing a crime or fraud that is reasonably certain to result in substantial injury to the financial interests or property of another and in furtherance of which the client has used or is using the lawyer's services;
3. to prevent, mitigate or rectify substantial injury to the financial interests or property of another that is reasonably certain to result or has resulted from the client's commission of a crime or fraud in furtherance of which the client has used the lawyer's services

In most instances, our knowledge of elder abuse on the part of our clients will involve serious bodily injury to the elder person, or a crime or fraud that is reasonably certain to result in substantial injury to the financial interests of property to another. However, in the latter case, the client must have used or be using the lawyer's services in furtherance of the crime or fraud. For example, he may have used our services to obtain the power of attorney he is now utilizing to effectuate the exploitation of the elder person.

---

25. *Id.*

The primary task of paralegals is to be attentive to signs of elder abuse and to report those signs to the attorney for whom they are working. Document any such signs thoroughly in the file. Bring a camera with you whenever visiting an elder client at home or in an institutional facility.

If you believe you are a mandated reporter under the applicable statute and the attorney directs you not to report, obtain independent legal advice before proceeding. The attorney's ethical obligations are not directly binding on you, but the statutes may be. Consult an attorney not associated with your attorney or the law office in which your attorney works. Remember that attorney has a firm obligation to keep what you tell her confidential. That attorney can advise you regarding protections to which you may be entitled, the proper authority to which you should report and the correct procedures for reporting. She will help you analyze the situation to determine whether you have the necessary facts, have properly interpreted the facts and validate your decision regarding the proper balancing of interests and integrity. Other members of your paralegal professional association may be helpful in locating the best attorney for this purpose.

CHAPTER ELEVEN

ETHICAL CONSIDERATIONS

We will conclude with a slight change of focus. Thus far we have been focused on working with the elder client. In doing so, we have frequently considered concerns and issues facing the client other than legal concerns in order to better understand the client. These concerns have included considerations of ethical problems the clients may face such as fairness to their children in distribution of their estate and the many ethical choices related to end-of-life healthcare.

In this chapter we will shift focus to working with the elder law attorney rather than the elder client. After all, in order to best serve and work with the elder client, we must understand the concerns of the attorney providing the primary legal services. We have already done much of this work in our review of the various substantive laws applicable to elder clients since the main focus of the attorney is that law. While focused on that law and providing services to the elder client, however, the attorney must also be mindful of her ethical obligations. The rules of professional conduct governing attorneys are not directly binding upon you, but they can still act as a guide as to what the right course of action is for you. Those rules directly bind your attorney and you cannot be an effective member of that attorney's legal team without understanding them.

Ethics, to my mind, is not a separate topic. It is an integral part of the everyday practice of law, regardless of the type of law being practiced or the clients being served. As a result, I have attempted to integrate discussion of ethical issues into every chapter in this book as an adjunct consideration to the law or other topic being considered. Now we will review and highlight those ethical considerations in their own right, rather than in conjunction with other topics. Thus this chapter presents anew materials collected from previous chapters. This will reinforce the importance of ethical considerations for attorneys serving elders client and provide easy access to those considerations for those who want to delve directly into ethical issues.

Keep in mind that my presentation of these issues is often just that—my presentation. It is not, and should not be taken as, legal advice. Often the correct advice depends on the particular facts involved in and the circumstances surrounding an issue, as well as the particular rules of professional conduct governing the jurisdiction in which an attorney is practicing. Finally, keep in mind that this presentation of issues is not intended to be comprehensive. It is just a sampling of ethical issues the elder law practitioner is likely to face.

A. Conflicts of Interest

Despite the often intense involvement of the family with our elder client, we must keep in mind exactly who our client is *and* communicate that fact clearly to everyone else. The paralegal should discuss exactly how and when this is to be done with the attorney. Even the most genuinely concerned members of the client's family are likely to have difficulty separating their own needs and concerns from that of the client. The bare fact of their connection to the client interferes with them maintaining the objectivity that the legal professional must maintain. This lack of objectivity is intensified by the stress brought on by the very age-related changes affecting our client that make legal assistance necessary.

Even if the client has a primary caregiver, each member of the family is likely to have an opinion about what should be done for the client and by the client. Each member of the family also has an interest in the work being done for the client by the legal team. Each member of the family will have expectations regarding how the client should be treated, how that member of the family should be treated, and how other members of the family should be treated by the legal professional. Each is likely to be voicing their opinion on the job the legal professional is doing.

Thus, it is important to establish and communicate ground rules at the initial interview. The client and each involved family member should clearly understand that she and only she is our client. As discussed in the next section, there are special considerations that must be given to confidentiality when dealing with an assisted elder client. The rules regarding confidentiality should also be explained clearly to the client and to the family.

Confusion regarding who the client is often arises when a caregiver makes the initial call to an attorney or arranges for the initial meeting. It is not at all unusual for an existing client to bring a parent to the "family attorney" and declare "My father wants to make a will." While this is a perfectly acceptable situation, it must be made clear at once—in a cordial and diplomatic way—that it is the father, not the child who is the client for purposes of making the will. The same is true when we are contacted to act on behalf of an elder client by a conservator or guardian.

Further, the legal professional must be careful to avoid a conflict of interest. The ethical rules in all jurisdictions have provisions covering representation of multiple clients when those clients *may* have conflicting interests. If a child who is already our client brings in a parent for legal services, that child may have an expectation that we will protect her interest in the course of providing those legal services. A conflict may arise, for example, if the parent wants to favor another child over that child or a stepparent over all of the children. The legal professionals have an obligation to reject matters in which they cannot maintain objectivity because of conflicts. There is also an obligation to disclose potential conflicts and obtain an informed, knowing waiver from the clients. That waiver should be in writing.

This point can be particularly difficult to maintain and explain when our client wishes to, or we are advising the client to, delegate authority through powers of attorney, advanced directives, trusts, or similar documents. Once the authority has been delegated, the agent will often act for the client. The agent's authority may extend to making legal decisions for the client and giving the legal professional direction with regard to those decisions. It is especially necessary in this situation for legal professionals to keep in mind who the client is.

While the agent speaks for the client, she is not the client. The elder person who delegated the authority must remain our primary concern and we have an obligation not to partake in decisions that are clearly not in the client's best interest. The agent owes certain fiduciary duties to the principal granting her authority. It may be necessary for the attorney to remind the agent of those duties. It is ethically required that the legal professionals not participate in acts that violate those duties.

My approach has been to make it clear to the agent that the principal is my client. To the extent that the agent works on behalf of the client, the attorney/client privilege extends to the agent. If, however, it is my determination is that the agent is violating his fiduciary duties—especially if the violation amounts to a crime or abuse of his authority—then the attorney/client privilege does not protect him. If a paralegal suspects that an agent is not acting in the best interest of the client, this fact should be discussed with the attorney immediately.

B. Confidentiality

The attorney/client privilege extends to agents of the attorney and the client. This only makes sense given the purpose of the privilege which is to encourage full disclosure without fear that the information will be revealed to others, so that clients receive the best and most competent legal advice and representation. We tend to think of this extension most often in terms of the attorney's staff—paralegals, secretaries, investigators and others who assist the attorney in providing the advice and representation. However, it applies also to the agents of the client who assist in the communication. This is most obvious in the case of corporate clients since all communication with corporations must be done through one or more of their agents.

We should take care to protect the attorney/client privilege when the client is assisted by another person during communications between the attorney and the client. While we understand the workings of the privilege, many clients and the assistant will not. Like so many other aspects of the legal process, we should take the time to explain at least the basics to both clients and their agents. In this case, the basics consist of the fact that for purposes of the communications that occur between the attorney and the client or the agent on the client's behalf, the third party is indeed the agent of the client. *Both the agent and client should understand and acknowledge the fact of the agency prior to the communications taking place.*

First, the client should clearly understand that there is no way to pre-screen statements made in front of the agent, so if there is any topic that the client does not want mentioned, the client should let the attorney and/or paralegal know in private. The logistics of this can be difficult, as once the two are in the room, it can be difficult and embarrassing for the client to ask that the agent leave. As discussed more fully in the next sub-section, I most often handled this by making it a general rule to ask the agent to leave at the very beginning of the meeting. I explain to both the client and the agent that I do this as a matter of policy so I can document the file for the benefit of all concerned, not because of anything related to their particular circumstances.

During my experience representing attorneys against whom ethics complaints had been brought, I became aware of several instances where failure to establish such a procedure resulted in the filing of complaints. In one such instance, the client came in to discuss settlement of a personal injury claim. Of course, this required the attorney to assess both the strengths and weaknesses of the case. One weakness was certain aspects of the client's past medical history that related to alcohol and drug abuse. The client had not been aware going into the conversation that this topic would come up and was quite upset that the agent had been informed. This problem could have been avoided if the agent had been asked to leave the room long enough for the attorney to outline the upcoming discussion.

Second, the agent should be aware of his or her obligation to maintain the confidentiality that underpins the attorney/client privilege. Many people do not understand just how important the confidentiality obligation is or how deep it runs. They must be made to understand that they cannot go home and discuss what they heard at the meeting with other members of the client's family, with their own family, their drinking buddies or their co-workers—even if they change the names and other information to protect identities.

I generally handle this by having both the client and the agent sign a Confidentiality Acknowledgement. This is a simple document written in terms the client and the agent can understand. Like any form, it should be adjusted for the particular practice and circumstances.

CONFIDENTIALITY ACKNOWLEDGEMENT

_____ (Agent) agrees to act as agent for _____ (Client) for purposes of helping communication between Client and his/her attorney and that attorney's staff only.

Client agrees that Agent is authorized to act as his/her agent for purposes of helping communication between Client and his/her attorney and that attorney's staff only.

Client understands this means that Agent will hear information that would otherwise be kept confidential between Client and the attorney and the attorney's staff. Since it is not possible to identify all the topics that might be covered in advance, Client understands that this could result in Agent hearing information not expected by Client.

Agent understands that he or she must keep everything he or she hears from the attorney or Client while acting as Client's agent absolutely confidential. He or she cannot repeat it to other members of Client's family, Agent's family, or any other person without the express permission of Client.

While this form will provide some protection in the event the client does file a complaint for breach of confidentiality, the goal of using it is primarily educational. It will help both the client and the agent focus on the status of their relationship in terms that they can understand for purposes we understand. This helps integrate all concerned into the legal team. Such integration facilitates the purposes of the legal team while minimizing the chances of complaints.

C. Preventing Undue Influence of Our Clients

Caregivers and Other Third-parties

A second difficulty caused when an elderly client is assisted to a law office is the possibility of undue influence being asserted on the client by the helper. The potential for undue influence is inherent in the very relationship that brings the two to the office together. This is true even if the two are not related by blood or marriage. The relationship with which we are concerned is the dependence relationship of the elderly person on the helper that is implied by the very fact that the elderly person needs the assistance provided by the helper.

The legal professional has an obligation to the client to be aware of the signs of undue influence and other elder abuse. This was discussed more extensively in the chapters dealing with an elder client's family and elder abuse. In this context, the paralegal can be especially helpful to the attorney as a "second set of eyes." Both the attorney and the paralegal should watch for signs that the helper is dominating the client, rather than assisting the client. These signs include

- The helper speaks for the client;
- The client repeatedly asks the helper to answer a question for him or her;
- The client consistently looks to the helper before answering a question;
- The client stops or changes an answer after the helper looks at, touches, or makes a movement towards the client;
- The helper frequently corrects the client's answers;
- The helper refuses or is reluctant to allow the client to speak privately with the attorney or paralegal;
- The client appears confused or influenced by medication or alcohol.

None of these signs is definitive. Many elderly clients are confused; need help remembering, and the like. However, a legal professional should proceed with caution when these signs appear.

As stated above, it is my general practice to insist upon meeting separately with the client in any situation where there may be a conflict between my client and the person with the client. I apply this policy to parent/child and husband/wife situations as well as elder client situations. However, I do tend to emphasize it more in cases involving elderly clients, especially when a child is bringing in a parent to prepare a will, create a trust, or transfer property.

As noted earlier, the logistics of this can be delicate as once the two are in the room it can be difficult and embarrassing for the client to ask that the agent leave. I handle this by taking the responsibility. I explain that it is my rule to ask the other person to leave at the very beginning of the meeting *before* there is any substantive discussion. I explain to both the client and the other person that I do this as a matter of policy so I can document the file for the benefit of all concerned, not because of anything related to their particular circumstances. The important thing from my perspective is (1) not to insult either the agent or the client by suggesting that the agent may be taking advantage of the client or that the client is not capable of independent thought, and (2) make it clear that I am the person responsible for this request, not the client. If an abusive relationship does exist, we do not want the abuser to blame the abused for this challenge to their dominance over the abused.

Once the other person is out of the room I look for changes in demeanor on the part of my client, ask questions intended only to determine competency, and inquire about the client's relationship with the other person. Generally the actual answers to the questions are not important. I am more interested in the client's reactions, demeanor, and any changes in their behavior might indicate a problem.

All of the law office staff should be given a clear understanding of to whom they can speak regarding the client. If the agency is established for one member of the family, it does not extend to other members of the family or members of the agent's family. For example, if a son is the agent, the staff should speak only to the son and not to the son's wife. This is not an unusual situation. The son brings the parent into the office for the legal services, but depends on the daughter-in-law to carry on the dialogue with the law office because the son works during the day and the daughter-in-law does not. If it is necessary, formally establish the daughter-in-law as an agent, but do not begin "stretching" the agency beyond that which is formally established.

This procedure provides practical benefits to the legal team while preserving the attorney/client privilege. It is important to limit the number of persons calling the office regarding the client. Even when the number of children or other interested parties is small, the number of phone calls or "drop-ins" can become overwhelming for the legal staff. Further, each of the callers is likely to have his or her own perspective on what is being done and what should be done. Even if they are all told the same thing, they may each hear it differently or put their own gloss on what is said. The legal team then has three or four often conflicting versions of what was said circulating among the family. As noted previously, many clients, and especially frail elder clients, will "feed" these conflicting versions in individual conversations in order to avoid upsetting the person with whom they are talking.

There is one danger to this focused approach to communication: a freer flow of information may better assist the legal professional in ascertaining abuse by the agent. In this respect it is good to keep in mind that there is nothing preventing that professional from *listening* to and using information from any source. Complaints by a person interested in our client's estate or the outcome of decisions being made by or for our client are somewhat suspect. Many attorneys discount such complaints when they come from someone with "an axe to grind." However, they should be considered and investigated.

One goal of the elder client's legal team is to minimize the stress, trauma, confusion, and frustration of and *conflict between* members of the client's family. The better we do keeping communications clear the more likely it is that we will have accomplished this goal.

Avoiding Unintentional Undue Influence by the Legal Professional

The importance of the various methods of making advance decisions is that *the client* can make the decision that best suits his own beliefs. Having a living will or an advanced health care directive does not compel a client to choose an approach in opposition to his own beliefs. It simply allows him to make the decision rather than leave it to someone else, someone who may not share his beliefs. Establishing a "fair" estate plan must be done using the client's conception of fairness, not ours.

We must be careful in discussing these options with clients so that we do not judge their decisions or let them feel we do not approve of their decision. As noted previously, the elderly, especially those who are seriously ill, can be particularly vulnerable to outside influences. While many people become less concerned about what others think of them as they grow older, some others suffer from loss of a sense of self that can make them more susceptible to such influence. Our role is to assist the client in determining and effectuating his wishes, not to judge, shame, or persuade the client to our way of thinking.

It is often difficult to gauge our own prejudices and the way they affect our demeanor and approach to client. It is important that we reflect carefully on our own preferences. For example, it is my belief that options for making decisions regarding end-of-life healthcare can be arranged in a descending order, i.e., that the first is better than the second, the second better than the third, and so on.

I view these options as belonging to one of three categories. In the first, the client makes as many health care decisions for herself in advance as she can and designates someone to make only those decisions which were not anticipated in advance. In the second, the client makes no decisions in advance except the designation of the person or persons who will make necessary decisions on her behalf. Finally, there is the option of taking no action. In this instance, the client should understand that taking no action is itself making a decision.

The client decides to allow someone designated by state law to make the decisions on her behalf. However, throughout the discussion we must keep in mind that the paralegal's role is to inform (and for the attorney to advise), not to convince or persuade a client, even unintentionally.

As noted in Chapter Eight, some clients, even once they are informed of the availability of advanced directives, will prefer to impose these most difficult decisions on others. Just as we should not judge our clients' ultimate decisions regarding, for example, the prolongation of life, we should not judge this decision. As noted in Chapter Five, perspectives in this regard vary with cultural, ethnic, and religious background. Instead, we should dispassionately make sure clients are fully informed regarding the consequences of leaving these decisions to other people. Once they are fully informed, the decision must be theirs.

Sometimes if the client has not or does not want to decide for himself, he may ask you what you would do. Avoid engaging in discussing your personal preferences. In the first place, expressing your preference may be taken as advice. Assuming such advice is to be given in a law office, it must come from the attorney. At most, explain that such personal decisions are best made in consultation with their priest or rabbi and their family. (Even this is advice of a sort. While it is not really legal advice, it still would best come from the attorney.)

D. Ensuring and Documenting Capacity of the Elder Client

A legal professional has an ethical obligation to ensure that his client is competent to execute legal documents before allowing the client to do so. Fulfilling that obligation means having a solid understanding of the competency standards and developing a procedure for ascertaining whether the client meets those standards. Then, in order to prevent disputes over the client's competency from interfering with the client's desires being effectuated, competency must be documented in the client file.

The Need for Documentation

It is not enough that our client be competent to execute a document. We must be able to show, if challenged, that the client was sufficiently competent to justify our conclusions regarding competency. As discussed in Chapter Four, we cannot assume that because a family is getting along when the document is executed they will still be getting along in the future, especially after our client dies. A quick run of any legal search engine with the words "will and testament undue influence" or "deed undue influence" will demonstrate this point all too well.

While paralegals can go through their entire careers without becoming witnesses in a legal proceeding, it is not unusual and every paralegal should be aware that each event of their day could lead to being called to testify. This means keeping good, comprehensive records of those events in each client file.

One difficulty is that on occasion what must be recorded is what *did not* happen, as in the story "Silver Blaze," in which Sherlock Holmes informs Inspector Gregory:

> Gregory: "Is there any other point to which you would wish to draw my attention?"
> Holmes: "To the curious incident of the dog in the night-time."
> Gregory: "The dog did nothing in the night-time."
> Holmes: "That was the curious incident."

Paralegals are not expected to record directly what did not happen. However, if one can show that records are regularly and comprehensively kept, the absence of a record becomes significant. For example, if a law office keeps a telephone log of every call that comes into the office, the absence of a call is evidence that none came in. This can be important when a client has filed a complaint or is claiming that you did not return a call. If you keep good records of your conversations with clients, the fact that you did not record a statement can be evidence that you did not give the client the legal advice she now claims you gave.

There are some times, though, when you should actually be recording the absence of problems through records of what was present. For example, in a will contest claiming either incompetency or undue influence, you may be called regarding the testator's demeanor, state of mind or clarity, but the absence of certain factors can also be important, e.g., the fact that the client arrived alone under her own power rather than with the primary beneficiary of the will as her attendant. Further, you may be called upon to testify many years after your actual interactions with the client. Or you may be unavailable and the record you make will have to speak for itself. Thus, the file should, at least, reflect the absence of abnormalities. Better yet, it will reflect that you asked questions or engaged in discussions specifically intended to elicit signs of incompetency or undue influence.

It will also reflect that the attorney asked any attendants to leave the room so that the client and the attorney could speak freely. If there are any concerns about possible incompetency or undue influence, those concerns and how they were dealt with will be part of the file. For example, if it appears the client is heavily dependent on an attendant to answer questions, those questions should be asked again and the client's ability in general should be investigated outside the presence of the attendant. In some cases it may be appropriate to require the client to undergo a medical evaluation before proceeding.

If you have concerns, report them to the attorney. The attorney will decide what steps to take after consulting with you. Your responsibilities will include noting the areas of concern, reporting them to the attorney and recording both the concerns and the steps taken to address them in a clear fashion that will be understandable to persons who may be reviewing the file without you or your knowledge of the background and context to assist them.

We ought not rely on the mere fact that a will was made self-proving (see Chapter Five) or that a notary notarized a deed, together with the presumption of capacity. This reliance is justified in the vast majority of cases. It will, indeed, be quite difficult for anyone to challenge the validity of a will when two witnesses sign the self-proving affidavits of a will attesting that they found the testatrix to be of sound mind at the time and place of signing the will. After all, any challenger will have to rely on evidence from before or after the signing while the degree of lucidity at the time of signing is what counts. However, we do not know which cases will be challenged or what evidence the challenger might have available. Our responsibility is to prepare every case as if it was the challenged case and the challenger has significant evidence, because every case *might be* that case. In addition, a properly documented the file may be instrumental in *preventing* a challenge from taking place, saving all parties to the dispute a great deal of stress, frustration, and money.

The How and What of Documentation

As our client executes a document, we will have an opinion as to the client's capacity to sign the document, but like Sergeant Friday of *Dragnet* our primary concern is "just the facts." Rule 701 of the Federal Rules of Evidence does provide for opinion testimony by lay (non-expert) witnesses when "limited to those opinions or inferences which are (a) *rationally based on the perception of the witness* and (b) helpful to a clear understanding of the witness' testimony or the determination of a fact in issue, and (c) not based on scientific, technical, or other specialized knowledge within the scope of Rule 702." (Emphasis added) This means we need to record *our perceptions* rather than (or as well as) the opinion we have drawn from those perceptions.[1] This principle is well stated in an opinion by the Pennsylvania Supreme Court:

---

1. In some instances the court will not allow the opinion itself to be expressed, but only the facts themselves. Rule 701(b) requires that the opinion be "helpful to a clear under-

We have said that a person's "mental capacity is best determined by his spoken words, his acts and conduct." These witnesses did outline and describe the words, acts and conduct of the appellant and, from their observation of such words, acts and conduct, they all concluded that the appellant *on those dates* did possess sufficient mental capacity to understand and appreciate the meaning and nature of the agreements which she executed. This conclusion, in a sense, was an *opinion* but "an opinion arrived at after an observation of facts, i.e., their sensory impression of [appellant's] words and actions," and "Their testimony was neither entirely factual nor entirely opinion but mixed opinion and factual." These three witnesses were not only the best but the sole living witnesses of how appellant spoke and how she acted on the critical days when these agreements were executed.[2] (Emphasis in original)

It would be best for your office to have a form upon which relevant information can be recorded and placed in each file with the document to which it refers. That form would provide places to record not only who was present, but *why*, i.e., what the connection is between those who are present and the person executing the document. We do not need the life story of the witnesses or the client in the file, but a brief notation of how the witnesses knew the client, whether they are interested (in the legal sense) in the document being executed, and the like can be helpful.

Such a form would also record the client's "spoken words, his acts and conduct." This need not be a transcript of the proceedings. Rather it is a short record of information pertinent to the task at hand. The *Girsh Trust* matter

---

standing of the witness' testimony or the determination of a fact in issue." If the fact-finder can assess the facts without help from the witness' opinion, then the opinion is not admissible under the rule. See, e.g. this case (which was not decided under Rule 701),

The testimony of two lay witnesses on the mental capacity, or lack thereof, of the testatrix was excluded. Each of them was a sister of the testatrix, and each of them happens to be one of the caveators. The rule is well established, as stated by Sykes, op. cit., Section 67, that: "A witness who is not an expert, an attending physician, nor a subscribing witness to the will, is not competent to express his opinion as to the capacity of the testator, without first stating facts upon which his opinion may be adequately founded." If such facts are not sufficient to support an opinion of the testator's lack of mental capacity, the witness should not be permitted to express such an opinion. All of the facts upon which these two witnesses would have based their opinions are among those enumerated upon which the caveators rest their claim of the testatrix' lack of mental capacity. We agree with the learned trial judge that they are not sufficient to warrant the expression of their opinion. *Sellers v. Qualls,* 110 A. 2d 73 (Md, 1954) (Internal citations omitted.)

2. *Girsh Trust,* 410 Pa. 455, 472 (1963) (Internal citations omitted.)

again provides us with an example of the types of information which are helpful to the court:

> Mr. Goldstein's arrival at the hotel apartment with the agreements, the discussion, sometimes in loud tones, between appellant and Mr. Goldstein of the contents of the agreements, the reading at length of the agreements by appellant, the execution of the separation agreement, the deletion by appellant from the trust agreement of references therein to a certain law firm and her refusal to execute the trust agreement until such references were deleted in a redrafted agreement, the execution on June 29 of the trust agreement redrafted to suit appellant's wishes, appellant's actions on both dates subsequent to Mr. Goldstein's departure, etc.[3]

Our task is often not just to record what happens but to ensure a *proper* record is made. That means designing the process and the discussion that occurs during that process to elicit the information you need. For example, we often see in movies or TV shows persons being asked who the president is or other such information to determine whether they are functioning mentally. When I spoke of Louisa Mae, I recounted her interest in and current knowledge of the Boston Red Sox. This information is indeed relevant and helpful, but not really designed to the task. Consider this comment from a Tennessee Court of Appeals case:

> It should be noted that the physician did not examine deceased for competency to execute the papers in question. His examination sought to determine slowness or impairment of mental function as a measure of the toxic effect of a nosebleed which had caused blood to enter the digestive system and overload the capacity of the liver to remove toxic matter from the blood which nourished the brain. His questions to the deceased included, "who is the president"; "count down from 100 by 7's". *There was no effort to ascertain whether deceased was aware of the identity of his relatives or estate or other facts relating to the competency to execute the instruments in question.*[4]

Thus, our form should be designed to prompt questions that will elicit information specifically addressed to the test for capacity related to the instrument the client will be executing. For a will, we will want to be able to elicit statements or affirmations from the client that he

---

3. *Id.* at 472–473.
4. *Roberts v Roberts*, 827 SW 2d 788—(Tenn, 1991)

- Clearly understood what a will was and expressed a desire to execute one for precisely the purpose one normally executes a will, i.e., to dispose of assets after death
- Was able to list the names of the normal beneficiaries of bounty, i.e., his sons
- Was able to state the nature of his property and his determination of how he wanted it to be distributed upon his death
- He appeared to be free from delusions that would affect the disposition of his property

This should not amount to a formulaic test for the clients to pass before they are allowed to execute the document. Rather, discussion of these topics can and should be worked into the normal preliminary chit-chat that takes place before and during the process of executing the document.

Witnesses can actually pose somewhat of a problem during this process in at least two respects. First, they may be asked to attest to the soundness of the client's mind without really knowing on what grounds a court will ultimately make that decision. I often make a short statement in this regard before the document is executed. This both informs the witnesses and highlights this part of the process for purposes of their later recollection. Second, the information necessary to show mental capacity must be elicited without putting or drawing forth information that might be subject to attorney/client confidentiality, or might be embarrassing to the client. Sometimes there are things about the natural beneficiaries of our bounty that we do not want others to know. While the confidentiality issue is lessened if the witnesses are all members of the attorney's staff and thus subject to the rules of confidentiality, these people are likely to be viewed as strangers by the client and thus not persons who should be privy to "family secrets."

Video Recordings

It has become increasing easy and inexpensive to record and store information electronically. There is some value to making a video recording of the execution of documents, especially wills. However, there are also dangers and concerns that should be kept in mind:

- Many elderly clients are not as familiar with or comfortable with new electronic technologies as are clients of younger generations. This unfamiliarity and discomfort can be misinterpreted by those viewing the record at a later date.
- Having a video record of the document being executed will not substitute for proper execution of the document and may actually record im-

proprieties in the execution. For example, most statutes require that wills be executed in the presence of the witnesses and that each witness also is present when the other(s) sign. A recording may show what appears to be one witness who slipped out to take a call on their cell phone at a crucial moment. Or a recording may show that the notary never actually asked if the client was executing the deed as "her free act and deed." If a recording is being done, it is especially important that there be an agenda (script) and that it be followed exactly by all participants.[5]

- Video recordings tend to emphasize certain features more than others. This is not helpful if those features make the client appear more ill, tired, or confused than they actually are.

- Unless your office makes it a general policy to record all such events, the fact that *this one* was recorded can lead to questions about why it was chosen for recording, e.g., whether the attorney herself have doubts about capacity. In most instances, the attorney anticipates a challenge, so it makes sense to have a recording, but this will not stop efforts to put a different "spin" on the decision to record.

Admissibility of such a recording in a proceeding to contest the validity of the executed document is governed by Article X of the Federal Rules of Evidence and comparable state rules.

In any case, just as we ought not to depend on the presumption of competence in lieu of other documentation, we ought not to depend on video recording as a substitute for traditional file documentation. Video recording, if used at all, should be used *in addition to* traditional file documentation, not *in lieu of* it.

E. Ensuring and Documenting the Integrity of Pre- and Post-nuptial Agreements

This is, in essence, another aspect of the obligation to avoid conflicts of interest. While all agreements are subject to claims of undue influence, fraud, and the like, marital agreements are particularly susceptible to such claims, especially with regard to the requirement of full disclosure. There are a number of steps we can take to reduce such claims and reduce the likelihood that any claims raised will be successful:

---

5. I once represented buyers at a real estate closing where one of the sellers responded to the notary's "free act and deed" inquiry by joking, "I've got to sign or my wife will be all over my ass!" The notary refused to notarize the deed. The closing was rescheduled for the next day before another notary and with a seller who stuck to the "script."

1. Make a full record of the disclosures. Obtain confirmation from the party to whom the disclosure has been made. Have financial disclosure statements attached to the agreement and acknowledged by both parties. Many states have mandatory financial disclosure forms that must be filed by the parties in the event of a divorce. Use of those forms or forms which disclose the same information may be useful in rebutting a claim that insufficient information was disclosed. They will not, of course, rebut a claim that false information was provided.

2. Avoid any appearance of a conflict of interest on the part of the legal team. Each party must have their own *independent* advice. While we cannot force one of the parties to obtain their own legal counsel, we must make it *absolutely clear* that we represent only one party and are acting only in that party's interest. This is true even if the two parties come into our office stating that they have worked out an agreement and simply want us to formalize it.

3. While we must encourage the party we do not represent to obtain their own legal counsel, we should not recommend or refer them to an attorney. Not only should the legal counsel be independent, but the process by which that counsel is selected should be independent.

4. If the one party is not represented by their own attorney, include an acknowledgment in the agreement itself that the person has been advised to seek independent counsel and that we represent only the other party. The acknowledgment should include a statement that the party is specifically waiving the right to independent counsel. This acknowledgement should not be hidden among the many, many provisions that are commonly made part of such an agreement. Include it in large bold-face type immediately above the signature lines.

5. Our clients should be encouraged to initiate discussion of prenuptial agreements sufficiently far in advance of the wedding to allow for full disclosure, careful consideration, and independent advice. While prenuptial agreements sprung upon the other party the night before the wedding have been enforced, they are particularly susceptible to be declared invalid by courts.

6. Make as many provisions of the agreement as possible reciprocal. Even if as a practical matter one spouse is giving up nothing by releasing their rights to the other spouse's property (because the other party has no property), the provision in the agreement should state that each party is releasing their interest in the other party's property as a matter of basic fairness. Of course, there will be instances when there are good reasons to have a provision be unilateral. When that is the case, the agreement should include a statement of those reasons.

Make sure the formalities for proper execution of the agreement are met before disinterested witnesses. We do not want the witnesses to Harry and Ruth's prenuptial agreement to be Harry's children or any of Harry's relatives. Have the agreement acknowledged as the parties' free act and deed before a notary, even if it is not required under state law.

F. Reporting Elder Abuse

This issue was discussed in Chapter Ten, so it is likely to be fresh in your mind. I will repeat some of that discussion here for those who have skipped to this chapter, but first let's take a look at a topic first addressed in Chapter Three – competency of the elder client to drive an automobile.

The Client Not Competent to Drive

We tend to think of competency solely in terms of mental capacity and in terms of acts such as signing wills or deeds, but there are other areas of great concern to the elderly. Perhaps the most important is the ability to obtain and keep a driver's license.

A driver's license is extremely important to an elderly person. Losing it means losing yet another part of their identity and it also means that their world becomes smaller. Their inability to move around freely in our mechanized mobile society limits their ability to socialize and to obtain services. In yet another respect, they become more dependent on others. Still the fact remains—as a person's vision, reaction time, and other physical and mental capacities decrease, they lose their competency to drive.

The American Bar Association website has an article dealing with this topic entitled, "Driving and the Older Adult." That article contains sound advice for attorneys dealing with this as a legal issue, "Like many other parts of an elder law practice, rather than having an immediate "legal" solution to give to our clients and their families regarding an older adult's continued driving, the elder law attorney must be willing to counsel clients and their families about what to look for with respect to impaired driving, steps to take to eliminate unacceptable risk, and the ramifications of impaired driving."[6]

---

6. Johanna Lyn Grama, "Driving and the Older Adult," *American Bar Association General Practice, Solo and Small Firms Division Law Trends and News,* May 2005. https://www.abanet.org/genpractice/newsletter/lawtrends/0506/family/drivingolderadult.html. (Last accessed May 25, 2010)

But what if the client and her family do not take the attorney's advice? Many states require physicians, emergency personnel, and law enforcement officials to report drivers who may not be competent to drive, but those laws seldom apply to attorneys. However, can an attorney ethically report a client who that attorney believes is not competent to drive? Can an attorney ethically *not* report a client who that attorney believes is not competent to drive? What if the only basis for the attorney's knowledge of the lack of competency is attorney/client communications?

One solution to this dilemma may lie in mandatory reporting requirements for elder abuse. If elder abuse includes self-neglect and self-neglect is the failure to provide for one's own safety, perhaps reporting the unsafe driver comes under those statutes. It may even be possible to report the client's family for neglect if they fail to take steps to keep the elder client from driving. Another solution may lie in ABA Model Rule 1.6.b provisions for revelation of otherwise confidential information that include allowing revelation of such information to prevent reasonably certain death or substantial bodily harm.

Ethics and Reporting of Elder Abuse

Some states mandate reporting by specific classes of people, usually healthcare professionals, social workers, and law enforcement personnel. Others cast a much broader net to include *anyone* who has reason to suspect elder abuse.

The Mississippi Vulnerable Adult Act, for example, contains a long list of identified classes of persons who must report, including health professionals (including those that rely solely on spiritual healing), accountants, and bank employees. However, the law clearly states that regardless of the list, "*any person* including, but not limited to, the following, who knows or suspects that a vulnerable adult has been or is being abused, neglected or exploited shall immediately report such knowledge or suspicion to the Department of Human Services or to the county department of human services where the vulnerable adult is located."[7] (Emphasis added.)

Of particular import for us is the fact that such statutes may apply to attorneys—indeed the Mississippi statute's first identified profession for mandatory reporting is the attorney profession. This appears to create an ethical dilemma for attorneys and their paralegals. The statutes require reporting even if the knowledge or suspicion comes to the attorney as part of attorney/client

---

7. Miss. Code Ann. 43-47-7 (LexisNexis current through 2009 3rd Extraordinary Session).

communications that would otherwise be considered confidential and subject to the attorney/client privilege.

The solution to this dilemma is likely to lie within the specific rules of professional conduct governing the jurisdiction in which the attorney practices. The ABA Model Rules of Professional Conduct, Rule 1.6.b.6 provides that an attorney may reveal privileged communications "to comply with other law or court order."[8] Thus, the rule allows attorneys to report in jurisdictions with mandatory reporting statutes. With regard to other professions, some commentator has suggested that failure to make a mandated report constitutes malpractice.[9] The same may be true of the legal profession.

A secondary concern is whether the attorney has an obligation to advise a client that the attorney/client privilege does not protect communications that may reveal elder abuse. In previous discussions, I noted that a power of attorney gives the agent authority to act on the principal's behalf, not to exploit the principal. If the principal is our client, there is no problem with reporting an agent who is exploiting the client. However, the issue is more complex if our client is the person doing the exploitation. They may confide in us on the assumption that what they say is confidential when, in some jurisdictions, we may be mandated to report. In these circumstances I believe the attorney has an obligation to advise the client of this exception to the attorney/client privilege before engaging in communications with the client.

The more dangerous territory is voluntary reporting. Reporting statutes often provide immunity from liability for reports made in good faith, and establish a presumption of good faith. Some statutes that provide for voluntary reporting provide that the reporter's identity may only be revealed as ordered by a court for good cause.[10] The content of the report is also usually confidential. All of this does not necessarily protect the legal professional if the report is a violation of the attorney/client privilege.

When we suspect a non-client is abusing our client, the obligation to report, even if reporting is not mandated, appears clear. This may not be the case, however, when the client directs us not to report. However, in circumstances of obvious abuse and exploitation, a direction not to report may be a form of self-neglect or undue influence. In such a case, I would err on the side of reporting unless there was some clear indication that reporting would vio-

---

8. Rule 1.6.b.6, ABA Model Rules of Professional Conduct (2004), http://www.law.cornell.edu/ethics/aba/current/ABA_CODE.HTM#Rule_1.6 (Last accessed May 25, 2010).

9. Ralph C. Brashier, *Mastering Elder Law*, 18 (Carolina Academic Press 2010).

10. *Id.*

late an ethical obligation. In my view, the overriding obligation is to act in the best interest of the client.

When we learn through privileged communications, however, that our client is the abuser, voluntary reporting must be carefully considered under the particular rules of professional conduct governing our jurisdiction. Under the ABA Model Rules, there appears to be enough leeway to make the voluntary report. Rule 1.6.b provisions for revelation of otherwise confidential information include:

Rule 1.6: Confidentiality of Information

b. A lawyer may reveal information relating to the representation of a client to the extent the lawyer reasonably believes necessary:
1. to prevent reasonably certain death or substantial bodily harm;
2. to prevent the client from committing a crime or fraud that is reasonably certain to result in substantial injury to the financial interests or property of another and in furtherance of which the client has used or is using the lawyer's services;
3. to prevent, mitigate or rectify substantial injury to the financial interests or property of another that is reasonably certain to result or has resulted from the client's commission of a crime or fraud in furtherance of which the client has used the lawyer's services

In most instances, our knowledge of elder abuse on the part of our clients will involve serious bodily injury to the elder person, or a crime or fraud that is reasonably certain to result in substantial injury to the financial interests of property to another. However, in the latter case, the client must have used or be using the lawyer's services in furtherance of the crime or fraud. For example, he may have used our services to obtain the power of attorney he is now utilizing to effectuate the exploitation of the elder person.

I believe that most rules of professional conduct allow attorneys to report self-neglect and suicidal intentions on the part of our clients, especially in states with mandatory reporting requirements. Certainly the case can be made under ABA Model Rule 1.6. However, not all commentators agree with this assessment, at least under the rules of some states.[11] The primary task of the paralegal is to be attentive to signs of elder abuse and to report those signs to the attorney for whom he is working. Document any such signs thoroughly in the file. Bring a camera with you whenever meeting a client at her home or in an institutional facility.

---

11. See, e.g., Weiss, *Evidence of Client's Contemplating Suicide: A Lawyer's Duty Not To Disclose*, http://www.abanet.org/cpr/comments/weiss16.pdf (Last accessed March 17, 2010).

If you believe you are a mandated reporter under the applicable statute and the attorney directs you not to report, obtain independent legal advice before proceeding. The attorney's ethical obligations are not directly binding on you, but the statutes may be. Consult an attorney not associated with your attorney or the law office in which your attorney works. Remember that attorney has a firm obligation to keep what you tell her confidential. That attorney can advise you regarding protections to which you may be entitled, the proper authority to which you should report and the correct procedures for reporting. She will help you analyze the situation to determine whether you have the necessary facts, have properly interpreted the facts and validate your decision regarding the proper balancing of interests and integrity. Other members of your paralegal professional association may be helpful in locating the best attorney for this purpose.

CONCLUSION

Empowerment does not come from the outside. It comes from within. It is not granted, it is earned. The empowered paralegal gains that power—and the confidence that comes with being professional—by being a competent, effective and efficient member of the legal team. *The Empowered Paralegal: Effective, Efficient and Professional* examined some clear, concise and easy-to-use techniques for empowering paralegals and put that knowledge to work in the context of litigation. Yet, the point of that book was more than just explanation and transmission of practical techniques. The point was in the basic underlying approach to all aspects of paralegal practices based on the concept that the paralegal can manage each aspect rather than being managed by it. The paralegal can and must do so as the professional they are.

The principles can and should be applied to every aspect of paralegal practice, in every type of office in which a paralegal works (law office, government office and corporate office), and in every area of law. The first principle is to recognize and to account for the fundamental *inter*relationships and responsibilities of paralegal practice:

- The interrelationship between the facts, the file, the docket and time
- The interrelationship between the client, the paralegal and the attorney
- The joint responsibility and involvement of all members of the legal team for the facts, the file and the docket in achieving a successful outcome.

The goal for the effective, empowered paralegal is the ability to understand and manage each of the key factors.

The second principle has to do with the way the paralegal approaches any and all aspects of paralegal practice. It is a proactive rather than reactive approach. It seeks to understand and manage even those aspects of practice that the paralegal cannot control. This principle involves taking a rational, empowered approach.

In this book, we applied those principles to working with the elder client. We examined the fundamental interrelationships and responsibilities in light of the dual nature of elder law and the dual nature of the elder client. Elder law is quite like any other kind of law and, at the same time, quite unlike any other area of law. Substantively the law is law—statutes, cases, rules, and regulations, all of which must be researched, analyzed, understood and applied. Elder law attorneys and their paralegals march through the same steps of legal research and analysis as other attorneys. They use the IRAC method of writing their memoranda and briefs. They need to manage their time, workloads, files, and dockets just as any other attorney/paralegal team.

Unlike any other type of law though, elder law is not about something a client is going through—a divorce, a bankruptcy, immigration, a criminal charge, a real estate transaction. Elder law is about whom and what the client *is*—elderly. Unlike other areas of law, elder law applies to everyone. Many people go through life without running a business, buying property, getting a divorce or being charged with a crime. But everyone goes through life with the certainty of growing old. Even those who do not survive long enough to confront old age (or their survivors) must deal with elder law issues—end-of-life decisions, death, disability, probate.

So, elder law is as much focused on "elder" as it is on "law." This book was thus focused primarily on the elder client rather than elder law. Our goal was to add knowledge and understanding of elder law clients and the issues they face to paralegal legal skills. These clients and their issues require some special accommodations. Managing their files requires slightly different methods, or at least slightly different focus, than other files. But all of these differences arise from the particular nature of the client—they are elderly.

The elderly, too, are dual natured. They have uniformity in that they are at approximately the same stage in life. That stage of life entails certain commonality of concerns as noted above—dying, death, planning for those left behind, physical changes, diminished mental capacity and vulnerability. There are even certain psychological factors that seem almost universal.

Yet, we cannot let this commonality mask the diversity of approaches to each of these concerns. Each client will perceive these issues and the law that relates to them from a unique perspective arising from years of personal experiences rooted in cultural, ethnic, religious and other influences. Thus, each will have his or her own perspective on aging, the elderly, the role of the family, dying, death, dead bodies and the other practical and legal issues that confront the elderly.

No one can hope to thoroughly understand the many different influences on our clients and their families, or the deeply personal perspective which result from those influences. However, the empowered paralegal will be aware of these differences and understand enough about them to appreciate how they affect the decisions that an elder law client will make.

When a paralegal applies these principles, that paralegal becomes empowered. The empowered paralegal is an essential member of the legal team in any office. In particular, the empowered paralegal not only survives, but thrives in the American law office.

INDEX